SLOW-COOKED CHAI TEA

A friend brought chai tea over to my mother's house. She told us that in India it is served every day. I had never had it before. I liked it so much I came up with a recipe to re-create it.
—Patty Crouse, Warren, PA

- -

Prep: 10 min. • **Cook:** 3 hours
Makes: 8 servings

6 cups water
1 cup sugar
1 cup nonfat dry milk powder
6 black tea bags
1 tsp. ground ginger
1 tsp. ground cinnamon
½ tsp. pepper
½ tsp. ground cardamom
½ tsp. ground cloves
½ tsp. vanilla extract

Place all ingredients in a 3- or 4-qt. slow cooker. Cook, covered, on high until heated through, 3-4 hours. Discard tea bags. Serve tea warm.
¾ cup: 131 cal., 0 fat (0 sat. fat), 2mg chol., 48mg sod., 30g carb. (30g sugars, 0 fiber), 3g pro.

CHIPOTLE HAM & CHEESE DIP

If you enjoy throwing dinner parties for friends, you can't beat a convenient slow-cooker recipe like this one. Who wants to be stuck in the kitchen? Just set the slow cooker on low and have fun visiting with guests.
—Lisa Renshaw, Kansas City, MO

- -

Prep: 15 min. • **Cook:** 1 hour
Makes: 7 cups

- 2 pkg. (8 oz. each) cream cheese, cubed
- 2 cups shredded Gouda cheese
- 1 can (12 oz.) evaporated milk
- 1 cup shredded cheddar cheese
- 2 Tbsp. chopped chipotle pepper in adobo sauce
- 1 tsp. ground cumin
- 2 cups diced fully cooked ham
  Fresh vegetables or tortilla chips

1. In a 3-qt. slow cooker, combine the first 6 ingredients. Cook, covered, on low 40 minutes.
2. Stir in ham; cook 20 minutes longer or until heated through. Serve warm with vegetables or chips.
¼ cup: 104 cal., 8g fat (5g sat. fat), 32mg chol., 261mg sod., 2g carb. (2g sugars, 0 fiber), 6g pro.

REUBEN SPREAD

You'll need only five ingredients to stir up this hearty dip that tastes like a Reuben sandwich. It's requested at all the gatherings we attend.
—Pam Rohr, Troy, OH

- -

Prep: 5 min. • **Cook:** 3 hours
Makes: 40 servings (5 cups)

- 2½ cups cubed cooked corned beef
- 1 can (14 oz.) sauerkraut, rinsed and well drained
- 2 cups shredded Swiss cheese
- 2 cups shredded cheddar cheese
- 1 cup mayonnaise
  Snack rye bread

In a 3-qt. slow cooker, combine the first 5 ingredients. Cover and cook on low for 3-4 hours or until heated through and the cheese is melted, stirring occasionally. Serve warm with rye bread.
2 Tbsp: 100 cal., 9g fat (3g sat. fat), 20mg chol., 233mg sod., 1g carb. (0 sugars, 0 fiber), 4g pro.

REUBEN SPREAD

Slow Cooker
THROUGH THE SEASONS

TASTE OF HOME BOOKS • RDA ENTHUSIAST BRANDS, LLC • MILWAUKEE, WI

Visit us at tasteofhome.com for other Taste of Home
books and products.

ISBN: 978-1-62145-758-9

Executive Editor: Mark Hagen
Senior Art Director: Raeann Thompson
Senior Editor: Christine Rukavena
Art Director: Maggie Conners
Senior Designer: Jazmin Delgado
Deputy Editor, Copy Desk: Dulcie Shoener
Copy Editor: Sara Strauss

Cover photography: Taste of Home Photo Studio

Pictured on front cover: Quinoa Chili, p. 248;
Simmered Turkey Enchiladas, p. 55; Secret's in the
Sauce BBQ Ribs, p. 125; Shredded Lamb Sliders,
p. 161

Pictured on spine: Cheddar Bacon Beer Dip, p. 237

Pictured on title page: Jalapeno Mac & Cheese,
p. 46; Root Beer Pulled Pork Nachos, p. 92; Slow-
Cooker Italian Sloppy Joes, p. 250; Cinnamon Roll
Casserole, p. 315

Pictured on back cover:
Root Vegetable Pot Roast, p. 276; Molten Mocha Cake,
p. 75; Slow-Cooked Cajun Corn, p. 142; Spicy Sausage
Meatball Sauce, p.197

Printed in USA
1 3 5 7 9 10 8 6 4 2

**PULLED BRISKET
SANDWICHES, P. 262**

CONTENTS

GET SOCIAL WITH US

TO FIND A RECIPE: tasteofhome.com
TO SUBMIT A RECIPE: tasteofhome.com/submit
TO FIND OUT ABOUT OTHER *TASTE OF HOME*
PRODUCTS: shop.tasteofhome.com

DON'T BE TEMPTED TO LIFT THE LID

BROWN YOUR MEAT IN A SKILLET

PREP INGREDIENTS THE NIGHT BEFORE

SLOW-COOK WITH CONFIDENCE

Follow these tips for slow-cooking success every time.

- **PLAN AHEAD TO PREP AND GO.** In most cases, you can prepare and load ingredients into the slow-cooker insert beforehand and store it in the refrigerator overnight. But an insert can crack if exposed to rapid temperature changes. Let the insert sit out just long enough to reach room temperature (20-30 minutes) before placing it in the slow cooker.

- **USE THAWED INGREDIENTS.** Although throwing frozen chicken breasts into the slow cooker may seem easy, it's not a smart shortcut. Thawing foods in a slow cooker can create the ideal environment for bacteria to grow, so thaw frozen meat and veggies ahead of time. The exception is if you're using a prepackaged slow-cooker meal kit and following the instructions as written.

- **TAKE THE TIME TO BROWN.** Give yourself a few extra minutes to brown the meat in a pan before placing it in the slow cooker. Doing so adds rich color and flavor to the dish.

- **MAKE USE OF SMART LAYERING.** Dense foods like potatoes can take a long time to cook. They are often layered in the bottom of the slow cooker, where they can be closer to the heat than an item that is layered on top. For best results, always follow any layering instructions a recipe provides.

- **ADJUST COOK TIME FOR HIGH ALTITUDE.** Slow-cooking will take longer at a high altitude. Add about 30 minutes for each hour of cooking that the recipe calls for; legumes will take about twice as long.

- **WANT YOUR FOOD READY SOONER?** Cooking 1 hour on high is roughly equal to 2 hours on low, so adjust the recipe to suit your schedule.

HOW TO KEEP YOUR COOKER CLEAN

ALLOW the stoneware insert to cool before rinsing it. Wash it in the dishwasher or in the sink with warm, soapy water.

DO NOT use abrasive cleansers.

USE a damp sponge to clean the metal base. Do not soak the base in water.

TO REMOVE white mineral stains from the insert, fill the cooker with hot water mixed with 1 cup white vinegar. Heat on high for 2 hours. Empty the insert, let it cool and wash as usual.

Taste *of* Home.

Slow Cooker
THROUGH THE SEASONS

PULLED PORK NACHOS

2. Remove roast; cool slightly. Strain cooking juices, reserving vegetables and ½ cup juices; discard remaining juices. Skim fat from reserved juices. Shred pork with 2 forks.

3. Return pork, reserved juices and vegetables to slow cooker. Stir in beans, barbecue sauce and cheese; heat through. Serve over chips with toppings as desired.

Freeze option: Freeze cooled pork mixture in freezer containers. To use, partially thaw in refrigerator overnight. Heat through in a saucepan, stirring occasionally; add a little broth or water if necessary.

½ cup pork mixture: 233 cal., 11g fat (5g sat. fat), 60mg chol., 416mg sod., 14g carb. (6g sugars, 2g fiber), 18g pro.

SLOW-COOKER SECRETS
Have only chicken on hand? Easily substitute 3 lbs. boneless skinless chicken breasts for the pork in these nachos. Cook

PULLED PORK NACHOS

While home from college, my daughter made these nachos—her first recipe ever. My son and I couldn't get enough.
—Carol Kurpjuweit, Humansville, MO

- -

Prep: 30 min. • **Cook:** 8 hours
Makes: 16 servings

- 1 tsp. garlic powder
- 1 tsp. mesquite seasoning
- ¼ tsp. pepper
- ⅛ tsp. celery salt
- 3 lbs. boneless pork shoulder butt roast
- 1 medium green pepper, chopped
- 1 medium sweet red pepper, chopped
- 1 medium onion, chopped
- 1 can (16 oz.) baked beans
- 1 cup barbecue sauce
- 1 cup shredded cheddar cheese
  Corn or tortilla chips
  Optional toppings: Chopped tomatoes, shredded lettuce and chopped green onions

1. In a small bowl, mix the seasoning ingredients. Place roast in a 5- or 6-qt. slow cooker; rub with seasonings. Add peppers and onion. Cook, covered, on low 8-10 hours.

SO-EASY
STICKY CHICKEN WINGS

My neighbor once shared these tangy wings with me at a potluck, and they have been a family favorite ever since.
—Jo Vanderwolf, Lillooet, BC

Prep: 20 min. • **Cook:** 3 hours
Makes: 40 pieces

- 4 **lbs. chicken wings**
- 1 **cup barbecue sauce**
- 1 **cup soy sauce**
- 6 **green onions, chopped, divided**
- 1 **Tbsp. sesame seeds**

Using a sharp knife, cut through the 2 wing joints; discard wing tips. Place remaining wing pieces in a 4- or 5-qt. slow cooker. Stir in barbecue sauce, soy sauce and ¼ cup chopped green onions. Cook, covered, on high 3-4 hours or until tender. Sprinkle with sesame seeds and remaining green onions.
1 piece: 68 cal., 4g fat (1g sat. fat), 14mg chol., 452mg sod., 3g carb. (2g sugars, 0 fiber), 6g pro.

ASIAN WRAPS

ASIAN WRAPS

This recipe is just like any other Asian wrap but with more flavor, a healthy twist and the convenience of a slow cooker. Instead of ordering Chinese, try making these yourself.
—Melissa Hansen, Ellison Bay, WI

Prep: 30 min. • **Cook:** 3½ hours
Makes: 1 dozen

- 2 **lbs. boneless skinless chicken breast halves**
- ¼ **cup reduced-sodium soy sauce**
- ¼ **cup ketchup**
- ¼ **cup honey**
- 2 **Tbsp. minced fresh gingerroot**
- 2 **Tbsp. sesame oil**
- 1 **small onion, finely chopped**
- 2 **Tbsp. cornstarch**
- 2 **Tbsp. cold water**
- 12 **round rice papers (8 in.)**
- 3 **cups broccoli coleslaw mix**
- ¾ **cup crispy chow mein noodles**

1. Place chicken in a 3-qt. slow cooker. In a small bowl, whisk the soy sauce, ketchup, honey, ginger and oil; stir in onion. Pour over chicken. Cook, covered, on low 3-4 hours or until chicken is tender. Remove chicken; shred with 2 forks and refrigerate until assembly.
2. Meanwhile, in a small bowl, mix cornstarch and water until smooth; gradually stir into honey mixture. Cook, covered, on high until the sauce is thickened, 20-30 minutes. Toss chicken with ¾ cup sauce; reserve remaining sauce for serving.
3. Fill a large shallow dish partway with water. Dip a rice paper wrapper into the water just until pliable, about 45 seconds (do not soften completely); allow excess water to drip off.
4. Place wrapper on a flat surface. Layer ¼ cup coleslaw, ⅓ cup chicken mixture and 1 Tbsp. noodles across bottom third of wrapper. Fold in both sides of wrapper; fold bottom over filling, then roll up tightly. Place on a serving plate, seam side down. Repeat with remaining ingredients. Serve with reserved sauce.

1 wrap with 1 tsp. sauce: 195 cal., 5g fat (1g sat. fat), 42mg chol., 337mg sod., 21g carb. (8g sugars, 1g fiber), 17g pro.
Diabetic exchanges: 2 lean meat, 1½ starch, ½ fat.

READER RAVE...
"This is a really good spring roll and not hard to make—even for an old man with stiff fingers!"
—KENNETHBALMAS, TASTEOFHOME.COM

CHICKEN
CORDON BLEU
SLIDERS

BLUEBERRY ICED TEA

I enjoy coming up with new ways to use my slow cooker in the kitchen. If it's going to take up space, it needs to earn its keep! Serve this refreshing tea over plenty of ice and garnish it with a few blueberries if desired. For fun, freeze blueberries in your ice cubes.
—Colleen Delawder, Herndon, VA

- -

Prep: 10 min. • **Cook:** 3 hours + cooling
Makes: 11 servings

- 12 cups water
- 2 cups fresh blueberries
- 1 cup sugar
- ¼ tsp. salt
- 4 family-sized tea bags
   Ice cubes
   Optional: Additional
   blueberries, lemon slices
   and fresh mint leaves

CHICKEN CORDON BLEU SLIDERS

Sandwiches are my favorite food, so I'm always searching for new ideas. I like sloppy joes and wondered if I could make a sloppy joe of sorts even better. This was one such experiment that met with my family's approval.
—Carolyn Eskew, Dayton, OH

- -

Prep: 20 min.
Cook: 2½ hours + standing
Makes: 2 dozen

- 1½ lbs. boneless skinless
   chicken breasts
- 1 garlic clove, minced
- ¼ tsp. salt
- ¼ tsp. pepper
- 1 pkg. (8 oz.) cream cheese, cubed
- 2 cups shredded Swiss cheese
- 1¼ cups finely chopped
   fully cooked ham
- 2 pkg. (12 oz. each) Hawaiian
   sweet rolls, split
   Chopped green onions

1. Place chicken in a greased 3-qt. slow cooker; sprinkle with garlic, salt and pepper. Top with cream cheese. Cook, covered, on low 2½-3 hours or until a thermometer inserted in chicken reads 165°. Remove the chicken; shred with 2 forks. Return to slow cooker.
2. Stir in Swiss cheese and ham. Cover and let stand 15 minutes or until cheese is melted. Stir before serving on rolls. Sprinkle with green onions.
1 slider: 209 cal., 10g fat (5g sat. fat), 53mg chol., 254mg sod., 17g carb. (6g sugars, 1g fiber), 14g pro.

1. In a 5-qt. slow cooker, combine water, blueberries, sugar and salt. Cover and cook on low heat 3 hours.
2. Turn off slow cooker; add tea bags. Cover and let stand 5 minutes. Discard tea bags; cool 2 hours. Strain and discard blueberries. Pour into pitcher; serve over ice cubes. If desired, top each serving with additional blueberries, lemon slices and fresh mint leaves.
1 cup: 73 cal., 0 fat (0 sat. fat), 0 chol., 61mg sod., 19g carb. (18g sugars, 0 fiber), 0 pro.

BLUEBERRY ICED TEA

SOUPS & SANDWICHES

PB&J PORK
SANDWICHES

PB&J PORK SANDWICHES

I came up with this recipe for one of my daughters who loves peanut butter and pork! The result has become a favorite—kids and grown-ups alike often request it for dinner.
—Jill Cox, Lincoln, NE

Prep: 15 min. • **Cook:** 6 hours
Makes: 6 servings

- 3 to 4 lbs. boneless pork shoulder butt roast
- 1 tsp. salt
- ½ tsp. pepper
- 1 can (14½ oz.) reduced-sodium chicken broth
- 1 cup creamy peanut butter
- ¾ cup apricot preserves
- ¼ cup packed brown sugar
- ¼ cup finely chopped onion
- ¼ cup cider vinegar
- 3 Tbsp. Dijon mustard
- 1 garlic clove, minced
- 2 Tbsp. butter, melted
- 6 ciabatta rolls, split
  Coleslaw, optional

1. Sprinkle roast with salt and pepper; transfer to a 5-qt. slow cooker. In a large bowl, whisk broth, peanut butter, preserves, brown sugar, onion, vinegar, mustard and garlic; pour over meat. Cook, covered, on low 6-8 hours or until the meat is tender.
2. Preheat broiler. Remove roast; cool slightly. Shred pork with 2 forks. Return the pork to slow cooker; heat through. Brush butter over cut sides of rolls. Place rolls, buttered side up, on an ungreased baking sheet. Broil 3-4 in. from heat 30-60 seconds or until golden brown. Using a slotted spoon, spoon pork mixture onto roll bottoms; top with coleslaw if desired. Replace tops.

1 sandwich: 862 cal., 49g fat (15g sat. fat), 145mg chol., 1207mg sod., 59g carb. (32g sugars, 3g fiber), 51g pro.

VEGAN CABBAGE SOUP

Comforting soups that simmer all day long are staples on busy days. For a heartier version of this vegan soup, simply stir in canned beans, like cannellini or navy.
—*Taste of Home* Test Kitchen

Prep: 15 min. • **Cook:** 6 hours
Makes: 10 servings (2½ qt.)

- 4 cups vegetable stock
- 1 can (14 oz.) Italian diced tomatoes
- 1 can (6 oz.) tomato paste
- 1 small head cabbage (about 1½ lbs.), shredded
- 4 celery ribs, chopped
- 2 large carrots, chopped
- 1 medium onion, chopped
- 2 garlic cloves, minced
- 2 tsp. Italian seasoning
- ½ tsp. salt
  Fresh basil, optional

In a 5- or 6-qt. slow cooker, whisk together stock, diced tomatoes and tomato paste. Stir in the vegetables, garlic, Italian seasoning and salt. Cook, covered, on low until vegetables are tender, 6-8 hours. If desired, top each serving with fresh basil.
1 cup: 110 cal., 0 fat (0 sat. fat), 0 chol., 866mg sod., 24g carb. (13g sugars, 6g fiber), 4g pro.

VEGAN
CABBAGE SOUP

SLOW-COOKER ITALIAN BEEF SANDWICHES

I have fond memories of my mother in the kitchen preparing her amazing beef dip sandwiches. They always made our house smell like an Old World Italian restaurant. And as good as the aroma was, somehow the flavor was even better! Set out a jar of giardiniera for spooning on top.
—Kira Vosk, Muskego, WI

Prep: 1 hour • **Cook:** 7 hours
Makes: 12 servings

- 4 **Tbsp. olive oil, divided**
- 1 **boneless beef chuck eye or other boneless beef chuck roast (4 to 5 lbs.)**
- 2¼ **tsp. salt, divided**
- 2¼ **tsp. pepper, divided**
- 2 **small onions, coarsely chopped**
- 9 **garlic cloves, chopped**
- ¾ **cup dry red wine**
- 4 **cups beef stock**
- 3 **fresh thyme sprigs**
- 4 **tsp. Italian seasoning**
- 1½ **tsp. crushed red pepper flakes**
- 4 **medium green peppers, cut into ½-in. strips**
- 1 **tsp. garlic powder**
- 12 **crusty submarine buns or hoagie buns, split partway**
- 12 **slices provolone or part-skim mozzarella cheese Giardiniera, optional**

1. In a 6-qt. stockpot, heat 3 Tbsp. oil over medium-high heat; brown roast on all sides. Sprinkle with 2 tsp. each salt and pepper. Carefully transfer to a 6-qt. slow cooker.

2. Add onions to stockpot; cook and stir until lightly browned, 2-3 minutes. Add garlic; cook 30 seconds longer. Add wine; cook 3-5 minutes, stirring to loosen browned bits from pan. Stir in stock, thyme, Italian seasoning and pepper flakes; transfer to slow cooker. Cook, covered, on low until beef is tender, 7-9 hours.

3. About ½ hour before serving, preheat oven to 350°. Place peppers in a 15x10x1-in. baking pan. Drizzle with the remaining oil. Sprinkle with garlic powder and remaining salt and pepper; toss to coat. Roast until the peppers are softened, 15-20 minutes, stirring halfway.

4. Remove roast; cool slightly. Strain cooking juices into a small saucepan, reserving strained mixture and removing thyme stems. Skim fat from juices; heat through and keep warm. Coarsely shred beef with 2 forks; stir in reserved strained mixture. If desired, moisten beef with the cooking juices.

5. To serve, preheat broiler. Arrange buns on baking sheets, cut sides up. Broil 3-4 in. from heat until lightly toasted. Remove from oven; top each bun with about ⅔ cup beef mixture and 1 slice cheese. Broil until cheese is melted, about 30 seconds.

6. Top with peppers and, if desired, giardiniera. Serve with cooking juices for dipping.

1 sandwich: 595 cal., 30g fat (11g sat. fat), 113mg chol., 1134mg sod., 38g carb. (6g sugars, 3g fiber), 44g pro.

**SLOW-COOKER
ITALIAN BEEF SANDWICHES**

POTATO & LEEK SOUP

Chock-full of veggies and bacon, with just a little tanginess from sour cream, bowls of this comforting soup taste just as terrific with sandwiches as they do with crackers.
—Melanie Wooden, Reno, NV

Prep: 20 min. • **Cook:** 8 hours
Makes: 8 servings (2 qt.)

- 4 cups chicken broth
- 3 medium potatoes,
     peeled and cubed
- 1½ cups chopped cabbage
- 2 medium carrots, chopped
- 1 medium leek
     (white portion only), chopped
- 1 medium onion, chopped
- ¼ cup minced fresh parsley
- ½ tsp. salt
- ½ tsp. caraway seeds
- ½ tsp. pepper
- 1 bay leaf
- ½ cup sour cream
- 1 lb. bacon strips,
     cooked and crumbled

1. Combine the first 11 ingredients in a 4- or 5-qt. slow cooker. Cover and cook on low until the vegetables are tender, 8-10 hours.
2. Before serving, combine the sour cream with 1 cup soup; return all to the slow cooker. Stir in bacon and discard bay leaf.

1 cup: 209 cal., 11g fat (4g sat. fat), 27mg chol., 1023mg sod., 18g carb. (4g sugars, 2g fiber), 10g pro.

SPLIT PEA & SAUSAGE SOUP

A big bowl of satisfying soup is the perfect antidote to the blues. Whether for a family meal or an informal get-together, I pull out my tried-and-true soup recipe, toss everything in the slow cooker and simply relax.
—Trisha Kruse, Eagle, ID

Prep: 25 min. • **Cook:** 7 hours
Makes: 6 servings (2¼ qt.)

- 1   lb. smoked sausage, sliced
- 1   medium potato, peeled and cubed
- 2   medium carrots, thinly sliced
- 2   celery ribs, thinly sliced
- 1   medium onion, chopped
- 2   Tbsp. butter
- 3   garlic cloves, minced
- ¼   tsp. dried oregano
- 1   cup dried green split peas
- 2½ tsp. chicken bouillon granules
- 1   bay leaf
- 5   cups water

1. Saute sausage, potato, carrots, celery and onion in butter in a large skillet until vegetables are crisp-tender. Add garlic and oregano; cook 2 minutes longer.
2. Transfer to a 5-qt. slow cooker. Add the peas, bouillon, bay leaf and water. Cover and cook on low for 7-8 hours or until peas are tender. Discard bay leaf.
1½ cups: 429 cal., 25g fat (11g sat. fat), 61mg chol., 1267mg sod., 33g carb. (7g sugars, 10g fiber), 20g pro.

PORK & RICE NOODLE SOUP

My husband and I are crazy for the Korean noodle bowls at our favorite restaurant. I created this recipe to enjoy the same flavors in a quick and easy meal. You can find rice noodles in the Asian section of the grocery store.
—Lisa Renshaw, Kansas City, MO

Prep: 15 min. • **Cook:** 6½ hours
Makes: 8 servings (3 qt.)

- 1½ lbs. boneless country-style pork ribs, cut into 1-in. cubes
- 6   garlic cloves, minced
- 2   Tbsp. minced fresh gingerroot
- 2   cans (14½ oz. each) reduced-sodium chicken broth
- 2   cans (13.66 oz. each) coconut milk
- ¼   cup reduced-sodium soy sauce
- 4   oz. uncooked thin rice noodles
- 2   cups frozen pepper strips, thawed
- 1   can (8 oz.) sliced water chestnuts, drained
- ¼   cup minced fresh cilantro
- 2   Tbsp. lime juice

1. In a 5-qt. slow cooker, combine the first 6 ingredients. Cook, covered, on low 6-8 hours or until meat is tender.
2. Add rice noodles, pepper strips and water chestnuts; cook 30-35 minutes longer or until the noodles are tender. If desired, skim the soup. Just before serving, stir in cilantro and lime juice.
1½ cups: 380 cal., 23g fat (18g sat. fat), 49mg chol., 677mg sod., 21g carb. (4g sugars, 1g fiber), 20g pro.

PORK & RICE NOODLE SOUP

SHREDDED BUFFALO CHICKEN SANDWICHES

VEGGIE MEATBALL SOUP FOR 3

This hearty soup is a snap to put together before I leave for work. I just add uncooked pasta when I get home, and then I have a few minutes to relax before supper is ready.
—Charla Tinney, Tyrone, OK

- -

Prep: 10 min. • **Cook:** 4¼ hours
Makes: 3 cups

- 1½ **cups reduced-sodium beef broth**
- 1 **cup frozen mixed vegetables, thawed**
- ¾ **cup canned stewed tomatoes**
- 9 **frozen fully cooked homestyle meatballs (½ oz. each), thawed**
- 2 **bay leaves**
- ⅛ **tsp. pepper**
- ½ **cup uncooked spiral pasta**

In a 1½-qt. slow cooker, combine first 6 ingredients. Cover and cook on low for 4-5 hours or until heated through. Stir in the pasta; cover and cook on high for 15-30 minutes or until tender. Discard bay leaves.

1 cup: 250 cal., 11g fat (5g sat. fat), 35mg chol., 671mg sod., 26g carb. (6g sugars, 5g fiber), 11g pro. **Diabetic exchanges:** 1½ starch, 1½ fat, 1 vegetable, 1 lean meat.

SLOW-COOKER SECRETS

Always thaw frozen meats before adding them to the slow cooker. This leads to even cooking, addresses many food safety issues and makes the recipe's cooking timelines more reliable.

SHREDDED BUFFALO CHICKEN SANDWICHES

My family loves Buffalo chicken wings, but frying makes them unhealthy. This recipe takes out some of the fat yet lets us enjoy the same amazing taste.
—Terri McKenzie, Wilmington, OH

- -

Prep: 10 min. • **Cook:** 3 hours
Makes: 6 servings

- 4 **boneless skinless chicken breast halves (6 oz. each)**
- 3 **celery ribs, chopped**
- 2 **cups Buffalo wing sauce**
- ½ **cup chicken stock**
- 2 **Tbsp. butter**
- 4 **tsp. ranch salad dressing mix**
- 6 **hoagie buns, toasted**
  Optional: Blue cheese or ranch salad dressing, and celery ribs

In a 3- or 4-qt. slow cooker, combine the first 6 ingredients. Cook, covered, on low until chicken is tender, 3-4 hours. Remove from slow cooker. Cool slightly; shred meat with 2 forks and return to slow cooker. Using tongs, serve on hoagie buns. If desired, top with dressing and serve with celery ribs.
1 sandwich: 398 cal., 12g fat (4g sat. fat), 73mg chol., 2212mg sod., 42g carb. (6g sugars, 2g fiber), 32g pro.

CAROLINA-STYLE VINEGAR BBQ CHICKEN

I live in Georgia, but I appreciate the tangy, sweet and slightly spicy taste of Carolina vinegar chicken. I make my version in the slow cooker. After the tempting aroma fills the house, your family is sure to be at the dinner table on time!
—Ramona Parris, Canton, GA

- -

Prep: 10 min. • **Cook:** 4 hours
Makes: 6 servings

- 2   **cups water**
- 1   **cup white vinegar**
- ¼   **cup sugar**
- 1   **Tbsp. reduced-sodium chicken base**
- 1   **tsp. crushed red pepper flakes**
- ¾   **tsp. salt**
- 1½   **lbs. boneless skinless chicken breasts**
- 6   **whole wheat hamburger buns, split, optional**

1. In a bowl, mix the first 6 ingredients. Place the chicken in a 3-qt. slow cooker; add vinegar mixture. Cook, covered, on low 4-5 hours or until chicken is tender.
2. Remove the chicken; cool slightly. Reserve 1 cup cooking juices; discard remaining juices. Shred chicken with 2 forks. Return meat and reserved cooking juices to slow cooker; heat through. If desired, serve chicken mixture on buns.

½ cup: 134 cal., 3g fat (1g sat. fat), 63mg chol., 228mg sod., 3g carb. (3g sugars, 0 fiber), 23g pro. **Diabetic exchanges:** 3 lean meat.

CHUNKY CREAMY
CHICKEN SOUP

CHUNKY CREAMY CHICKEN SOUP

I am a stay-at-home mom who relies on my slow cooker for fast, nutritious meals with minimal prep time and cleanup. I knew this recipe was a hit when I didn't have any leftovers and my husband asked me to make it again.
—Nancy Clow, Mallorytown, ON

Prep: 15 min. • **Cook:** 4½ hours
Makes: 7 servings

- 1½ lbs. boneless skinless chicken breasts, cut into 2-in. strips
- 2 tsp. canola oil
- ⅔ cup finely chopped onion
- 2 medium carrots, chopped
- 2 celery ribs, chopped
- 1 cup frozen corn
- 2 cans (10¾ oz. each) condensed cream of potato soup, undiluted
- 1½ cups chicken broth
- 1 tsp. dill weed
- 1 cup frozen peas
- ½ cup half-and-half cream

1. In a large skillet over medium-high heat, brown chicken in oil. Transfer to a 5-qt. slow cooker; add the onion, carrots, celery and corn.
2. In a large bowl, whisk soup, broth and dill until blended; stir into slow cooker. Cover and cook on low until chicken and vegetables are tender, about 4 hours.
3. Stir in the peas and cream. Cover and cook until heated through, about 30 minutes longer.
1 cup: 229 cal., 7g fat (3g sat. fat), 66mg chol., 629mg sod., 17g carb. (5g sugars, 3g fiber), 24g pro.

LOADED POTATO-LEEK SOUP

While I was growing up, my mother made potato and onion soup because it was affordable and fast. I've trimmed the calories, and it's still a comforting family favorite.
—Courtney Stultz, Weir, KS

Prep: 20 min. • **Cook:** 6 hours
Makes: 6 servings (about 1½ qt.)

- 1 medium leek
- 1½ lbs. potatoes (about 2 large), peeled and finely chopped
- 2 cups fresh cauliflowerets
- ¾ tsp. rubbed sage
- ½ tsp. salt
- ¼ tsp. pepper
- 4 cups reduced-sodium chicken or vegetable broth
- 2 tsp. olive oil
- 2 tsp. lemon juice
  Sour cream, optional

1. Finely chop white portion of leek. Cut leek greens into thin strips; reserve for topping. In a 3- or 4-qt. slow cooker, combine the potatoes, cauliflowerets, seasonings, broth and chopped leek. Cook, covered, on low 6-8 hours or until the vegetables are tender.
2. In a small skillet, heat oil over medium-high heat. Add reserved leek greens; cook 3-5 minutes. Puree soup using an immersion blender. Or cool soup slightly and puree in batches in a blender. Stir in lemon juice. Top with leek greens and, if desired, sour cream.
1 cup: 108 cal., 2g fat (0 sat. fat), 0 chol., 593mg sod., 20g carb. (3g sugars, 2g fiber), 4g pro. **Diabetic exchanges:** 1 starch, ½ fat.

SHREDDED
CHICKEN GYROS

ITALIAN BEEF VEGETABLE SOUP

This hearty beef soup features a ton of fresh vegetables, making it the perfect dish to use fresh garden produce. It's also fantastic during cooler weather. Consider serving this Italian soup with some breadsticks, rolls or flaky biscuits.
—Courtney Stultz, Weir, KS

Prep: 20 min. • **Cook:** 5 hours
Makes: 6 servings (1½ qt.)

½   lb. lean ground beef (90% lean)
¼   cup chopped onion
2   cups chopped cabbage
2   medium carrots, chopped
1   cup fresh Brussels sprouts, quartered
1   cup chopped fresh kale
1   celery rib, chopped
1   Tbsp. minced fresh parsley
½   tsp. pepper
½   tsp. dried basil
¼   tsp. salt
3   cups beef stock
1   can (14½ oz.) Italian diced tomatoes, undrained

1. In a large skillet, cook beef with onion over medium-high heat until browned, about 4-5 minutes, breaking meat into crumbles. Transfer to a 3- or 4-qt. slow cooker. Stir in remaining ingredients.
2. Cook, covered, on low 5-6 hours or until carrots are tender.
Freeze option: Freeze cooled soup in freezer containers. To use, partially thaw in refrigerator overnight. Heat through in a saucepan, stirring occasionally.
1 cup: 127 cal., 3g fat (1g sat. fat), 24mg chol., 617mg sod., 14g carb. (9g sugars, 3g fiber), 11g pro. **Diabetic exchanges:** 1 starch, 1 lean meat.

SHREDDED CHICKEN GYROS

Our family always has such a wonderful time at the annual Salt Lake City Greek Festival. One of my favorite parts is all the awesome food. This meal is a good way to mix up our menu, and my kids are big fans.
—Camille Beckstrand, Layton, UT

Prep: 20 min. • **Cook:** 3 hours
Makes: 8 servings

2   medium onions, chopped
6   garlic cloves, minced
1   tsp. lemon-pepper seasoning
1   tsp. dried oregano
½   tsp. ground allspice
½   cup water
½   cup lemon juice
¼   cup red wine vinegar
2   Tbsp. olive oil
2   lbs. boneless skinless chicken breasts
8   whole pita breads
    Optional toppings: Tzatziki sauce, torn romaine, and sliced tomato, cucumber and onion

1. In a 3-qt. slow cooker, combine the first 9 ingredients; add chicken. Cook, covered, on low 3-4 hours or until chicken is tender (a thermometer should read at least 165°).
2. Remove chicken from slow cooker. Shred with 2 forks; return to slow cooker. Using tongs, place chicken mixture on pita breads. If desired, serve with toppings.
1 gyro: 337 cal., 7g fat (1g sat. fat), 63mg chol., 418mg sod., 38g carb. (2g sugars, 2g fiber), 29g pro. **Diabetic exchanges:** 3 lean meat, 2½ starch, ½ fat.

ITALIAN BEEF
VEGETABLE SOUP

PINEAPPLE-DIJON HAM SANDWICHES

My kids adore ham; the challenge is finding new ways to prepare it. I like to slow-cook it with pineapple and Dijon. The cooking juices make an amazing dipping sauce.
—Camille Beckstrand, Layton, UT

- -

Prep: 20 min. • **Cook:** 3 hours
Makes: 10 servings

- 2 lbs. fully cooked ham, cut into ½-in. cubes
- 1 can (20 oz.) crushed pineapple, undrained
- 1 medium green pepper, finely chopped
- ¾ cup packed brown sugar
- ¼ cup finely chopped onion
- ¼ cup Dijon mustard
- 1 Tbsp. dried minced onion
- 10 hamburger buns, split
- 10 slices Swiss cheese
  Additional Dijon mustard, optional

1. In a greased 4-qt. slow cooker, combine the first 7 ingredients. Cook, covered, on low 3-4 hours or until heated through.
2. Preheat broiler. Place bun bottoms and tops on baking sheets, cut sides up. Using a slotted spoon, place ham mixture on bottoms; top with cheese. Broil 3-4 in. from heat 1-2 minutes or until cheese is melted and tops are toasted. Replace tops. If desired, serve with additional mustard.
1 sandwich: 396 cal., 8g fat (3g sat. fat), 67mg chol., 1283mg sod., 52g carb. (30g sugars, 2g fiber), 28g pro.

LOADED BROCCOLI-CHEESE POTATO CHOWDER

LOADED BROCCOLI-CHEESE POTATO CHOWDER

For anyone who loves baked potatoes or broccoli-cheese soup, this is the best of both worlds. If you have bacon lovers, offer crumbled cooked bacon as a topping. Then everyone is happy, carnivore or not!
—Vivi Taylor, Middleburg, FL

- -

Prep: 15 min. • **Cook:** 6 hours 10 min.
Makes: 8 servings (about 2 qt.)

- 1 pkg. (20 oz.) refrigerated O'Brien hash brown potatoes
- 1 garlic clove, minced
- 2 cups reduced-fat sour cream
- ¼ cup all-purpose flour
- ½ tsp. pepper
- ⅛ tsp. ground nutmeg
- 3 cups vegetable stock
- 1 pkg. (12 oz.) frozen broccoli florets, thawed
- 4 cups shredded cheddar cheese, divided
- ½ cup finely chopped green onions

1. Combine the hash browns and garlic in a 5- or 6-qt. slow cooker. In a large bowl, whisk the sour cream, flour, pepper and nutmeg until smooth; stir in stock. Pour into slow cooker; stir to combine. Cook, covered, on low until hash browns are tender, 6-8 hours.
2. Add the broccoli and 3 cups cheese; cover and cook until cheese is melted, about 10 minutes longer. Serve with green onions and remaining cheese.
1 cup: 386 cal., 23g fat (13g sat. fat), 62mg chol., 921mg sod., 26g carb. (6g sugars, 2g fiber), 20g pro.

SWEET & SPICY PINEAPPLE CHICKEN SANDWICHES

My kids often ask for chicken sloppy joes, and this version has a bonus of sweet pineapple. It is a perfect recipe to double for a potluck. Try topping the sandwiches with smoked Gouda.
—Nancy Heishman, Las Vegas, NV

Prep: 15 min. • **Cook:** 2¾ hours
Makes: 8 servings

- 2½ lbs. boneless skinless chicken breasts
- 1 bottle (18 oz.) sweet and spicy barbecue sauce, divided
- 2 Tbsp. honey mustard
- 1 can (8 oz.) unsweetened crushed pineapple, undrained
- 8 hamburger buns, split and toasted
  Optional: Bibb lettuce leaves and thinly sliced red onion

1. Place chicken breasts in a 4-qt. slow cooker. Combine ¼ cup barbecue sauce and mustard; pour over chicken. Cover and cook on low 2½-3 hours or until chicken is tender.
2. Remove chicken; discard liquid. Shred chicken with 2 forks; return to slow cooker. Add crushed pineapple and remaining barbecue sauce; cover and cook on high for 15 minutes.
3. Serve on toasted buns with lettuce and onion if desired.

Freeze option: Place shredded chicken in freezer containers. Cool and freeze. To use, partially thaw in refrigerator overnight. Heat through in a covered saucepan, stirring occasionally; add broth if necessary.

1 sandwich: 415 cal., 6g fat (1g sat. fat), 78mg chol., 973mg sod., 56g carb. (30g sugars, 2g fiber), 34g pro.

SWEET & SPICY PINEAPPLE
CHICKEN SANDWICHES

SLOW-COOKED SPLIT PEA SOUP

I've been making this soup for years. After any holiday meal where ham is served, the hostess sends me home with the ham bone and a bag of peas so I can cook up this family favorite.
—Susan Simons, Eatonville, WA

Prep: 15 min. • **Cook:** 7 hours
Makes: 8 servings (about 3 qt.)

- 1 meaty ham bone or 2 lbs. smoked ham hocks
- 1 pkg. (16 oz.) dried green split peas
- 1 lb. potatoes, peeled and cubed (about 3 cups)
- 1 large onion, chopped
- 2 medium carrots, chopped
- 1 Tbsp. dried celery flakes
- ½ tsp. garlic powder
- ½ tsp. dried thyme
- ½ tsp. dried basil
- ¼ tsp. lemon-pepper seasoning
- ⅛ tsp. dried marjoram
- 1 bay leaf
- 6 cups reduced-sodium chicken broth

1. In a 4- or 5-qt. slow cooker, combine all ingredients. Cook, covered, on low 7-9 hours or until peas are tender.
2. Remove ham bone from soup. When cool enough to handle, remove meat from bone; discard bone. Cut meat into cubes and return to soup or save meat for another use. Remove bay leaf.

Freeze option: Freeze cooled soup in freezer containers. To use, partially thaw in refrigerator overnight. Heat through in a saucepan, stirring occasionally; add a little broth if necessary.

1⅔ cups: 312 cal., 2g fat (1g sat. fat), 21mg chol., 883mg sod., 50g carb. (7g sugars, 16g fiber), 25g pro.

SLOW-COOKER CHEESY BROCCOLI SOUP

Whenever I order soup at a restaurant, I go for the broccoli-cheese option. I finally put my slow cooker to the test and made my own. It took a few tries, but now the soup is exactly how I like it.
—Kristen Hills, Layton, UT

Prep: 15 min. • **Cook:** 3 hours
Makes: 4 servings

- 2 **Tbsp. butter**
- 1 **small onion, finely chopped**
- 2 **cups finely chopped fresh broccoli**
- 3 **cups reduced-sodium chicken broth**
- 1 **can (12 oz.) evaporated milk**
- ½ **tsp. pepper**
- 1 **pkg. (8 oz.) Velveeta, cubed**
- 1½ **cups shredded extra-sharp cheddar cheese**
- 1 **cup shredded Parmesan cheese Additional shredded extra-sharp cheddar cheese**

1. In a small skillet, heat the butter over medium-high heat. Add onion; cook and stir 3-4 minutes or until tender. Transfer to a 3- or 4-qt. slow cooker. Add broccoli, broth, milk and pepper.
2. Cook, covered, on low 3-4 hours or until the broccoli is tender. Stir in Velveeta until melted. Add the next 2 ingredients; stir until melted. Just before serving, stir soup to combine. Top servings with additional shredded cheddar cheese.
1¾ cups: 675 cal., 49g fat (30g sat. fat), 165mg chol., 1964mg sod., 21g carb. (15g sugars, 2g fiber), 39g pro.

TANDOORI CHICKEN PANINI

The tandoori-style spices in this chicken give it a bold flavor that's so hard to resist. It tastes incredible tucked between pieces of naan, then grilled for an Indian-inspired panini.
—Yasmin Arif, Manassas, VA

Prep: 25 min. • **Cook:** 3 hours
Makes: 6 servings

- 1½ **lbs. boneless skinless chicken breasts**
- ¼ **cup reduced-sodium chicken broth**
- 2 **garlic cloves, minced**
- 2 **tsp. minced fresh gingerroot**
- 1 **tsp. paprika**
- ¼ **tsp. salt**
- ¼ to ½ **tsp. cayenne pepper**
- ¼ **tsp. ground turmeric**
- 6 **green onions, chopped**
- 6 **Tbsp. chutney**
- 6 **naan flatbreads**

1. Place the first 8 ingredients in a 3-qt. slow cooker. Cook, covered, on low until chicken is tender, 3-4 hours.
2. Shred chicken with 2 forks. Stir in green onions.
3. Spread chutney over 1 side of each naan. Top chutney side of 3 naan with chicken mixture; top with remaining naan, chutney side down.
4. Cook sandwiches on a panini maker or indoor grill until golden brown, 6-8 minutes. Cut each sandwich in half before serving.
½ sandwich: 351 cal., 6g fat (2g sat. fat), 68mg chol., 830mg sod., 44g carb. (12g sugars, 2g fiber), 27g pro.
Diabetic exchanges: 3 starch, 3 lean meat.

SOPA DE CAMARONES
(SHRIMP SOUP)

SOPA DE CAMARONES (SHRIMP SOUP)

My daughter and I came up with this soup recipe when she was younger, and it's been a favorite with family and friends ever since. It may even be tastier as leftovers the next day!
—Patti Fair, Valdosta, GA

- -

Prep: 20 min. • **Cook:** 2 hours
Makes: 4 servings

- 3 **Tbsp. butter**
- 3 **celery ribs, sliced**
- 1 **small onion, chopped**
- ⅓ **cup lemon juice**
- 6 **garlic cloves, minced**
- 1 **to 2 Tbsp. sugar**
- 2 **cans (14½ oz. each) Mexican petite diced tomatoes, undrained**
- 1 **lb. peeled and deveined cooked shrimp (61-70 per lb.)**
- 1 **can (6 oz.) tomato paste**
  Hot cooked rice
  Optional: Lime wedges and chopped cilantro

1. In a large skillet, heat butter over medium heat. Add celery and onion; cook and stir until crisp-tender, 3-4 minutes. Add lemon juice, garlic and sugar; cook 1 minute longer.
2. Transfer to a 3- or 4-qt. slow cooker. Add undrained tomatoes, shrimp and tomato paste. Cook, covered, on low until heated through, 2-3 hours. Serve with rice and, if desired, lime wedges and chopped cilantro.

1½ cups: 313 cal., 11g fat (6g sat. fat), 195mg chol., 712mg sod., 26g carb. (16g sugars, 4g fiber), 28g pro.

SLOW-COOKER SECRETS
For a thicker bean soup with a particularly velvety texture, try mashing half the beans first before adding them all to the slow cooker.

PESTO BEAN SOUP

PESTO BEAN SOUP

This is one of my favorite vegetarian recipes. I like to make large batches and freeze it. Homemade pesto is tasty, but you can use store-bought to make the recipe really simple. Serve the soup with garlic toast and a green salad.
—Liz Bellville, Tonasket, WA

Prep: 10 min. • **Cook:** 4 hours
Makes: 8 servings (2½ qt.)

- 1 **carton (32 oz.) reduced-sodium vegetable broth**
- 1 **large white onion, chopped**
- 4 **garlic cloves, minced**
- 2½ **cups sliced baby portobello mushrooms**
- 3 **cans (15 to 15½ oz. each) cannellini beans, rinsed and drained**
- ¾ **cup prepared pesto, divided**
- ¼ **cup grated Parmigiano-Reggiano cheese**
  Optional: Additional pesto and cheese

In a 4-qt. slow cooker, combine the first 5 ingredients. Stir in ½ cup pesto. Cook, covered, on low until vegetables are tender, 4-6 hours. Before serving, stir in the remaining pesto and the cheese. If desired, serve with additional pesto and cheese.

1¼ cups: 244 cal., 9g fat (2g sat. fat), 2mg chol., 586mg sod., 30g carb. (3g sugars, 8g fiber), 9g pro. **Diabetic exchanges:** 2 starch, 1½ fat, 1 lean meat.

SESAME PULLED PORK
SANDWICHES

SESAME PULLED PORK SANDWICHES

I wanted to build a better-tasting pork sandwich, and this Asian-style filling was a huge hit with my husband and coworkers. Bring on the wasabi mayo.
—Jennifer Berry, Lexington, OH

Prep: 15 min. • **Cook:** 4½ hours
Makes: 12 servings

- 3 **pork tenderloins (1 lb. each)**
- 1¾ **cups reduced-fat sesame ginger salad dressing, divided**
- ¼ **cup packed brown sugar**

SLAW
- 1 **pkg. (14 oz.) coleslaw mix**
- 4 **green onions, chopped**
- ¼ **cup minced fresh cilantro**
- 2 **Tbsp. reduced-fat sesame ginger salad dressing**
- 2 **tsp. sesame oil**
- 1 **tsp. sugar**
- 1 **tsp. reduced-sodium soy sauce**

TO SERVE
- 12 **multigrain hamburger buns, split**
  Wasabi mayonnaise, optional

1. Place the tenderloins in a 5-qt. slow cooker coated with cooking spray; pour ¾ cup salad dressing over pork, turning to coat. Cook, covered, on low until meat is tender, 4-5 hours.
2. Remove pork; cool slightly. Shred meat into bite-sized pieces; return to slow cooker. Stir in brown sugar and the remaining salad dressing. Cook, covered, until heated through, 30-45 minutes longer.
3. Combine slaw ingredients. Serve pork on buns with slaw and, if desired, wasabi mayonnaise.

1 sandwich: 324 cal., 9g fat (2g sat. fat), 64mg chol., 756mg sod., 33g carb. (14g sugars, 3g fiber), 27g pro. **Diabetic exchanges:** 3 lean meat, 2 starch.

HEARTY MANHATTAN CLAM CHOWDER

This veggie-packed clam chowder is savory and satisfying. Butter up some crusty bread and you'll have yourself a complete meal.
—Carol Bullick, Royersford, PA

- -

Prep: 20 min. • **Cook:** 7 hours
Makes: 6 servings (about 2¼ qt.)

- 1½ **lbs. potatoes (about 3 medium), peeled and cut into ¾-in. cubes**
- 1 **large onion, chopped**
- 2 **medium carrots, shredded (about ¾ cup)**
- 3 **celery ribs, sliced**
- 4 **cans (6½ oz. each) chopped clams, undrained**
- 5 **bacon strips, cooked and crumbled**
- 1 **Tbsp. dried parsley flakes**
- 1 **bay leaf**
- 1½ **tsp. dried thyme**
- ¼ **tsp. coarsely ground pepper**
- 1 **can (28 oz.) diced tomatoes, undrained**

Place all ingredients in a 4- or 5-qt. slow cooker. Cook, covered, on low until vegetables are tender, 7-9 hours. Remove bay leaf before serving.
1½ cups: 203 cal., 4g fat (1g sat. fat), 50mg chol., 995mg sod., 29g carb. (8g sugars, 5g fiber), 15g pro.

SLOW-COOKED LOADED POTATO SOUP

I like to put twists on my grandmother's recipes, which is what I did with this one. I look forward to passing my own tasty comfort food recipes to my kids.
—Jamie Chase, Rising Sun, IN

- -

Prep: 30 min. • **Cook:** 8¼ hours
Makes: 12 servings (4 qt.)

- 5 **lbs. potatoes, peeled and cubed (about 10 cups)**
- 1 **medium onion, finely chopped**
- 5 **cans (14½ oz. each) chicken broth**
- 1 **garlic clove, minced**
- 1½ **tsp. salt**
- ¼ **tsp. pepper**
- 2 **pkg. (8 oz. each) cream cheese, softened and cubed**
- 1 **cup half-and-half cream**
- ¼ **cup butter, cubed**

TOPPINGS
- 1 **lb. bacon strips, cooked and crumbled**
- ¾ **cup shredded sharp cheddar cheese**
- ¼ **cup minced chives**

1. Place potatoes and onion in a 6-qt. slow cooker; add broth, garlic, salt and pepper. Cook, covered, on low 8-10 hours or until potatoes are tender.
2. Mash potatoes to desired consistency. Stir in cream cheese, cream and butter. Cook, covered, 15 minutes longer or until heated through.
3. Just before serving, whisk soup to combine. Top servings with bacon, cheese and chives.
1⅓ cups: 447 cal., 27g fat (14g sat. fat), 86mg chol., 1512mg sod., 37g carb. (5g sugars, 4g fiber), 14g pro.

SLOW-COOKED LOADED POTATO SOUP

SLOW-COOKED CHICKEN CAESAR WRAPS

I first made this recipe for our daughter who loves Caesar salads, then later for our extended family while on vacation. It's such an easy meal—perfect for times when you'd rather be outside than inside cooking all day.
—Christine Hadden, Whitman, MA

- -

Prep: 10 min. • **Cook:** 3 hours
Makes: 6 servings

1½	lbs. boneless skinless chicken breast halves
2	cups chicken broth
¾	cup creamy Caesar salad dressing
½	cup shredded Parmesan cheese
¼	cup minced fresh parsley
½	tsp. pepper
6	flour tortillas (8 in.)
2	cups shredded lettuce
	Optional: Salad croutons, cooked crumbled bacon and additional shredded Parmesan cheese

1. Place chicken and broth in a 1½- or 3-qt. slow cooker. Cook, covered, on low 3-4 hours or until a thermometer inserted in chicken reads 165°. Remove chicken and discard cooking juices. Shred chicken with 2 forks; return to slow cooker.

2. Stir in dressing, Parmesan, parsley and pepper; heat through. Serve in tortillas with lettuce and, if desired, salad croutons, crumbled bacon and additional shredded Parmesan cheese.

1 wrap: 472 cal., 25g fat (5g sat. fat), 79mg chol., 795mg sod., 29g carb. (1g sugars, 2g fiber), 31g pro.

SLOW-COOKED CHICKEN CAESAR WRAPS

READER RAVE...
"This is so simple but so tasty. I added bacon, but that's the only thing. I'll definitely make this again. Even my picky eaters enjoyed it."
—STEPHANIE647, TASTEOFHOME.COM

ENTREES

SLOPPY JOE TATER TOT CASSEROLE

SLOPPY JOE TATER TOT CASSEROLE

This simple casserole is an easy dinner for both you and the kids. Serve with carrot and celery sticks for a fuss-free feast. You can also stir in some spicy brown mustard if the adults want a little more zing.
—Laura Wilhelm,
West Hollywood, CA

- -

Prep: 20 min. • **Cook:** 4 hours + standing
Makes: 10 servings

- 1 bag (32 oz.) frozen Tater Tots, divided
- 2 lbs. ground beef or turkey
- 1 can (15 oz.) tomato sauce
- 1 bottle (8 oz.) sweet chili sauce
- 2 Tbsp. packed brown sugar
- 1 Tbsp. Worcestershire sauce
- 1 Tbsp. dried minced garlic
- 1 Tbsp. dried minced onion
- ½ tsp. salt
- ½ tsp. pepper
- 1¼ cups shredded Colby-Monterey Jack cheese
- ¼ tsp. paprika

1. Place half the Tater Tots in bottom of a 5-qt. slow cooker.
2. In a large skillet, cook beef over medium-high heat until no longer pink, 5-6 minutes, breaking into crumbles. Drain. Stir in the next 8 ingredients; reduce heat and simmer 2-3 minutes. Place beef mixture in slow cooker; top with remaining Tater Tots. Cook, covered, on low 4 hours.
3. Top with the cheese. Sprinkle with the paprika. Let stand, uncovered, about 15 minutes before serving.
1 cup: 466 cal., 24g fat (9g sat. fat), 69mg chol., 1332mg sod., 41g carb. (18g sugars, 4g fiber), 22g pro.

SLOW-ROASTED LEMON DILL CHICKEN

SLOW-ROASTED LEMON DILL CHICKEN

The lemon and dill in this recipe give this spring chicken a bright, fresh taste. Pair the entree with a side of noodles or a mixed green salad.
—Lori Lockrey, Pickering, ON

- -

Prep: 20 min. • **Cook:** 4 hours + standing
Makes: 6 servings

- 2 medium onions, coarsely chopped
- 2 Tbsp. butter, softened
- ¼ tsp. grated lemon zest
- 1 broiler/fryer chicken (4 to 5 lbs.)
- ¼ cup chicken stock
- 4 sprigs fresh parsley
- 4 fresh dill sprigs
- 3 Tbsp. lemon juice
- 1 tsp. salt
- 1 tsp. paprika
- ½ tsp. dried thyme
- ¼ tsp. pepper

1. Place onions on bottom of a 6-qt. slow cooker. In a small bowl, mix butter and lemon zest.
2. Tuck wings under chicken; tie drumsticks together. With fingers, carefully loosen skin from chicken breast; rub butter mixture under the skin. Secure skin to underside of breast with toothpicks. Place chicken over onions, breast side up. Add stock, parsley and dill.
3. Drizzle lemon juice over chicken; sprinkle with seasonings. Cook, covered, on low setting 4-5 hours (a thermometer inserted in thigh should read at least 170°).
4. Remove chicken from slow cooker; tent with foil. Let stand 15 minutes before carving.
5 oz. cooked chicken: 429 cal., 26g fat (9g sat. fat), 149mg chol., 565mg sod., 1g carb. (0 sugars, 0 fiber), 44g pro.

SLOW-COOKED BEEF BURRITOS WITH GREEN CHILES

I created this recipe years ago, and it has become such a favorite that the wonderful aroma as it cooks makes my family instantly happy. It is hearty, flavorful and easy to prepare, and it uses the long, slow cooking method that truly defines comfort food.
—Sally Pahler, Palisade, CO

- -

Prep: 20 min. • **Cook:** 7 hours
Makes: 14 servings

2   garlic cloves, minced
1   tsp. salt
2   tsp. ground cumin
1   tsp. cayenne pepper
1   boneless beef
    chuck roast (4 lbs.)
1   can (28 oz.) diced tomatoes
4   cans (7 oz. each) whole
    green chiles, drained and
    coarsely chopped
1   large onion, diced
14 whole wheat tortillas
    (8 in.), warmed
    Optional toppings: Shredded
    cheddar cheese, salsa, sour
    cream, sliced ripe olives

1. Combine garlic, salt, cumin and cayenne; rub over roast. Place in a 5- or 6-qt. slow cooker. Add tomatoes, chiles and onion. Cook, covered, on low 7-8 hours or until meat is tender.
2. Remove roast from slow cooker; shred with 2 forks. Remove vegetables with a slotted spoon; discard the cooking juices. Return beef and vegetables to slow cooker and heat through. Serve in tortillas, with toppings as desired.

1 burrito: 355 cal., 13g fat (5g sat. fat), 84mg chol., 499mg sod., 28g carb. (4g sugars, 4g fiber), 30g pro. **Diabetic exchanges:** 4 lean meat, 2 starch.

SLOW-COOKER SECRETS
Not only does the coarse texture of hand-chopped chiles add flair, but the larger pieces also hold up well in the slow cooker. If you're tight on time, use canned diced green chiles instead.

SLOW-COOKED BEEF BURRITOS WITH GREEN CHILES

CRAZY DELICIOUS BABY BACK RIBS

My husband often craves baby back ribs, so we cook them multiple ways. This low and slow method with a tangy sauce is the best we've found.
—Jan Whitworth, Roebuck, SC

Prep: 15 min. • **Cook:** 5¼ hours
Makes: 8 servings

- 2 **Tbsp. smoked paprika**
- 2 **tsp. chili powder**
- 2 **tsp. garlic salt**
- 1 **tsp. onion powder**
- 1 **tsp. pepper**
- ½ **tsp. cayenne pepper**
- 4 **lbs. pork baby back ribs**

SAUCE

- ½ **cup Worcestershire sauce**
- ½ **cup mayonnaise**
- ½ **cup yellow mustard**
- ¼ **cup reduced-sodium soy sauce**
- 3 **Tbsp. hot pepper sauce**

1. In a small bowl, combine the first 6 ingredients. Cut ribs into serving-size pieces; rub with seasoning mixture. Place ribs in a 6-qt. slow cooker. Cook, covered, on low until meat is tender, 5-6 hours.

2. Preheat oven to 375°. In a small bowl, whisk the sauce ingredients. Transfer ribs to a foil-lined 15x10x1-in. baking pan; brush with some of the sauce. Bake until browned, 15-20 minutes, turning once and brushing occasionally with sauce. Serve with remaining sauce.

1 serving: 420 cal., 33g fat (9g sat. fat), 86mg chol., 1082mg sod., 6g carb. (2g sugars, 2g fiber), 24g pro.

ITALIAN SHRIMP & PASTA

This dish will remind you a bit of classic shrimp Creole, but it has a surprise Italian twist.
—Karen Edwards, Sanford, ME

Prep: 20 min. • **Cook:** 7½ hours
Makes: 6 servings

- 1   lb. boneless skinless chicken thighs, cut into 2x1-in. strips
- 2   Tbsp. canola oil
- 1   can (28 oz.) crushed tomatoes
- 2   celery ribs, chopped
- 1   medium green pepper, cut into 1-in. pieces
- 1   medium onion, coarsely chopped
- 2   garlic cloves, minced
- 1   Tbsp. sugar
- ½   tsp. salt
- ½   tsp. Italian seasoning
- ⅛ to ¼ tsp. cayenne pepper
- 1   bay leaf
- 1   cup uncooked orzo or other small pasta
- 1   lb. peeled and deveined cooked shrimp (31-40 per lb.)

1. In a large skillet, brown chicken in oil; transfer to a 3-qt. slow cooker. Stir in tomatoes, celery, pepper, onion, garlic, sugar and seasonings. Cook, covered, on low 7-8 hours or until the chicken is just tender.
2. Discard bay leaf. Stir in pasta; cook, covered, on high until pasta is tender, about 15 minutes. Stir in shrimp; cook, covered, until heated through, about 5 minutes longer.

1½ cups: 418 cal., 12g fat (2g sat. fat), 165mg chol., 611mg sod., 40g carb. (10g sugars, 4g fiber), 36g pro. **Diabetic exchanges:** 5 lean meat, 2½ starch, 1 fat.

CANTONESE PORK

This Cantonese-style recipe is our favorite way to prepare pork loin. We love it with fried rice and veggies, but it's also delicious sliced and served cold as an appetizer. Try dipping it in soy sauce, hot mustard, plum sauce or sesame seeds.
—Carla Mendres, Winnipeg, MB

Prep: 10 min. + marinating
Cook: 3 hours • **Makes:** 10 servings

- 3   Tbsp. honey
- 2   Tbsp. soy sauce
- 1   Tbsp. sesame oil
- 1   Tbsp. Chinese cooking wine or mirin (sweet rice wine)
- 4   garlic cloves, crushed
- 1   tsp. minced fresh gingerroot
- 1   tsp. hoisin sauce
- 1   tsp. oyster sauce
- 1   tsp. Chinese five-spice powder
- 1   tsp. salt
- 1   tsp. red food coloring, optional
- 1   boneless pork loin roast (about 4 lbs.)

1. In a large shallow bowl, combine the first 10 ingredients and, if desired, red food coloring. Cut pork roast lengthwise in half. Add pork to bowl; turn to coat. Cover and refrigerate at least 24 hours.
2. Transfer the pork and marinade to a 5-qt. slow cooker. Cook, covered, on low 3-4 hours or until a thermometer inserted in roast reads 145° and meat is tender. Let roast stand for 10-15 minutes before slicing.

5 oz. cooked pork: 262 cal., 10g fat (3g sat. fat), 91mg chol., 498mg sod., 6g carb. (5g sugars, 0 fiber), 36g pro. **Diabetic exchanges:** 5 lean meat.

CANTONESE PORK

CHICKEN IN COCONUT
PEANUT SAUCE

CHICKEN IN COCONUT PEANUT SAUCE

My youngest son has been out of the country for several years teaching English. When he returned to the United States, I made this home-cooked meal for him that combined Asian and American cuisine. He loved it!
—Sheila Joan Suhan, Scottdale, PA

Prep: 15 min. • **Cook:** 5 hours
Makes: 6 servings

- ½ cup coconut milk
- ½ cup creamy peanut butter
- 1 can (28 oz.) crushed tomatoes
- 1 medium onion, finely chopped
- 2 to 3 jalapeno peppers, seeded and finely chopped
- 2 Tbsp. brown sugar
- 3 garlic cloves, minced
- 2 tsp. ground cumin
- 1 tsp. salt
- 1 tsp. pepper
- 12 boneless skinless chicken thighs (about 3 lbs.)
  Minced fresh cilantro
  Hot cooked rice, optional

In a 5-qt. slow cooker, whisk coconut milk and peanut butter until smooth. Stir in tomatoes, onion, peppers, brown sugar, garlic and seasonings. Add the chicken; cook, covered, on low 5-6 hours or until chicken is tender. Stir before serving. Sprinkle with cilantro; if desired, serve with rice.
Note: Wear disposable gloves when cutting hot peppers; the oils can burn skin. Avoid touching your face.
2 chicken thighs with 1 cup sauce: 559 cal., 31g fat (10g sat. fat), 151mg chol., 865mg sod., 22g carb. (14g sugars, 4g fiber), 50g pro.

MEATBALL TORTELLINI

I combined some favorite staples from our freezer and pantry to come up with an easy dish. It uses just a few ingredients and requires little preparation.
—Tracie Bergeron, Chauvin, LA

Prep: 10 min. • **Cook:** 3 hours
Makes: 6 servings

- 1 pkg. frozen fully cooked Italian meatballs (12 oz.), thawed
- 2 cups uncooked dried cheese tortellini
- 2 cans (10¾ oz. each) condensed cream of mushroom soup, undiluted
- 2¼ cups water
- 1 tsp. Creole seasoning
- 1 pkg. (16 oz.) frozen California-blend vegetables, thawed

1. In a 3-qt. slow cooker, combine meatballs and tortellini. In a large bowl, whisk the soup, water and Creole seasoning. Pour over meatball mixture; stir well.
2. Cook, covered, on low until tortellini are tender, 3-4 hours. Add vegetables during last half-hour of cooking.
Note: If you don't have Creole seasoning in your cupboard, you can make your own using ¼ tsp. each salt, garlic powder and paprika, and a pinch each of dried thyme, ground cumin and cayenne pepper.
1 cup: 408 cal., 23g fat (10g sat. fat), 55mg chol., 1592mg sod., 35g carb. (3g sugars, 6g fiber), 16g pro.

FRUITY PORK ROAST

I like using the slow cooker because it gives me time for other preparations and frees up the oven. Plus, it usually doesn't matter if you serve the food later than planned. This pork roast, which I created by adapting other recipes, gets a special flavor from the fruit.

—Mary Jeppesen-Davis, St. Cloud, MN

Prep: 25 min. • **Cook:** 5 hours + standing
Makes: 8 servings

- ½   **medium lemon, sliced**
- ½   **cup dried cranberries**
- ⅓   **cup golden raisins**
- ⅓   **cup unsweetened apple juice**
- 3   **Tbsp. sherry or additional unsweetened apple juice**
- 1   **tsp. minced garlic**
- ½   **tsp. ground mustard**
- 1   **boneless pork loin roast (3 lbs.)**
- ½   **tsp. salt**
- ¼   **tsp. pepper**
- ⅛   **to ¼ tsp. ground ginger**
- 1   **medium apple, peeled and sliced**
- ½   **cup packed fresh parsley sprigs**

1. In a small bowl, combine the first 7 ingredients. Cut roast in half; sprinkle with salt, pepper and ginger.
2. Transfer to a 5-qt. slow cooker. Pour fruit mixture over roast. Place apple and parsley around roast. Cover and cook on low until meat is tender, 5-6 hours.
3. Transfer meat to a serving platter. Let stand for 10-15 minutes before slicing.

5 oz. cooked pork with ¼ cup fruit mixture: 272 cal., 8g fat (3g sat. fat), 85mg chol., 200mg sod., 15g carb. (12g sugars, 1g fiber), 33g pro. **Diabetic exchanges:** 5 lean meat, 1 fruit.

SLOW-COOKER HONEY TERIYAKI CHICKEN

SLOW-COOKER HONEY TERIYAKI CHICKEN

This recipe is a snap to whip up on a work day, and tastes just like Chinese takeout! My kids love it, and they don't even know it's healthy.
—Rachel Ruiz, Fort Walton Beach, FL

- -

Prep: 20 min. • **Cook:** 3¾ hours
Makes: 8 servings

- 2 **lbs. boneless skinless chicken thighs**
- 1 **medium onion, thinly sliced**
- 4 **garlic cloves, minced**
- 1 **Tbsp. minced fresh gingerroot**
- 1 **cup chicken broth**
- ¼ **cup soy sauce**
- ¼ **cup honey**
- ½ **to 1 tsp. crushed red pepper flakes**
- ¼ **tsp. pepper**
- 3 **Tbsp. cornstarch**
- 3 **Tbsp. cold water**
  Hot cooked rice
  Minced fresh cilantro and sesame seeds, optional

1. Place chicken in a 3- or 4-qt. slow cooker. Top with onion, garlic and ginger. Combine broth, soy sauce, honey, pepper flakes and pepper; pour over chicken. Cook, covered, on low until chicken is no longer pink, 3½-4 hours.
2. In a small bowl, mix cornstarch and water until smooth; gradually stir into slow cooker. Cook, covered, on high until sauce is thickened, 15-30 minutes. When chicken is cool enough to handle, shred chicken with 2 forks; return to slow cooker. Serve with rice. Garnish with cilantro and sesame seeds as desired.
⅔ cup: 223 cal., 8g fat (2g sat. fat), 76mg chol., 647mg sod., 14g carb. (9g sugars, 0 fiber), 22g pro. **Diabetic exchanges:** 3 lean meat, 1 starch.

PEPPERY CHICKEN WITH POTATOES

We like this recipe because the chicken cooks while we're in church on Sundays and is ready for us when we get home.
—Lori Draves, Highland, WI

Prep: 20 min. • **Cook:** 5 hours + standing
Makes: 4 servings

- 1   **lb. red potatoes (about 6 medium), cut into wedges**
- 1   **large onion, chopped**
- 2   **tsp. salt**
- 1   **tsp. paprika**
- ½   **tsp. onion powder**
- ½   **tsp. garlic powder**
- ½   **tsp. dried thyme**
- ½   **tsp. white pepper**
- ½   **tsp. cayenne pepper**
- ¼   **tsp. pepper**
- 1   **broiler/fryer chicken (3½ to 4 lbs.)**

1. Place potatoes and onion in a 6-qt. slow cooker. In a small bowl, mix seasonings. Tuck wings under chicken; tie drumsticks together. Rub seasoning mixture over outside and inside of chicken. Place chicken over vegetables.
2. Cook, covered, on low 5-6 hours or until a thermometer inserted in thickest part of thigh reads 170°-175°. Remove chicken from slow cooker; tent with foil. Let stand 15 minutes before carving.
3. Transfer vegetables to a platter; keep warm. If desired, skim fat and thicken cooking juices for gravy. Serve with the chicken.

8 oz. cooked chicken with ¾ cup potato mixture: 616 cal., 30g fat (8g sat. fat), 183mg chol., 1346mg sod., 23g carb. (3g sugars, 3g fiber), 61g pro.

JALAPENO MAC & CHEESE

JALAPENO MAC & CHEESE

Many years ago after I had knee surgery, a friend brought me a big casserole of mac and cheese along with the recipe. I have fiddled with the recipe over the years, most recently adding jalapenos at the request of my son. What an awesome spicy twist!
—Teresa Gustafson, Elkton, MD

Prep: 25 min. • **Cook:** 3 hours
Makes: 15 servings

- 1   **pkg. (16 oz.) uncooked elbow macaroni**
- 6   **Tbsp. butter, divided**
- 4   **jalapeno peppers, seeded and finely chopped**
- 3   **cups shredded cheddar cheese**
- 2   **cups shredded Colby-Monterey Jack cheese**
- 2   **cups whole milk**
- 1   **can (10¾ oz.) condensed cream of onion soup, undiluted**
- 1   **can (10¾ oz.) condensed cheddar cheese soup, undiluted**
- ½   **cup mayonnaise**
- ¼   **tsp. pepper**
- 1   **cup crushed Ritz crackers (about 25 crackers)**

1. Cook macaroni according to package directions for al dente; drain. Transfer to a greased 5-qt. slow cooker.
2. Melt 2 Tbsp. butter in a large skillet over medium-high heat. Add jalapenos; cook and stir until crisp-tender, about 5 minutes. Add to slow cooker. Stir in the cheeses, milk, soups, mayonnaise and pepper.
Cook, covered, on low 3 hours or until cheese is melted and mixture is heated through. Melt remaining 4 Tbsp. butter; stir in crackers. Sprinkle over macaroni mixture.

¾ cup: 428 cal., 27g fat (13g sat. fat), 53mg chol., 654mg sod., 33g carb. (5g sugars, 2g fiber), 14g pro.

FAVORITE BEEF ROAST DINNER

This is our family's favorite slow-cooked beef roast. My two children adore it and always want seconds. I love putting together new flavor combinations in the kitchen.
—Sheryl Padilla, Peyton, CO

Prep: 15 min. • **Cook:** 6 hours
Makes: 8 servings

- 4   medium potatoes, peeled and quartered
- ½   lb. fresh baby carrots
- 1   boneless beef chuck roast (3 to 4 lbs.)
- 4½ tsp. dried minced onion
- 3   garlic cloves, minced
- 1   Tbsp. Worcestershire sauce
- 1   tsp. garlic salt
- 1   tsp. celery seed
- 1   tsp. dried oregano
- 1   tsp. dried thyme
- 1   tsp. pepper

1. Place the potatoes, carrots and roast in a 6-qt. slow cooker. Sprinkle with remaining ingredients. Cover and cook on low for 6-8 hours or until meat and vegetables are tender.
2. Skim fat from cooking juices; serve with roast and vegetables.

5 oz. cooked beef with ¾ cup vegetables and 3 Tbsp. cooking juices: 368 cal., 16g fat (6g sat. fat), 111mg chol., 342mg sod., 19g carb. (3g sugars, 2g fiber), 35g pro.

FAVORITE BEEF ROAST DINNER

SLOW-COOKER TROPICAL PORK CHOPS

Pork and fruit go so nicely together. Cook them slowly, then add fresh herbs right before serving to get this light and bright main dish.
—Roxanne Chan, Albany, CA

Prep: 15 min. • **Cook:** 3 hours
Makes: 4 servings

- 2   jars (23½ oz. each) mixed tropical fruit, drained and chopped
- ¾   cup thawed limeade concentrate
- ¼   cup sweet chili sauce
- 1   garlic clove, minced
- 1   tsp. minced fresh gingerroot
- 4   bone-in pork loin chops (¾ in. thick and 5 oz. each)
- 1   green onion, finely chopped
- 2   Tbsp. minced fresh cilantro
- 2   Tbsp. minced fresh mint
- 2   Tbsp. slivered almonds, toasted
- 2   Tbsp. finely chopped crystallized ginger, optional
- ½   tsp. grated lime zest

1. In a 3-qt. slow cooker, combine the first 5 ingredients. Add pork, arranging chops to sit snugly in fruit mixture. Cook, covered, on low until meat is tender (a thermometer inserted in pork should read at least 145°), 3-4 hours.
2. In a small bowl, mix remaining ingredients. To serve, remove pork chops from slow cooker. Using a slotted spoon, serve fruit over pork. Sprinkle with herb mixture.

1 serving: 572 cal., 13g fat (4g sat. fat), 69mg chol., 326mg sod., 91g carb. (86g sugars, 3g fiber), 24g pro.

HUNGARIAN TREASURE (SZEKELY GULYAS)

ZA'ATAR CHICKEN

It's hard to find a dinner that both my husband and kids will enjoy—and even harder to find one that's fast and easy. This is it! No matter how much I make of this dish, it's gone to the last bite.
—Esther Erani, Brooklyn, NY

- -

Prep: 20 min. • **Cook:** 5 hours
Makes: 6 servings

- ¼ cup za'atar seasoning
- ¼ cup olive oil
- 3 tsp. dried oregano
- 1 tsp. salt
- ½ tsp. ground cumin
- ½ tsp. ground turmeric
- 3 lbs. bone-in chicken thighs
- 1 cup pimiento-stuffed olives
- ½ cup dried apricots
- ½ cup pitted dried plums (prunes)
- ¼ cup water
  Hot cooked basmati rice, optional

1. In a large bowl, combine the first 6 ingredients. Add chicken; toss to coat.
2. Arrange olives, apricots and plums on the bottom of a 4- or 5-qt. slow cooker. Add water; top with chicken. Cook, covered, on low until chicken is tender, 5-6 hours. If desired, serve with basmati rice.

1 serving: 484 cal., 32g fat (7g sat. fat), 107mg chol., 1367mg sod., 18g carb. (10g sugars, 2g fiber), 30g pro.

READER RAVE...

"I made this on the stovetop, cooking it low and slow for three hours. It was delicious. Definitely keeping this one in the rotation."

—JANINELANZA, TASTEOFHOME.COM

HUNGARIAN TREASURE (SZEKELY GULYAS)

This combination of pork, sauerkraut, sour cream and paprika is heavenly served on buttery egg noodles with or without poppy seeds. Here's to great comfort food.
—*Taste of Home* Test Kitchen

- -

Prep: 25 min. • **Cook:** 3 hours
Makes: 6 servings

- 1½ lbs. pork tenderloin, cubed
- ¼ tsp. salt
- ¼ tsp. pepper
- 1 Tbsp. olive oil
- 2 Tbsp. butter
- 1 large onion, chopped
- 6 garlic cloves, minced
- ½ tsp. smoked paprika
- 2 pkg. (1 lb. each) sauerkraut, rinsed and well drained
- ½ cup water
- 1½ cups sour cream
- ½ tsp. poppy seeds
  Hot cooked buttered egg noodles

1. Sprinkle pork with salt and pepper. In a large skillet, heat oil over medium-high heat; brown meat. Transfer meat to a 4- or 5-qt. slow cooker. In the same skillet, melt butter over medium-high heat. Add onion; cook and stir until tender, 6-8 minutes. Add garlic and paprika; cook 1 minute longer. Pour over meat. Add sauerkraut and water.
2. Cook, covered, on low until the pork is tender, 3-4 hours. Stir in the sour cream; sprinkle with poppy seeds. Serve with noodles.

1⅓ cups: 369 cal., 25g fat (12g sat. fat), 79mg chol., 1181mg sod., 12g carb. (6g sugars, 5g fiber), 26g pro.

ZA'ATAR
CHICKEN

ASPARAGUS TUNA NOODLE CASSEROLE

I updated a traditional tuna casserole using spring-fresh asparagus. This is so different and delicious. Use frozen asparagus when fresh is not in season.
—Nancy Heishman, Las Vegas, NV

Prep: 20 min. • **Cook:** 5 hours
Makes: 8 servings

- 2 **cups uncooked elbow macaroni**
- 2 **cans (10½ oz. each) condensed cream of asparagus soup, undiluted**
- 2 **cups sliced fresh mushrooms**
- 1 **medium sweet red pepper, chopped**
- 1 **small onion, chopped**
- ¼ **cup lemon juice**
- 1 **Tbsp. dried parsley flakes, divided**
- 1½ **tsp. smoked paprika, divided**
- 1 **tsp. garlic salt**
- ½ **tsp. pepper**
- 2 **lbs. fresh asparagus, cut into 1-in. pieces**
- 2 **pouches (6.4 oz. each) light tuna in water**
- 1½ **cups shredded Colby cheese**
- 1 **cup multigrain snack chips, crushed**
- 4 **bacon strips, cooked and crumbled**

1. Cook macaroni according to package directions for al dente; drain. Transfer to a 4- or 5-qt. greased slow cooker. Stir in soup, mushrooms, red pepper, onion, lemon juice, 1½ tsp. parsley, 1 tsp. paprika, garlic salt and pepper. Cook, covered, on low 4 hours.

2. Stir in asparagus and tuna. Cook, covered, on low until asparagus is crisp-tender, 1 hour longer. Sprinkle with remaining 1½ tsp. parsley and ½ tsp. paprika. Serve with cheese, crushed chips and bacon.

1⅓ cups: 338 cal., 15g fat (6g sat. fat), 44mg chol., 1110mg sod., 30g carb. (5g sugars, 5g fiber), 22g pro.

SLOW-COOKER SECRETS

This is a great addition to a potluck or bring-a-dish buffet. When taking your slow cooker to such an event, pack an extension cord so you can easily plug in your cooker without hassling the hostess.

ASPARAGUS TUNA
NOODLE CASSEROLE

SPICY LIME CHICKEN

I've been turning this spicy lime chicken into tacos for years, but it was my son Austin who put it on cooked rice with all his favorite taco toppings. A family favorite was created out of leftovers!
—Christine Hair, Odessa, FL

Prep: 10 min. • **Cook:** 3 hours
Makes: 6 servings

- 1½ **lbs. boneless skinless chicken breast halves (about 4)**
- 2 **cups chicken broth**
- 3 **Tbsp. lime juice**
- 1 **Tbsp. chili powder**
- 1 **tsp. grated lime zest**
  Fresh cilantro leaves

1. Place chicken in a 3-qt. slow cooker. Combine broth, lime juice and chili powder; pour over chicken. Cook, covered, on low until chicken is tender, about 3 hours.
2. Remove chicken. When cool enough to handle, shred meat with 2 forks; return to slow cooker. Stir in lime zest. Serve with cilantro if desired.

1 serving: 132 cal., 3g fat (1g sat. fat), 64mg chol., 420mg sod., 2g carb. (1g sugars, 1g fiber), 23g pro. **Diabetic exchanges:** 3 lean meat.

TOMATO-TOPPED ITALIAN PORK CHOPS

Time to bring out the slow cooker! You're only seven ingredients away from a delicious meal.
—Krystle Chasse,
Radium Hot Springs, BC

Prep: 25 min. • **Cook:** 8 hours
Makes: 6 servings

- 6 **bone-in pork loin chops (7 oz. each)**
- 1 **Tbsp. canola oil**
- 1 **small onion, chopped**
- ½ **cup chopped carrot**
- 1 **can (14½ oz.) diced tomatoes, drained**
- ¼ **cup reduced-fat balsamic vinaigrette**
- 2 **tsp. dried oregano**

1. In a large skillet, brown chops in oil in batches. Transfer to a 4- or 5-qt. slow cooker coated with cooking spray. Saute onion and carrot in drippings until tender. Stir in the tomatoes, vinaigrette and oregano; pour over chops.
2. Cover and cook on low for 8-10 hours or until meat is tender.
1 pork chop: 267 cal., 12g fat (3g sat. fat), 86mg chol., 234mg sod., 7g carb. (4g sugars, 2g fiber), 31g pro. **Diabetic exchanges:** 4 lean meat, 1 vegetable, 1 fat.

SLOW-COOKER MEAT LOAF

An old standby, meat loaf gets fun Mexican flair and an easy preparation method with this slow-cooked recipe. Boost the flavor by serving it with taco sauce or salsa.
—Julie Sterchi, Campbellsville, KY

Prep: 10 min. • **Cook:** 6 hours
Makes: 8 servings

- 1 **large egg, beaten**
- ⅓ **cup taco sauce**
- 1 **cup coarsely crushed corn chips**
- ⅓ **cup shredded Mexican cheese blend or cheddar cheese**
- 2 **Tbsp. taco seasoning**
- ½ **tsp. salt, optional**
- 2 **lbs. lean ground beef (90% lean)**
  Additional taco sauce or salsa

In a large bowl, combine the first 5 ingredients and, if desired, salt. Crumble beef over mixture and mix lightly but thoroughly. Shape into a round loaf; place in a 3-qt. slow cooker. Cover and cook on low until a thermometer reads 160°, 6-8 hours. Serve with taco sauce or salsa.
1 piece: 258 cal., 11g fat (5g sat. fat), 86mg chol., 471mg sod., 14g carb. (1g sugars, 1g fiber), 24g pro.

SLOW-COOKER
MEAT LOAF

SQUASH & LENTIL LAMB STEW

My family lived in New Zealand many years ago. Every Sunday my mother made a lamb stew—it was Dad's favorite! I changed the recipe to suit my family's more modern palates, but it seems just as exotic and delicious.
—Nancy Heishman, Las Vegas, NV

Prep: 30 min. • **Cook:** 6 hours
Makes: 8 servings (2½ qt.)

- 1 can (13.66 oz.) coconut milk
- ½ cup creamy peanut butter
- 2 Tbsp. red curry paste
- 1 Tbsp. hoisin sauce
- 1 tsp. salt
- ½ tsp. pepper
- 1 can (14½ oz.) chicken broth
- 3 tsp. olive oil, divided
- 1 lb. lamb or beef stew meat (1½-in. pieces)
- 2 small onions, chopped
- 1 Tbsp. minced fresh gingerroot
- 3 garlic cloves, minced
- 1 cup dried brown lentils, rinsed
- 4 cups cubed peeled butternut squash (about 1 lb.)
- 2 cups chopped fresh spinach
- ¼ cup minced fresh cilantro
- ¼ cup lime juice

SQUASH & LENTIL LAMB STEW

1. In a 5- or 6-qt. slow cooker, whisk together the first 7 ingredients. In a large skillet, heat 2 tsp. oil over medium heat; brown lamb in batches. Add to the slow cooker.

2. In same skillet, saute onions in remaining 1 tsp. oil over medium heat until tender, 4-5 minutes. Add ginger and garlic; cook and stir 1 minute. Add to slow cooker. Stir in lentils and squash.

3. Cook, covered, on low 6-8 hours, until meat and lentils are tender. Stir in spinach until wilted. Stir in cilantro and lime juice.

Freeze option: Freeze cooled stew in freezer containers. To use, partially thaw in refrigerator overnight. Heat through in a saucepan, stirring occasionally; add broth if necessary.

1¼ cups: 411 cal., 21g fat (11g sat. fat), 38mg chol., 777mg sod., 34g carb. (7g sugars, 6g fiber), 23g pro.

SLOW-COOKER SECRETS
No peeking! Opening the slow cooker allows steam to escape, causing the temperature to drop. You may need to add as much as 20-30 minutes to the cook time for each time the lid is lifted.

FLAVORFUL LEMON CHICKEN

This easy, attractive meal is bound to become a staple in your home. There's nothing complicated or fancy about this delicious find, which relies on everyday ingredients.
—Elizabeth Hokanson, Arborg, MB

Prep: 20 min. • **Cook:** 4¼ hours
Makes: 6 servings

- 1 **tsp. dried oregano**
- ½ **tsp. seasoned salt**
- ¼ **tsp. pepper**
- 6 **boneless skinless chicken breast halves (6 oz. each)**
- 2 **tsp. chicken bouillon granules**
- ¼ **cup boiling water**
- 3 **Tbsp. lemon juice**
- 1½ **tsp. minced garlic**
- 1½ **cups sour cream**
- 2 **tsp. minced fresh parsley**
  Hot cooked brown rice, optional

1. Combine the oregano, seasoned salt and pepper; rub over chicken. Place in a 3-qt. slow cooker.
2. In a small bowl, dissolve bouillon in boiling water. Stir in lemon juice and garlic. Pour over chicken. Cover and cook on low until chicken is tender, 4-5 hours.
3. Remove chicken and keep warm. Stir in the sour cream and parsley; cover and cook until heated through, about 15 minutes. Serve chicken with sauce and, if desired, rice.

1 chicken breast half with about ⅓ cup sauce: 309 cal., 14g fat (8g sat. fat), 134mg chol., 509mg sod., 4g carb. (2g sugars, 0 fiber), 36g pro.

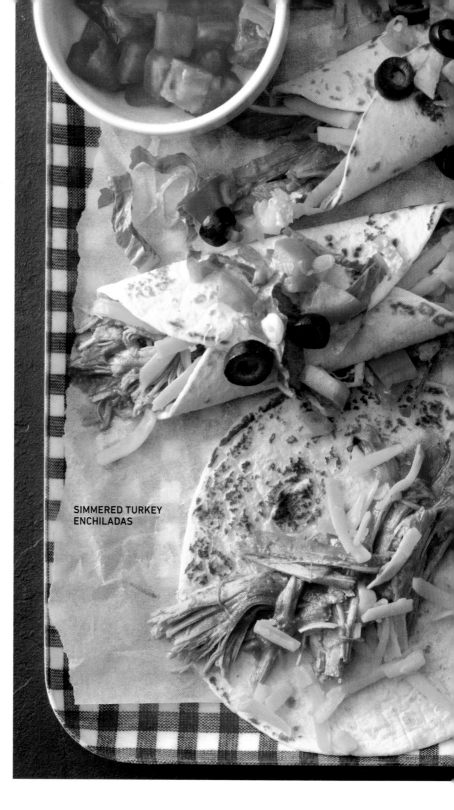

SIMMERED TURKEY ENCHILADAS

SIMMERED TURKEY ENCHILADAS

I discovered a different way to serve economical turkey thighs. I simmer them in tomato sauce, green chiles and seasonings until they're tender and flavorful. Then I serve them in tortillas with our family's favorite fresh toppings.
—Stella Schams, Tempe, AZ

Prep: 10 min. • **Cook:** 6 hours
Makes: 4 servings

- 2 lbs. turkey thighs or drumsticks
- 1 can (8 oz.) tomato sauce
- 1 can (4 oz.) chopped green chiles
- 1/3 cup chopped onion
- 2 Tbsp. Worcestershire sauce
- 1 to 2 Tbsp. chili powder
- 1/4 tsp. garlic powder
- 8 flour tortillas (6 in.), warmed
  Optional toppings: Chopped green onions, sliced ripe olives, chopped tomatoes, shredded cheddar cheese, sour cream and shredded lettuce

1. Remove skin from turkey; place turkey in a 5-qt. slow cooker. In a small bowl, combine the tomato sauce, chiles, onion, Worcestershire sauce, chili powder and garlic powder; pour over turkey. Cover and cook on low until turkey is tender, 6-8 hours.
2. Remove turkey; shred meat with a fork and return to the slow cooker. Heat through.
3. Spoon about 1/2 cup turkey mixture down the center of each tortilla. Fold bottom of tortilla over filling and roll up. Add toppings of your choice.
Freeze option: Individually wrap cooled enchiladas in paper towels and foil; freeze in a freezer container. To use, remove foil; place paper towel-wrapped enchilada on a microwave-safe plate. Microwave on high until heated through, 3-4 minutes, turning once. Let stand about 20 seconds.
2 enchiladas: 497 cal., 20g fat (4g sat. fat), 114mg chol., 1028mg sod., 34g carb. (3g sugars, 2g fiber), 45g pro.

SWEDISH MEATBALLS ALFREDO

I'm a big fan of this potluck-perfect dish. It takes much less time than many other slow-cooker recipes. Plus, it's easy. I'm all for the easy!
—Carole Bess White, Portland, OR

Prep: 10 min. • **Cook:** 2 hours
Makes: 10 servings

- 2 jars (15 oz. each) roasted garlic Alfredo sauce
- 2 cups heavy whipping cream
- 2 cups sour cream
- 3/4 tsp. hot pepper sauce
- 1/2 tsp. garlic powder
- 1/2 tsp. dill weed
- 1/8 tsp. pepper
- 1 pkg. (32 oz.) frozen fully cooked Swedish meatballs, thawed
  Paprika
  Hot cooked egg noodles

1. In a 5-qt. slow cooker, combine the first 7 ingredients. Stir in meatballs. Cook, covered, on low until meatballs are heated through, 2-3 hours.
2. Sprinkle with paprika. Serve with hot cooked noodles.
1 cup: 766 cal., 67g fat (38g sat. fat), 238mg chol., 1357mg sod., 16g carb. (7g sugars, 2g fiber), 21g pro.

SLOW-COOKED THAI
DRUNKEN NOODLES

SLOW-COOKER ASIAN SHORT RIBS

My slow cooker is my best friend.
I use it at least three times a week. This
recipe is one of my favorites. The sauce
can be used for other cuts of meat, too.
—Carole Resnick, Cleveland, OH

Prep: 15 min. • **Cook:** 6 hours
Makes: 6 servings

- ¾ **cup sugar**
- ¾ **cup ketchup**
- ¾ **cup reduced-sodium soy sauce**
- ⅓ **cup honey**
- ¼ **cup lemon juice**
- 3 **Tbsp. hoisin sauce**
- 1 **Tbsp. ground ginger**
- 2 **garlic cloves, minced**
- 4 **lbs. bone-in beef short ribs**
   **Optional: Hot cooked ramen
   noodles, sesame seeds, julienned
   green onions and carrots, sliced
   cucumber, radish, mushrooms
   and red chili pepper**

In a greased 4- or 5-qt. slow cooker,
whisk together the first 8 ingredients.
Add short ribs and turn to coat; cook,
covered, on low 6-7 hours or until meat
is tender. If desired, serve with ramen
noodles and optional toppings.
1 serving: 460 cal., 15g fat (6g sat. fat),
73mg chol., 1706mg sod., 56g carb. (51g
sugars, 0 fiber), 27g pro.

> **SLOW-COOKER SECRETS**
> Round out either of these two
> entrees (and keep the kitchen
> cool) with frozen egg rolls,
> made easily in the air fryer,
> and a tossed green salad.

SLOW-COOKED THAI DRUNKEN NOODLES

I really love pad kee mao and was
inspired to try my recipe in the slow
cooker on a really busy day. It came out
tasting great! I was so happy to have it
ready to go when we got home. You can
easily substitute chicken, turkey or
beef for the pork.
—Lori McLain, Denton, TX

Prep: 25 min. • **Cook:** 5 hours + standing
Makes: 6 servings

- 1 **lb. boneless pork ribeye
   chops, chopped**
- 1 **medium onion, halved and sliced**
- 1 **can (8¾ oz.) whole baby
   corn, drained, optional**
- 1 **small sweet red pepper, sliced**
- 1 **small green pepper, sliced**
- 1¾ **cups sliced fresh mushrooms**
- ½ **cup chicken broth**
- ½ **cup soy sauce**
- ¼ **cup honey**
- 2 **garlic cloves, minced**
- 2 **tsp. Sriracha chili sauce**
- ¼ **tsp. ground ginger**
- 8 **oz. thick rice noodles or linguine**
- 1 **cup fresh snow peas
   Thinly sliced fresh basil**

1. Place pork, onion, corn, if desired,
peppers and mushrooms in a 6- or
7-qt. slow cooker. Whisk broth, soy
sauce, honey, garlic, Sriracha chili
sauce and ginger until blended; pour
over top. Cook, covered, on low for
5-6 hours or until the pork is cooked
through and vegetables are tender.
2. Meanwhile, cook pasta according
to package directions; do not overcook.
Drain noodles and rinse under cold
water. Stir noodles and peas into slow
cooker; let stand 15 minutes. Garnish
with basil.
1½ cups: 360 cal., 9g fat (3g sat. fat),
44mg chol., 1467mg sod., 47g carb. (14g
sugars, 2g fiber), 21g pro.

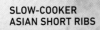
SLOW-COOKER
ASIAN SHORT RIBS

SIDES

DREAMY
POLENTA

DREAMY POLENTA

I grew up eating polenta, so it's a must at my holiday gatherings. Traditional recipes require constant stirring, but using my handy slow cooker allows me to turn my attention to the lineup of other foods on my spread.
—Ann Voccola, Milford, CT

- -

Prep: 10 min. • **Cook:** 5 hours
Makes: 12 servings

- 1 **Tbsp. butter**
- 5 **cups whole milk**
- 4 **cups half-and-half cream**
- 12 **Tbsp. butter, divided**
- 2 **cups yellow cornmeal**
- ¾ **tsp. salt**
- ½ **tsp. minced fresh rosemary**
- ¼ **tsp. pepper**
- 2 **cups shredded Asiago cheese**

1. Generously grease a 5-qt. slow cooker with 1 Tbsp. butter. Add milk, cream, 6 Tbsp. butter, cornmeal, salt, rosemary and pepper; stir to combine.
2. Cook, covered, on low 5-6 hours or until polenta is thickened, whisking every hour. Just before serving, whisk again; stir in cheese and remaining butter. Garnish with additional rosemary if desired.
¾ cup: 444 cal., 29g fat (18g sat. fat), 100mg chol., 379mg sod., 29g carb. (9g sugars, 1g fiber), 13g pro.

SLOW-COOKED POTATOES
WITH SPRING ONIONS

SLOW-COOKED POTATOES WITH SPRING ONIONS

I love the simplicity of this recipe, as well as its ease of preparation with my slow cooker. Everyone always enjoys roasted potatoes, even my pickiest child! If desired, top with shredded or crumbled cheese.
—Theresa Gomez, Stuart, FL

- -

Prep: 5 min. • **Cook:** 6 hours
Makes: 12 servings

- 4 **lbs. small red potatoes**
- 8 **green onions, chopped (about 1 cup)**
- 1 **cup chopped sweet onion**
- ¼ **cup olive oil**
- ½ **tsp. salt**
- ½ **tsp. pepper**

In a 5- or 6-qt. slow cooker, combine all ingredients. Cook, covered, on low until potatoes are tender, 6-8 hours.
1 serving: 157 cal., 5g fat (1g sat. fat), 0 chol., 110mg sod., 26g carb. (2g sugars, 3g fiber), 3g pro. **Diabetic exchanges:** 1½ starch, 1 fat.

READER RAVE...
"I found this recipe to be not only easy but simply tasty, too!
—SQUEAKYMOUSE, TASTEOFHOME.COM

CHEESE-STUFFED SWEET ONIONS

These onions are cooked in vegetable broth and stuffed with a delicious blend of cheeses. Experiment to find the blend you like. Instead of goat cheese, try cream cheese or mascarpone. You could substitute Gorgonzola cheese for the blue cheese, and in place of Romano, you could use Parmesan. Any blend is delicious!
—Sonya Labbe, West Hollywood, CA

- -

Prep: 25 min. • **Cook:** 4 hours
Makes: 8 servings

- 4 large Vidalia or other sweet onions
- ¾ cup crumbled goat cheese
- ¾ cup crumbled blue cheese
- 1 tsp. minced fresh thyme
- 2 cups vegetable stock
- 1 Tbsp. olive oil
- ¼ tsp. salt
- ⅛ tsp. pepper
- ¼ cup grated Romano or Parmesan cheese
  Fresh thyme leaves

1. Peel onions. Cut a ½-in. slice off top of each onion; remove centers with a melon baller, leaving ½-in. shells. Chop removed onion, reserving 3 cups (save remaining onion for another use). Mix goat and blue cheeses, minced thyme and reserved onion; spoon into onions.
2. Place onions and stock in a 6-qt. slow cooker; drizzle with oil. Sprinkle with salt, pepper and Romano cheese. Cook, covered, on low 4-5 hours or until onions are tender. Cut in half to serve; sprinkle with thyme leaves.
½ stuffed onion: 137 cal., 9g fat (5g sat. fat), 23mg chol., 471mg sod., 8g carb. (3g sugars, 2g fiber), 7g pro.

SLOW-COOKER BOILED EGGS

This is my go-to method when I need to make hard-boiled eggs for a crowd. It's a lifesaver and perfect for Easter! I love the walk-away convenience.
—Rashanda Cobbins, Milwaukee, WI

- -

Prep: 5 min. • **Cook:** 2 hours + chilling
Makes: 12 servings

- 12 large eggs
  Cold water

1. Gently place eggs in bottom of 6-qt. slow cooker. Cover with water. Cook, covered, on high 2-3 hours.
2. Remove eggs from slow cooker; rinse eggs in cold water and place in ice water until completely cooled. Drain and refrigerate. Remove shells; if desired, cut eggs before serving.
1 egg: 72 cal., 5g fat (2g sat. fat), 186mg chol., 71mg sod., 0 carb. (0 sugars, 0 fiber), 6g pro. **Diabetic exchanges:** 1 medium-fat meat.

SLOW-COOKER SECRETS
Slow cookers heat differently and can be impacted by capacity. To ensure your eggs are cooked properly, add an extra egg or a "tester" to the batch. This way it can be easily removed and cracked to check for doneness.

SLOW-COOKER
BOILED EGGS

CREAMY RICE

This wonderful side dish goes well with any meat stew. I use whatever fresh herbs I have on hand along with chopped parsley for even more flavor.
—Laura Crane, Leetonia, OH

Prep: 25 min. • **Cook:** 2½ hours
Makes: 8 servings

- 3 cups cooked rice
- 2 large eggs, lightly beaten
- 1 can (12 oz.) evaporated milk
- 1 cup shredded Swiss cheese
- 1 cup shredded cheddar cheese
- 1 medium onion, chopped
- ½ cup minced fresh parsley
- 6 Tbsp. water
- 2 Tbsp. canola oil
- 1 garlic clove, minced
- 1½ tsp. salt
- ¼ tsp. pepper

In a 3-qt. slow cooker, combine all ingredients. Cover and cook on low for 2½-3 hours or until a thermometer reads 160°.

¾ cup: 290 cal., 15g fat (8g sat. fat), 94mg chol., 624mg sod., 24g carb. (6g sugars, 1g fiber), 13g pro.

SLOW-COOKER VEGAN BAKED BEANS

This version of baked beans doesn't need an oven. The slow cooker makes it the ultimate hands-off party dish.
—*Taste of Home* Test Kitchen

- -

Prep: 10 min. + soaking • **Cook:** 9 hours
Makes: 8 servings

- 1 **lb. dried navy beans**
- 2 **cups water**
- 1 **medium onion, chopped**
- ½ **cup molasses**
- ⅓ **cup packed brown sugar**
- 2 **Tbsp. ketchup**
- 2 **tsp. ground mustard**
- ½ **tsp. liquid smoke, optional**
- ½ **tsp. salt**
- ½ **tsp. pepper**
- ¼ **tsp. ground nutmeg**
- ¼ **tsp. ground cloves**

1. Sort beans and rinse in cold water. Place beans in a large bowl; add enough water to cover by 2 in. Let beans stand, covered, overnight.
2. Drain and rinse beans, discarding liquid. Transfer beans to a greased 3-qt. slow cooker. In a small bowl, combine remaining 11 ingredients. Stir into the slow cooker.
3. Cook, covered, on low 9-10 hours or until beans are tender.
Freeze option: Freeze cooled beans in freezer containers. To use, partially thaw in refrigerator overnight. Heat through in a saucepan, stirring occasionally; add water if necessary.
½ cup: 294 cal., 1g fat (0 sat. fat), 0 chol., 161mg sod., 60g carb. (27g sugars, 9g fiber), 13g pro.

SLOW-COOKER POLENTA

This Italian classic is so easy to make, and now you can prepare it any day of the week.
—Elisabeth Matelski, Boston, MA

- -

Prep: 10 min. • **Cook:** 6 hours
Makes: 12 servings

- 13 **cups reduced-sodium chicken broth, divided**
- 3 **cups cornmeal**
- 1 **medium onion, finely chopped**
- 3 **garlic cloves, minced**
- 2 **bay leaves**
- 2 **tsp. salt**
- 1 **cup half-and-half cream**
- 1 **cup shredded Parmesan cheese**
- ¼ **cup butter, cubed**
- 1 **tsp. pepper**
   Additional shredded Parmesan cheese

In a 6-qt. slow cooker, combine 12 cups broth, the cornmeal, onion, garlic, bay leaves and salt. Cook, covered, on low 6-8 hours, until liquid is absorbed and polenta is creamy. Remove bay leaves. Stir in cream, cheese, butter, pepper and remaining broth. If desired, serve with additional cheese.
1 cup: 255 cal., 8g fat (5g sat. fat), 25mg chol., 1168mg sod., 34g carb. (3g sugars, 2g fiber), 9g pro.

SLOW-COOKER POLENTA

CHUTNEY-GLAZED CARROTS

Carrots slow-cooked with chutney, Dijon and ginger make a zippy side for a spring gathering or summer barbecue. We love serving these carrots with grilled chicken or beef.
—Nancy Heishman, Las Vegas, NV

Prep: 15 min. • **Cook:** 4 hours
Makes: 4 servings

- ⅓ cup mango chutney
- 2 Tbsp. sugar
- 2 Tbsp. minced fresh parsley
- 2 Tbsp. white wine or unsweetened apple juice
- 1 Tbsp. Dijon mustard
- 1 Tbsp. butter, melted
- 1 garlic clove, minced
- ½ tsp. salt
- ¼ tsp. ground ginger
- ¼ tsp. pepper
- 1 lb. fresh carrots, cut into ¼-in. slices (about 4 cups)

1. Place the first 10 ingredients in a 3-qt. slow cooker. Add carrots; toss to combine.
2. Cook, covered, on low 4-5 hours or until the carrots are tender. Stir before serving.
¾ cup: 183 cal., 3g fat (2g sat. fat), 8mg chol., 714mg sod., 36g carb. (24g sugars, 3g fiber), 1g pro.

GREEN BEANS IN
BACON CHEESE SAUCE

GREEN BEANS IN BACON CHEESE SAUCE

I like to take this side dish to potlucks because it is easy to prep and feeds a crowd. It's always popular.
—Karen Lewis, Pleasant Grove, AL

Prep: 10 min. • **Cook:** 5 hours
Makes: 10 servings

- 2 pkg. (16 oz. each) frozen french-style green beans, thawed
- 1 can (10¾ oz.) condensed cream of mushroom soup, undiluted
- 1 can (10¾ oz.) condensed cheddar cheese soup, undiluted
- ¾ cup chopped onion
- ¾ cup bacon bits
- ½ cup shredded cheddar cheese
- 1 jar (4½ oz.) sliced mushrooms, drained
- 1 jar (4 oz.) diced pimientos, drained
- ½ tsp. pepper

In a 3- or 4-qt. slow cooker, combine all ingredients. Cover and cook on low for 5-6 hours or until beans are tender.
¾ cup: 137 cal., 6g fat (3g sat. fat), 16mg chol., 817mg sod., 14g carb. (5g sugars, 3g fiber), 7g pro.

SMOKY WHITE BEANS
& HAM

VEGETABLES WITH CHEESE SAUCE

Who can pass up veggies smothered in cheese? No one I know! This is an inviting recipe to serve kids who normally shy away from vegetables.
—Teresa Flowers, Sacramento, CA

Prep: 5 min. • **Cook:** 3 hours
Makes: 6 servings

- 1 **pkg. (16 oz.) frozen Italian vegetables, thawed**
- 3 **cups frozen broccoli florets, thawed**
- 1 **pkg. (8 oz.) cubed Velveeta**
- 1½ **cups frozen cut kale, thawed and squeezed dry**
- ⅓ **cup chicken broth**
- 1 **Tbsp. butter**
- ¼ **tsp. salt**
- ¼ **tsp. pepper**

Place all ingredients in a 3- or 4-qt. slow cooker. Cook, covered, on low 3-4 hours or until cheese is melted. Stir before serving.

¾ cup: 209 cal., 16g fat (7g sat. fat), 42mg chol., 704mg sod., 14g carb. (6g sugars, 4g fiber), 10g pro.

SLOW-COOKER SECRETS

Substitute an equal amount of mozzarella cheese, or even cream cheese if that's what you happen to have on hand, for the Velveeta.

SMOKY WHITE BEANS & HAM

I had never made or eaten this dish before meeting my husband here in Kentucky. Now I make it at least once a week. I serve it with some homemade sweet cornbread. Delicious!
—Christine Duffy, Sturgis, KY

Prep: 15 min. + soaking • **Cook:** 6 hours
Makes: 10 servings

- 1 **lb. dried great northern beans**
- 3 **smoked ham hocks (about 1½ lbs.)**
- 1 **large onion, chopped**
- 3 **cans (14½ oz. each) reduced-sodium chicken or beef broth**
- 2 **cups water**
- 1 **Tbsp. onion powder**
- 1 **Tbsp. garlic powder**
- 2 **tsp. pepper**
  Thinly sliced green onions, optional

1. Rinse and sort beans; soak according to package directions.

2. Drain and rinse beans, discarding liquid. Transfer beans to a 6-qt. slow cooker. Add ham hocks. Stir in onion, broth, water and seasonings. Cook, covered, on low 6-8 hours or until the beans are tender.

3. Remove meat from bones when cool enough to handle; cut ham into small pieces and return to slow cooker. Serve with a slotted spoon. Sprinkle servings with onions if desired.

⅔ cup: 195 cal., 2g fat (0 sat. fat), 8mg chol., 505mg sod., 32g carb. (2g sugars, 10g fiber), 15g pro. **Diabetic exchanges:** 2 starch, 2 lean meat.

VEGETABLES WITH
CHEESE SAUCE

PARSLEY SMASHED POTATOES

I love potatoes but hate the work involved in making mashed potatoes from scratch. I came up with a simple spring side dish that was made even easier thanks to my slow cooker. Save the leftover broth for soup the next day!
—Katie Hagy, Blacksburg, SC

Prep: 20 min. · **Cook:** 6 hours
Makes: 8 servings

- 16 **small red potatoes (about 2 lbs.)**
- 1 **celery rib, sliced**
- 1 **medium carrot, sliced**
- ¼ **cup finely chopped onion**
- 2 **cups chicken broth**
- 1 **Tbsp. minced fresh parsley**
- 1½ **tsp. salt, divided**
- 1 **tsp. pepper, divided**
- 1 **garlic clove, minced**
- 2 **Tbsp. butter, melted**
   Additional minced fresh parsley

1. Place potatoes, celery, carrot and onion in a 4-qt. slow cooker. In a small bowl, mix broth, parsley, 1 tsp. salt, ½ tsp. pepper and garlic; pour over vegetables. Cook, covered, on low 6-8 hours or until potatoes are tender.

2. Transfer potatoes from slow cooker to a 15x10x1-in. pan; discard cooking liquid and vegetables (or save for another use). Using the bottom of a measuring cup, flatten potatoes slightly. Transfer to a large bowl; drizzle with butter. Sprinkle with remaining salt and pepper; toss to coat. Sprinkle with additional parsley.

2 smashed potatoes: 114 cal., 3g fat (2g sat. fat), 8mg chol., 190mg sod., 20g carb. (2g sugars, 2g fiber), 2g pro. **Diabetic exchanges:** 1 starch, ½ fat.

**PARSLEY
SMASHED POTATOES**

SWEET ONION CREAMED CORN

A friend gave me this recipe. She was from the South, and whenever I cook it, I remember her fondly.
—Nancy Heishman, Las Vegas, NV

Prep: 25 min. • **Cook:** 3 hours 10 min.
Makes: 8 servings

- 5 bacon strips, chopped
- 1 large sweet onion, chopped
- 1 medium sweet red pepper, chopped
- 5 cups frozen corn (about 24 oz.), thawed
- 2 cups cubed fully cooked ham
- ½ cup half-and-half cream
- 1 Tbsp. brown sugar
- 1 Tbsp. dried parsley flakes
- 1 tsp. smoked paprika
- ½ tsp. salt
- ½ tsp. pepper
- 1 pkg. (8 oz.) cream cheese, cubed and softened

1. In a large skillet, cook bacon over medium heat until crisp, stirring occasionally. Remove with a slotted spoon, leaving drippings in pan; drain on paper towels.
2. Cook and stir the onion and red pepper in bacon drippings over medium-high heat until tender, 5-6 minutes.
3. In a greased 4-qt. slow cooker, combine corn, ham, cream, brown sugar, parsley, paprika, salt, pepper, bacon and onion mixture. Cook, covered, on low until heated through, 3-4 hours. Stir in cream cheese; cook, covered, 10 minutes longer. Stir before serving.
¾ cup: 336 cal., 20g fat (10g sat. fat), 68mg chol., 791mg sod., 26g carb. (8g sugars, 3g fiber), 15g pro.

LEMONY SPRING VEGGIES

These spuds do a slow simmer with carrots and onion for a comfort side that bucks up any entree. Finish the dish with a sprinkle of chives.
—*Taste of Home* Test Kitchen

Prep: 10 min. • **Cook:** 4 hours 10 min.
Makes: 8 servings

- 4 medium carrots, halved lengthwise and cut into 1-in. pieces
- 1 large sweet onion, coarsely chopped
- 1½ lbs. baby red potatoes, quartered
- 3 Tbsp. butter, melted
- ¾ tsp. salt
- ¼ tsp. pepper
- 1 cup frozen peas, thawed
- 1 tsp. grated lemon zest
- ¼ cup minced fresh chives

1. Place carrots and onion in a 4-qt. slow cooker; top with potatoes. Drizzle with melted butter; sprinkle with salt and pepper. Cook, covered, on low until vegetables are tender, 4-5 hours.
2. Add the peas to slow cooker. Cook, covered, on high until heated through, 10-15 minutes. Stir in the lemon zest. Sprinkle with chives.
¾ cup: 141 cal., 5g fat (3g sat. fat), 11mg chol., 298mg sod., 23g carb. (5g sugars, 3g fiber), 3g pro. **Diabetic exchanges:** 1½ starch, 1 fat.

SLOW-COOKED GREEN BEANS

I spent hours in search of sides for a cooking demo to present to women from my church. These easy green beans became my star attraction.
—Alice White, Willow Spring, NC

Prep: 10 min. • **Cook:** 2 hours
Makes: 12 servings

- 16 cups frozen french-style green beans (about 48 oz.), thawed
- ½ cup butter, melted
- ½ cup packed brown sugar
- 1½ tsp. garlic salt
- ¾ tsp. reduced-sodium soy sauce

Place beans in a 5-qt. slow cooker. Mix remaining ingredients; pour over beans and toss to coat. Cook, covered, on low until heated through, 2-3 hours. Serve with a slotted spoon.

⅔ cup: 143 cal., 8g fat (5g sat. fat), 20mg chol., 320mg sod., 17g carb. (12g sugars, 3g fiber), 1g pro.

HONEY-BUTTER PEAS & CARROTS

HONEY-BUTTER PEAS & CARROTS

The classic combination of peas and carrots is made even better with a few simple flavor enhancers. Slow-cooking allows the ingredients to meld for maximum richness.
—Theresa Kreyche, Tustin, CA

Prep: 15 min. • **Cook:** 5¼ hours
Makes: 12 servings

- 1 lb. carrots, sliced
- 1 large onion, chopped
- ¼ cup water
- ¼ cup butter, cubed
- ¼ cup honey
- 4 garlic cloves, minced
- 1 tsp. salt
- 1 tsp. dried marjoram
- ⅛ tsp. white pepper
- 1 pkg. (16 oz.) frozen peas

In a 3-qt. slow cooker, combine the first 9 ingredients. Cook, covered, on low 5 hours. Stir in peas. Cook, covered, on high 15-25 minutes longer or until the vegetables are tender.

½ cup: 106 cal., 4g fat (2g sat. fat), 10mg chol., 293mg sod., 16g carb. (10g sugars, 3g fiber), 3g pro. **Diabetic exchanges:** 1 starch, 1 fat.

GARLIC-DILL SODA BREAD

It's amazing how bread can be made in a slow cooker, which is why this recipe is so awesome—who knew it could be so easy! Let the inviting aroma of dill and cheese fill your kitchen.
—Melissa Hansen, Ellison Bay, WI

- -

Prep: 15 min. • **Cook:** 1½ hours
Makes: 1 loaf (12 pieces)

4   **cups all-purpose flour**
2   **Tbsp. dried parsley flakes**
1   **Tbsp. dried minced onion**
2   **tsp. garlic powder**
1½ **tsp. dill weed**
1   **tsp. salt**
1   **tsp. baking soda**
1   **tsp. ground mustard**
1¾ **cups buttermilk**
1   **cup shredded**
     sharp cheddar cheese

1. In a bowl, whisk first 8 ingredients. Add buttermilk and cheese; stir just until moistened. Turn onto a lightly floured surface; knead gently 6-8 times or just until the dough comes together. Shape dough into a 6-in. round loaf. Using a sharp knife, score surface with 1-in.-deep cuts in a crisscross pattern. Place in a greased 5-qt. slow cooker.
2. Cook, covered, on high 1½-2 hours or until a thermometer reads 190°-200°.
3. Preheat broiler. Remove bread; place on a baking sheet. Broil bread 6-8 in. from heat 2-3 minutes or until golden brown. Remove bread to a wire rack to cool completely.

1 wedge: 209 cal., 4g fat (2g sat. fat), 11mg chol., 434mg sod., 35g carb. (2g sugars, 1g fiber), 8g pro.

SLOW-COOKER SECRETS

It's key that slow-cooked breads reach the correct internal temperature before being removed from the slow cooker. If the bread does not reach that temperature during the suggested timeline, continue cooking it, checking the internal temperature every 30 minutes.

GARLIC-DILL
SODA BREAD

ROSEMARY BEETS

We're a family of beet eaters. For a simple side dish, I use a slow cooker and let the beets mellow with rosemary and thyme.
—Nancy Heishman, Las Vegas, NV

Prep: 20 min. • **Cook:** 6 hours
Makes: 8 servings

- ⅓ cup honey
- ¼ cup white balsamic vinegar
- 1 Tbsp. minced fresh rosemary or 1 tsp. dried rosemary, crushed
- 2 tsp. minced fresh thyme or ¾ tsp. dried thyme
- 1 Tbsp. olive oil
- 2 garlic cloves, minced
- ¾ tsp. salt
- ½ tsp. Chinese five-spice powder
- ½ tsp. coarsely ground pepper
- 5 large fresh beets (about 3½ lbs.), peeled and trimmed
- 1 medium red onion, chopped
- 1 medium orange, peeled and chopped
- 1 cup crumbled feta cheese

1. In a bowl, whisk the first 9 ingredients until blended. Place beets in a greased 4-qt. slow cooker. Add the onion and orange. Pour honey mixture over top.
2. Cook, covered, on low 6-8 hours or until beets are tender. Remove beets; cut into wedges. Return to slow cooker. Serve warm, or refrigerate and serve cold. Serve beets with a slotted spoon; sprinkle with cheese.
¾ cup: 200 cal., 4g fat (2g sat. fat), 8mg chol., 511mg sod., 37g carb. (31g sugars, 5g fiber), 6g pro. **Diabetic exchanges:** 2 vegetable, 1 starch, 1 fat.

GARDEN GREEN BEANS & POTATOES

Fresh green beans paired with red potatoes make for an easy and filling side dish. To make it even better, add crumbled bacon!
—Kelly Zinn, Cicero, IN

Prep: 10 min. • **Cook:** 6 hours
Makes: 16 servings

- 2 lbs. fresh green beans, trimmed
- 1½ lbs. red potatoes, quartered
- 1 medium onion, chopped
- ½ cup beef broth
- 1½ tsp. salt
- 1 tsp. dried thyme
- ½ tsp. pepper
- ¼ cup butter, softened
- 1 Tbsp. lemon juice

In a 6-qt. slow cooker, combine the first 7 ingredients. Cook, covered, on low until beans are tender, 6-8 hours. Stir in butter and lemon juice. Remove with a slotted spoon.
¾ cup: 77 cal., 3g fat (2g sat. fat), 8mg chol., 278mg sod., 12g carb. (2g sugars, 3g fiber), 2g pro. **Diabetic exchanges:** 1 vegetable, ½ starch, ½ fat.

GARDEN GREEN BEANS & POTATOES

SLOW-COOKER CREAMED CORN

I'm a teacher, and this is one of my go-to recipes for faculty potlucks. It's perfect when you need a comforting dish.
—Shelby Winters, Bonner Springs, KS

Prep: 15 min. • **Cook:** 3 hours
Makes: 8 servings

- ½ cup butter, cubed
- 1 medium onion, finely chopped
- ¼ cup finely chopped sweet red pepper
- 6 cups frozen corn (about 30 oz.), thawed
- 1 pkg. (8 oz.) cream cheese, cubed
- 1 can (4 oz.) chopped green chiles
- 1 tsp. salt
- ½ tsp. garlic powder
- ¼ tsp. pepper

In a large skillet, heat butter over medium-high heat. Add onion and red pepper; cook and stir 3-4 minutes or until tender. Transfer to a greased 3-qt. slow cooker. Stir in remaining ingredients. Cook, covered, on low 3-4 hours or until heated through. Stir just before serving.

⅔ cup: 302 cal., 22g fat (13g sat. fat), 59mg chol., 536mg sod., 25g carb. (4g sugars, 3g fiber), 5g pro.

SLOW-COOKER CORN PUDDING

Sweet and creamy, my corn pudding couldn't be simpler to prepare. It's so satisfying with so little effort—this dish never disappoints!
—Kay Chon, Sherwood, AR

- -

Prep: 10 min. • **Cook:** 4 hours
Makes: 8 servings

- 2 cans (11 oz. each) whole kernel corn, undrained
- 2 pkg. (8½ oz. each) cornbread mix
- 1 can (14¾ oz.) cream-style corn
- 1 cup sour cream
- ½ cup butter, melted
- 3 bacon strips, cooked and crumbled

In a greased 3- or 4-qt. slow cooker, combine all ingredients. Cook, covered, on low until set, 4-5 hours.
¾ cup: 504 cal., 27g fat (13g sat. fat), 42mg chol., 1009mg sod., 59g carb. (19g sugars, 6g fiber), 9g pro.

GARLIC GREEN BEANS WITH GORGONZOLA

I updated this green bean side dish by adding a touch of white wine, fresh thyme and green onions. It's delicious and simple to make, and my family absolutely loves it!
—Nancy Heishman, Las Vegas, NV

- -

Prep: 20 min. • **Cook:** 3 hours
Makes: 10 servings

- 2 lbs. fresh green beans, trimmed and halved
- 1 can (8 oz.) sliced water chestnuts, drained
- 4 green onions, chopped
- 5 bacon strips, cooked and crumbled, divided
- ⅓ cup white wine or chicken broth
- 2 Tbsp. minced fresh thyme or 2 tsp. dried thyme
- 4 garlic cloves, minced
- 1½ tsp. seasoned salt
- 1 cup sour cream
- ¾ cup crumbled Gorgonzola cheese

1. Place green beans, water chestnuts, green onions and ¼ cup cooked bacon in a 4-qt. slow cooker. In a small bowl, mix wine, thyme, garlic and seasoned salt; pour over top. Cook, covered, on low until beans are crisp-tender, 3-4 hours. Drain liquid from beans.
2. Just before serving, stir in sour cream; sprinkle with cheese and remaining bacon.
¾ cup: 142 cal., 9g fat (5g sat. fat), 17mg chol., 431mg sod., 11g carb. (4g sugars, 4g fiber), 6g pro.

GARLIC GREEN BEANS WITH GORGONZOLA

BACON
LIMA BEANS

GLAZED CARROTS WITH GREEN GRAPES

After receiving a slow cooker many years ago and not knowing what to do with the thing, I finally branched out and read up on what it was all about. This is one of the recipes I make that is really enjoyed by all. It is so colorful, and it's a delightful side for any meal.
—Lorraine Caland, Shuniah, ON

- -

Prep: 20 min. • **Cook:** 3½ hours
Makes: 7 servings

- 8 medium carrots, sliced (14 oz.)
- ⅓ cup orange marmalade
- 2 Tbsp. water
- ¼ tsp. salt
- 1 cup halved green grapes
- 1 Tbsp. butter
   Chopped fresh parsley, optional

In a 3-qt. slow cooker, combine the carrots, marmalade, water and salt. Cook, covered, on low heat until carrots are almost tender, 2¾ hours. Add the grapes and butter. Cover and cook on low until tender, 45 minutes longer. If desired, sprinkle with parsley.
½ cup: 98 cal., 2g fat (1g sat. fat), 4mg chol., 157mg sod., 21g carb. (16g sugars, 2g fiber), 1g pro.

BACON LIMA BEANS

An unusual twist on traditional baked beans, this sweet and spicy version is easy to make and is a surefire crowd pleaser at any time of the year!
—Bette Banjack, Norristown, PA

- -

Prep: 15 min. + soaking • **Cook:** 6 hours
Makes: 8 servings

- 1 lb. dried lima beans
- ½ lb. bacon strips, cooked and crumbled
- 1 can (10¾ oz.) condensed tomato soup, undiluted
- 1⅓ cups water
- 1 cup packed brown sugar
- 1 garlic clove, minced
- 1 tsp. salt
- 1 tsp. paprika
- ½ tsp. ground mustard

Rinse and sort beans; soak according to package directions. Drain and rinse beans, discarding liquid. In a 3-qt. slow cooker, combine beans and remaining ingredients. Cook, covered, on low until beans are tender, 6-8 hours.
¾ cup: 375 cal., 5g fat (1g sat. fat), 10mg chol., 635mg sod., 69g carb. (35g sugars, 12g fiber), 16g pro.

DESSERTS

APPLE PIE
OATMEAL DESSERT

APPLE PIE OATMEAL DESSERT

This warm and comforting dessert brings back memories of times spent with my family around the kitchen table. I serve the dish with sweetened whipped cream or vanilla ice cream as a topper.
—Carol Greer, Earlville, IL

Prep: 15 min. • **Cook:** 4 hours
Makes: 6 servings

- 1 cup quick-cooking oats
- ½ cup all-purpose flour
- ⅓ cup packed brown sugar
- 2 tsp. baking powder
- 1½ tsp. apple pie spice
- ¼ tsp. salt
- 3 large eggs
- 1⅔ cups 2% milk, divided
- 1½ tsp. vanilla extract
- 3 medium apples, peeled and finely chopped
  Vanilla ice cream, optional

1. In a large bowl, whisk oats, flour, brown sugar, baking powder, pie spice and salt. In a small bowl, whisk eggs, 1 cup milk and vanilla until blended. Add to oat mixture, stirring just until moistened. Fold in apples.
2. Transfer to a greased 3-qt. slow cooker. Cook, covered, on low until the apples are tender and top is set, 4-5 hours.
3. Stir in remaining milk. Serve warm or cold, with ice cream if desired.
¾ cup: 238 cal., 5g fat (2g sat. fat), 111mg chol., 306mg sod., 41g carb. (22g sugars, 3g fiber), 8g pro.

MOLTEN
MOCHA CAKE

MOLTEN MOCHA CAKE

When I first made my decadent slow-cooker chocolate cake, my husband's and daughter's expressions said it all. Now it's one of my daughter's favorites. Later, I gave one of these cakes to our next-door neighbors. Turns out their teenage son, who'd answered the door, ate the whole thing without telling anyone about it!
—Aimee Fortney, Fairview, TN

Prep: 10 min. • **Cook:** 2½ hours
Makes: 6 servings

- 4 large eggs
- 1½ cups sugar
- ½ cup butter, melted
- 1 Tbsp. vanilla extract
- 1 cup all-purpose flour
- ½ cup baking cocoa
- 1 Tbsp. instant coffee granules
- ¼ tsp. salt
  Optional: Vanilla ice cream and fresh raspberries

1. Whisk together the first 4 ingredients. In another bowl, whisk together the flour, cocoa, coffee granules and salt; gradually beat into the egg mixture. Transfer mixture to a greased 1½-qt. slow cooker.
2. Cook, covered, on low until a toothpick inserted in center comes out with moist crumbs, 2½-3 hours. Serve warm. If desired, serve with vanilla ice cream and raspberries.
1 serving: 482 cal., 19g fat (11g sat. fat), 165mg chol., 269mg sod., 71g carb. (51g sugars, 2g fiber), 8g pro.

COCONUT-MANGO MALVA PUDDING

My friend shared this amazing malva pudding recipe with me. Malva pudding is a dense, spongy cake drenched in a rich, sticky butter sauce. My slow-cooked tropical spin incorporates a creamy coconut sauce and juicy mangoes. Yum!
—Carmell Childs, Orangeville, UT

Prep: 20 min.
Cook: 2½ hours + standing
Makes: 12 servings

- 4 **large eggs, room temperature**
- 1½ **cups sugar**
- ¼ **cup apricot preserves**
- 2 **Tbsp. butter, melted**
- 1 **can (13.66 oz.) coconut milk**
- 2 **tsp. vanilla extract**
- 2 **tsp. white vinegar**
- 2 **cups all-purpose flour**
- 1¼ **tsp. baking soda**
- 1 **tsp. salt**

SAUCE
- 1 **cup canned coconut milk**
- ½ **cup butter, melted**
- ½ **cup sugar**
- 2 **Tbsp. apricot preserves**
- ½ **tsp. coconut extract**
- 2 **medium mangoes, peeled and chopped**
- ¼ **cup sweetened shredded coconut, toasted**
- 1 **container (8 oz.) frozen whipped topping, thawed**

1. In large bowl, beat eggs, sugar, apricot preserves and butter until combined. Add coconut milk, vanilla and vinegar; stir to combine (batter will be thin). In another bowl, whisk flour, baking soda and salt. Gradually stir flour mixture into batter just until moistened. Transfer to a greased 5-qt. slow cooker. Cook, covered, on high until a toothpick inserted in cake comes out with moist crumbs, 2½-3 hours.

2. Meanwhile, for sauce, whisk together the coconut milk, butter, sugar, apricot preserves and extract until smooth. Poke holes in warm cake with a skewer or chopstick. Pour mixture evenly over pudding; let stand to allow pudding to absorb sauce, 15-20 minutes. Serve with chopped mango, coconut and a dollop of whipped topping.

1 piece: 518 cal., 24g fat (19g sat. fat), 87mg chol., 452mg sod., 71g carb. (52g sugars, 2g fiber), 6g pro.

SLOW-COOKER SECRETS
This recipe can also be made with store-bought apricot jam instead of preserves.

COCONUT-MANGO
MALVA PUDDING

KEY LIME FONDUE

Love fondue but want something other than milk chocolate? Dip into this white chocolate Key lime fondue with graham crackers, fresh fruit, cookies and cubed pound cake.
—Elisabeth Larsen, Pleasant Grove, UT

Prep: 5 min. • **Cook:** 50 min.
Makes: 3 cups

- 1 **can (14 oz.) sweetened condensed milk**
- 12 **oz. white baking chocolate, finely chopped**
- ½ **cup Key lime or regular lime juice**
- 1 **Tbsp. grated lime zest**
  Graham crackers, macaroon cookies, fresh strawberries and sliced ripe bananas

1. In a 1½-qt. slow cooker, combine milk, white chocolate and lime juice.
2. Cook, covered, on low 50-60 minutes or until chocolate is melted. Stir in lime zest. Serve with the graham crackers, cookies and fruit.
¼ cup: 251 cal., 11g fat (8g sat. fat), 11mg chol., 62mg sod., 37g carb. (36g sugars, 0 fiber), 5g pro.

SALTY-SWEET PEANUT TREAT

Who knew slow-cooking could transform chocolate, peanuts and pretzels? When the clusters are done, we tuck them into mini muffin papers for a takeaway treat.
—Elizabeth Godecke, Chicago, IL

Prep: 10 min. • **Cook:** 1 hour + chilling
Makes: about 6 dozen

- 24 oz. milk chocolate, coarsely chopped
- 2 cups salted peanuts
- ¼ cup packed brown sugar
- 1 tsp. vanilla extract
- 2 cups crushed pretzels

In a 3-qt. slow cooker, combine chocolate, peanuts and brown sugar. Cook, covered, on low, stirring halfway through cooking, until chocolate is melted, about 1 hour. Stir in vanilla. Add pretzels; stir to combine. Drop mixture by tablespoonfuls onto waxed paper-lined baking sheets. Refrigerate until set, 10-15 minutes. Store in an airtight container.
1 treat: 84 cal., 5g fat (2g sat. fat), 2mg chol., 53mg sod., 9g carb. (6g sugars, 0 fiber), 2g pro.

TROPICAL ORANGE CAKE

TROPICAL ORANGE CAKE

Inspired by the fruity tropical flavors of my all-time favorite yogurt, this makes for a fresh, fun and comforting treat. Try it for a beautiful spring dessert that is ridiculously easy to prepare!
—Lisa Renshaw, Kansas City, MO

Prep: 15 min. • **Cook:** 4 hours + standing
Makes: 8 servings

- 3 cups cold 2% milk
- 1 pkg. (3.4 oz.) instant coconut cream pudding mix
- 1 pkg. orange cake mix (regular size)
- ¾ cup unsweetened pineapple tidbits
- 2 cups toasted coconut marshmallows, quartered

1. In a large bowl, whisk milk and pudding mix 2 minutes. Transfer to a greased 5-qt. slow cooker. Prepare cake mix batter according to package directions, folding pineapple into batter. Pour into slow cooker.
2. Cook, covered, on low until edges of cake are golden brown, about 4 hours.
3. Remove slow-cooker insert; sprinkle the cake with the marshmallows. Let cake stand, uncovered, 10 minutes before serving.
1 serving: 518 cal., 20g fat (6g sat. fat), 77mg chol., 596mg sod., 73g carb. (50g sugars, 1g fiber), 9g pro.

SLOW-COOKER CINNAMON ROLL

Come home to the heavenly aroma of fresh-baked cinnamon rolls! This healthier slow-cooked version tastes just as decadent as a traditional cinnamon roll but smartly sneaks in some whole grains.
—Nick Iverson, Denver, CO

Prep: 15 min. + rising • **Cook:** 3½ hours
Makes: 12 servings

1 pkg. (¼ oz.) active dry yeast
¾ cup warm water (110° to 115°)
½ cup quick-cooking oats
½ cup whole wheat flour
¼ cup packed brown sugar
2 Tbsp. butter, melted
1 large egg, room temperature
1 tsp. salt
1¾ to 2¼ cups all-purpose flour

FILLING
3 Tbsp. butter, softened
⅓ cup sugar
2 tsp. ground cinnamon

ICING
1 cup confectioners' sugar
2 Tbsp. half-and-half cream
4 tsp. butter, softened

1. Dissolve the yeast in warm water. Add the next 6 ingredients plus 1 cup all-purpose flour. Beat on medium speed until smooth. Stir in enough remaining flour to form a soft dough (dough will be sticky).

2. Turn onto a lightly floured surface; knead until smooth and elastic, about 6-8 minutes. Roll into an 18x12-in. rectangle. For filling, spread dough with butter, then combine the sugar and cinnamon; sprinkle over dough to within ½ in. of edges.

3. Roll up jelly-roll style, starting with a long side; pinch seam to seal. Cut crosswise in half to form 2 rolls. Place the rolls side by side; pinch top ends together to seal. Using a sharp knife, cut rolls lengthwise in half; loosely twist strips around each other. Pinch bottom ends together to seal. Shape into a coil; place on parchment. Transfer to a 6-qt. slow cooker. Let rise until doubled, about 1 hour.

4. Cook, covered, on low until bread is lightly browned, 3½-4 hours. Remove from slow cooker and cool slightly. Beat icing ingredients until smooth. Spread over warm roll.

1 slice: 240 cal., 7g fat (4g sat. fat), 33mg chol., 254mg sod., 41g carb. (20g sugars, 2g fiber), 4g pro.

SLOW-COOKER CINNAMON ROLL

STRAWBERRY RHUBARB
SAUCE

STRAWBERRY RHUBARB SAUCE

This tart and tangy fruit sauce is excellent over pound cake or ice cream. I have served this topping many times and have gotten rave reviews from friends, family and all who try it.
—Judith Wasman, Harkers Island, NC

Prep: 10 min. • **Cook:** 6 hours
Makes: 10 servings

- 6 **cups chopped rhubarb (½-in. pieces)**
- 1 **cup sugar**
- ½ **tsp. grated orange zest**
- ½ **tsp. ground ginger**
- 1 **cinnamon stick (3 in.)**
- ½ **cup white grape juice**
- 2 **cups halved unsweetened strawberries**
  Angel food cake, pound cake or vanilla ice cream

1. Place rhubarb in a 3-qt. slow cooker. Combine sugar, orange zest and ginger; sprinkle over rhubarb. Add cinnamon stick and grape juice. Cover and cook on low for 5-6 hours or until rhubarb is tender.
2. Stir in the strawberries; cook 1 hour longer. Discard cinnamon stick. Serve with cake or ice cream.

½ cup: 111 cal., 0 fat (0 sat. fat), 0 chol., 5mg sod., 28g carb. (24g sugars, 2g fiber), 1g pro.

SLOW-COOKER CHOCOLATE POTS DE CREME

SLOW-COOKER CHOCOLATE POTS DE CREME

Lunch on the go just got a whole lot sweeter. Tuck jars of this rich chocolate custard into lunch bags for a midday treat. These desserts in a jar are fun for picnics, too.
—Nick Iverson, Denver, CO

Prep: 20 min. • **Cook:** 4 hours + chilling
Makes: 8 servings

- 2 **cups heavy whipping cream**
- 8 **oz. bittersweet chocolate, finely chopped**
- 1 **Tbsp. instant espresso powder**
- 4 **large egg yolks, room temperature**
- ¼ **cup sugar**
- ¼ **tsp. salt**
- 1 **Tbsp. vanilla extract**
- 3 **cups hot water**
  Optional: Whipped cream, grated chocolate and fresh raspberries

1. Place cream, chocolate and espresso in a microwave-safe bowl; microwave on high until chocolate is melted and cream is hot, about 4 minutes. Whisk to combine.
2. In a large bowl, whisk egg yolks, sugar and salt until blended but not foamy. Slowly whisk in cream mixture; stir in extract.
3. Ladle egg mixture into eight 4-oz. jars. Center lids on jars and screw on bands until fingertip tight. Add hot water to a 7-qt. slow cooker; place jars in slow cooker. Cook, covered, on low 4 hours or until set. Carefully remove jars from slow cooker; cool on counter for 30 minutes. Refrigerate until cold, about 2 hours.
4. If desired, top with whipped cream, grated chocolate and raspberries.

1 serving: 424 cal., 34g fat (21g sat. fat), 160mg chol., 94mg sod., 13g carb. (11g sugars, 1g fiber), 5g pro.

SECRET'S IN THE SAUCE
BBQ RIBS,
PAGE 125

SUMMER

SNACKS & APPETIZERS

**SLOW-COOKER
CHEESEBURGER DIP**

SLOW-COOKER CHEESEBURGER DIP

This fun dip recipe uses ingredients I always have in the fridge, so it's easy to throw together on short notice.
—Cindi DeClue, Anchorage, AK

Prep: 25 min. • **Cook:** 1¾ hours
Makes: 16 servings

- 1 lb. lean ground beef (90% lean)
- 1 medium onion, chopped
- 1 pkg. (8 oz.) cream cheese, cubed
- 2 cups shredded cheddar cheese, divided
- 1 Tbsp. Worcestershire sauce
- 2 tsp. prepared mustard
- ¼ tsp. salt
- ⅛ tsp. pepper
- 1 medium tomato, chopped
- ¼ cup chopped dill pickles
  Tortilla chips or crackers

1. In a large skillet, cook beef and onion over medium-high heat until beef is no longer pink and onion is tender, 6-8 minutes, breaking beef into crumbles; drain. Transfer to a greased 1½- or 3-qt. slow cooker. Stir in the cream cheese, 1½ cups cheddar cheese, Worcestershire, mustard, salt and pepper. Sprinkle with remaining cheese.
2. Cook the mixture, covered, on low 1¾-2¼ hours or until dip is heated through and cheese is melted. Top with chopped tomato and pickles. Serve with tortilla chips or crackers.
¼ cup: 157 cal., 12g fat (6g sat. fat), 46mg chol., 225mg sod., 2g carb. (1g sugars, 0 fiber), 10g pro.

ORANGE BLOSSOM
MINT REFRESHER

ORANGE BLOSSOM MINT REFRESHER

I came up with this recipe because I'm not a fan of regular iced tea. This tea has the perfect combination of freshness and sweetness. The orange blossom water gives it a distinctive flavor. People often request the recipe after just one sip.
—Juliana Gauss, Centennial, CO

Prep: 10 min. + chilling • **Cook:** 6 hours
Makes: 20 servings

- 20 cups water
- 1 bunch fresh mint (about 1 cup)
- 1 cup sugar
- 1 large navel orange
- 1 to 2 Tbsp. orange blossom water or 1½ to 2½ tsp. orange extract
  Optional: Orange slices and additional fresh mint

1. Place water and mint in a 6-qt. slow cooker. Cover; cook on high 6 hours or until heated through. Strain tea; discard mint.
2. Whisk in sugar until dissolved. Cut orange in half; squeeze out juice. Stir in juice and orange blossom water. Transfer to a pitcher. Refrigerate for 4-6 hours. Serve over ice, with orange slices and additional mint if desired.
1 cup: 43 cal., 0 fat (0 sat. fat), 0 chol., 0 sod., 11g carb. (11g sugars, 0 fiber), 0 pro.

LIP-SMACKING PEACH & WHISKEY WINGS

These sweet, spicy, sticky chicken wings are lip-smacking good! You could use fresh peaches in place of canned, but if doing so, I would add a few tablespoons of brown sugar.
—Sue Falk, Sterling Heights, MI

Prep: 20 min. • **Cook:** 4¼ hours
Makes: 2 dozen pieces

- 3 **lbs. chicken wings (about 1 dozen)**
- 1 **tsp. salt**
- ½ **tsp. pepper**
- 1 **can (29 oz.) sliced peaches in extra-light syrup, undrained**
- ½ **cup whiskey**
- ¼ **cup honey**
- 1 **Tbsp. lime juice**
- 1 **Tbsp. Louisiana-style hot sauce**
- 3 **garlic cloves, minced**
- 4 **tsp. cornstarch**
- 2 **Tbsp. cold water**
  Minced chives, optional

1. Pat chicken wings dry. Using a sharp knife, cut through the 2 wing joints; discard wing tips. Season wings with salt and pepper. Place in a 3- or 4-qt. slow cooker.

2. Pulse peaches with syrup in a food processor until pureed. Add the next 5 ingredients; pulse to combine. Pour over wings; toss to coat. Cook, covered, on low until chicken is tender, 4-6 hours. Combine cornstarch and water until smooth; stir into slow cooker. Cook, covered, on high until the sauce is thickened, about 15 minutes. Preheat broiler. Remove wings to a 15x10x1-in. pan; arrange in a single layer. Broil wings 3-4 in. from heat until lightly browned, 2-3 minutes. Brush with sauce before serving. Serve with the remaining sauce and, if desired, chives.

1 piece: 93 cal., 4g fat (1g sat. fat), 18mg chol., 140mg sod., 8g carb. (7g sugars, 0 fiber), 6g pro.

SLOW-COOKER SECRETS
Even though the alcohol will cook off as these wings simmer, it's always best to use a high-quality liquor, beer or wine when such ingredients are called for in a slow-cooker recipe.

LIP-SMACKING PEACH & WHISKEY WINGS

JALAPENO POPPER & SAUSAGE DIP

My workplace had an appetizer contest, and I won it with this quick, easy jalapeno and cheese dip. Every time I take it anywhere, folks always empty the slow cooker.
—Bev Slabik, Dilworth, MN

- -

Prep: 15 min. • **Cook:** 3 hours
Makes: 24 servings

- 1 **lb. bulk spicy pork sausage**
- 2 **pkg. (8 oz. each) cream cheese, cubed**
- 4 **cups shredded Parmesan cheese (about 12 oz.)**
- 1 **cup sour cream**
- 1 **can (4 oz.) chopped green chiles, undrained**
- 1 **can (4 oz.) diced jalapeno peppers, undrained**
  Assorted fresh vegetables

1. In a large skillet, cook sausage over medium heat 6-8 minutes or until no longer pink, breaking it into crumbles. Using a slotted spoon, transfer sausage to a 3-qt. slow cooker.
2. Stir in cream cheese, Parmesan cheese, sour cream, chiles and peppers. Cook, covered, on low 3-3½ hours or until heated through. Stir before serving. Serve dip with assorted vegetables.

¼ cup: 180 cal., 15g fat (8g sat. fat), 44mg chol., 399mg sod., 2g carb. (1g sugars, 0 fiber), 8g pro.

SUN-DRIED TOMATO SPINACH-ARTICHOKE DIP

Fresh veggies and crackers will disappear quickly when they're next to this cheesy slow-cooked dip. With smoked Gouda, it has an extra level of flavor that keeps everyone guessing.
—Katie Stanczak, Hoover, AL

Prep: 10 min. • **Cook:** 2 hours
Makes: 3 cups

- 1 pkg. (10 oz.) frozen chopped spinach, thawed and squeezed dry
- 1 pkg. (8 oz.) cream cheese, softened
- 1 cup shredded smoked Gouda cheese
- ½ cup shredded fontina cheese
- ½ cup chopped water-packed artichoke hearts
- ¼ to ½ cup soft sun-dried tomato halves (not packed in oil), chopped
- ⅓ cup finely chopped onion
- 1 garlic clove, minced
  Assorted fresh vegetables and crackers

In a 1½-qt. slow cooker, mix spinach, cheeses, artichoke hearts, sun-dried tomatoes, onion and garlic. Cook, covered, on low 2-3 hours or until cheese is melted. Stir before serving. Serve with vegetables and crackers.
¼ cup: 134 cal., 11g fat (6g sat. fat), 35mg chol., 215mg sod., 4g carb. (2g sugars, 1g fiber), 6g pro.

SUMMER PEACH SALSA

SUMMER PEACH SALSA

Summer-fresh peaches and tomatoes make my salsa a winner over store-bought versions any day.
—Peggi Stahnke, Cleveland, OH

Prep: 20 min. • **Cook:** 3 hours + cooling
Makes: 11 cups

- 4 lbs. tomatoes (about 12 medium), chopped
- 1 medium onion, chopped
- 4 jalapeno peppers, seeded and finely chopped
- ½ to ⅔ cup packed brown sugar
- ¼ cup minced fresh cilantro
- 4 garlic cloves, minced
- 1 tsp. salt
- 4 cups chopped peeled fresh peaches (about 4 medium), divided
- 1 can (6 oz.) tomato paste

1. In a 5-qt. slow cooker, combine the first 7 ingredients; stir in 2 cups peaches. Cook, covered, on low 3-4 hours or until onion is tender.
2. Stir tomato paste and remaining peaches into slow cooker. Cool. Transfer to covered containers. (If freezing, use freezer-safe containers and fill to within ½ in. of tops.) Refrigerate up to 1 week or freeze up to 12 months. Thaw frozen salsa in the refrigerator before serving.
Note: Wear disposable gloves when cutting hot peppers; the oils can burn skin. Avoid touching your face.
¼ cup: 28 cal., 0 fat (0 sat. fat), 0 chol., 59mg sod., 7g carb. (5g sugars, 1g fiber), 1g pro. **Diabetic exchanges:** ½ starch.

CHINESE MEATBALLS

These were a huge hit at a summer cookout I attended recently. You can use two tablespoons of chopped crystallized ginger in place of the fresh ginger if you'd like.
—Pat Barnes, Panama City, FL

- -

Prep: 35 min. • **Cook:** 3 hours
Makes: 6 dozen

- **2 large eggs, lightly beaten**
- **2 Tbsp. soy sauce**
- **1 tsp. salt**
- **6 green onions, sliced**
- **2 lbs. lean ground pork**
- **2 cans (8 oz. each) sliced water chestnuts, drained and chopped**
- **1 cup dry bread crumbs**

SAUCE
- **¼ cup cornstarch**
- **1 cup pineapple juice**
- **⅓ cup sugar**
- **4 tsp. minced fresh gingerroot**
- **1 can (10½ oz.) condensed beef consomme, undiluted**
- **½ cup white vinegar**

1. Preheat oven to 400°. In a large bowl, combine first 4 ingredients. Add pork, water chestnuts and bread crumbs; mix lightly but thoroughly. Shape mixture into 1-in. balls. Place in a greased 15x10x1-in. pan. Bake 15 minutes.

2. In a 5- or 6-qt. slow cooker, mix the cornstarch and juice until smooth. Stir in remaining ingredients. Add meatballs; stir gently to coat. Cook, covered, on low 3-4 hours or until meatballs are cooked through and sauce is thickened.

Freeze option: Freeze cooled meatball mixture in freezer containers. To use, partially thaw in refrigerator overnight. Heat through in a covered saucepan, stirring occasionally; add a little broth if necessary.

1 meatball: 41 cal., 2g fat (1g sat. fat), 12mg chol., 109mg sod., 4g carb. (2g sugars, 0 fiber), 3g pro.

SLOW-COOKER SECRETS
Stir 1 teaspoon crushed red pepper flakes into the sauce mixture to give these meatballs Sichuan flair.

CHINESE
MEATBALLS

CARIBBEAN CHIPOTLE
PORK SLIDERS

CARIBBEAN CHIPOTLE PORK SLIDERS

One of our favorite summer pulled pork recipes combines the heat of chipotle peppers with a cool tropical coleslaw. The robust flavors make these sliders a big hit with guests.
—Kadija Bridgewater, Boca Raton, FL

- -

Prep: 35 min. • **Cook:** 8 hours
Makes: 20 servings

- 1 **large onion, quartered**
- 1 **boneless pork shoulder butt roast (3 to 4 lbs.)**
- 2 **finely chopped chipotle peppers in adobo sauce plus 3 Tbsp. sauce**
- ¾ **cup honey barbecue sauce**
- ¼ **cup water**
- 4 **garlic cloves, minced**
- 1 **Tbsp. ground cumin**
- 1 **tsp. salt**
- ¼ **tsp. pepper**

COLESLAW
- 2 **cups finely chopped red cabbage**
- 1 **medium mango, peeled and chopped**
- 1 **cup pineapple tidbits, drained**
- ¾ **cup chopped fresh cilantro**
- 1 **Tbsp. lime juice**
- ¼ **tsp. salt**
- ⅛ **tsp. pepper**
- 20 **Hawaiian sweet rolls, split and toasted**

1. Place onion in a 5-qt. slow cooker. Cut roast in half; place over onion. In a small bowl, combine chipotle peppers, adobo sauce, barbecue sauce, water, garlic, cumin, salt and pepper; pour over meat. Cook, covered, on low 8-10 hours or until meat is tender.
2. Remove roast; cool slightly. Skim fat from cooking juices. Shred pork with 2 forks. Return pork to slow cooker; heat through.
3. For coleslaw, in a large bowl, combine cabbage, mango, pineapple, cilantro, lime juice, salt and pepper. Place ¼ cup pork mixture on each roll bottom; top with 2 Tbsp. coleslaw. Replace tops.
1 sandwich: 265 cal., 10g fat (4g sat. fat), 55mg chol., 430mg sod., 27g carb. (15g sugars, 2g fiber), 16g pro.

SAUSAGE JALAPENO DIP

SAUSAGE JALAPENO DIP

This creamy dip cooks like a dream in the slow cooker. Scoop it up with crunchy tortilla chips or raw veggies.
—Gina Fensler, Cincinnati, OH

- -

Prep: 15 min. • **Cook:** 5½ hours
Makes: 6 cups

- 1 **lb. bulk Italian sausage**
- 2 **large sweet red peppers, finely chopped**
- 3 **jalapeno peppers, finely chopped**
- 1 **cup whole milk**
- 2 **pkg. (8 oz. each) cream cheese, softened**
- 1 **cup shredded part-skim mozzarella cheese Tortilla chips**

1. In a large skillet, cook the sausage over medium heat 6-8 minutes or until no longer pink, breaking it into crumbles; drain.
2. Place red peppers, jalapenos and sausage in a 3-qt. slow cooker; add milk. Cook, covered, on low 5-6 hours or until peppers are tender.
3. Stir in cheeses. Cook, covered, on low 30 minutes longer or until cheese is melted. Serve with tortilla chips.
Note: Wear disposable gloves when cutting hot peppers; the oils can burn skin. Avoid touching your face.
¼ cup: 137 cal., 12g fat (6g sat. fat), 33mg chol., 211mg sod., 3g carb. (2g sugars, 0 fiber), 5g pro.

ROOT BEER PULLED PORK NACHOS

I count on my slow cooker to do the honors when I have a house full of summer guests. Teenagers especially love DIY nachos. Try cola, ginger ale or lemon-lime soda if you're simply not into root beer.

—James Schend, Pleasant Prairie, WI

Prep: 20 min. • **Cook:** 8 hours
Makes: 12 servings

- 1 **boneless pork shoulder butt roast (3 to 4 lbs.)**
- 1 **can (12 oz.) root beer or cola**
- 12 **cups tortilla chips**
- 2 **cups shredded cheddar cheese**
- 2 **medium tomatoes, chopped**
  Optional: Pico de gallo, chopped green onions and sliced jalapeno peppers

1. In a 4- or 5-qt. slow cooker, combine pork roast and root beer. Cook, covered, on low 8-9 hours, until meat is tender.
2. Remove roast; cool slightly. When cool enough to handle, shred meat with 2 forks. Return to slow cooker; keep meat warm.
3. To serve, drain pork. Layer tortilla chips with pork, cheese, tomatoes and optional toppings as desired. Serve nachos immediately.

1 serving: 391 cal., 23g fat (8g sat. fat), 86mg chol., 287mg sod., 20g carb. (4g sugars, 1g fiber), 25g pro.

SLOW-COOKER SECRETS
The cooked, cooled meat can be frozen for up to 4 months. Just be sure the cooking liquid covers the meat so it doesn't dry out. To use, partially thaw in refrigerator overnight, then reheat in the microwave or on the stovetop.

ROOT BEER
PULLED PORK NACHOS

ITALIAN MEATBALLS & SAUSAGES

Here's a wonderful nibble for a tailgate or any family function. The snack is so easy to prepare and also very tasty. I have doubled and even tripled the recipe for large groups. No matter how much I make, I always come home with an empty slow cooker.
—Jan Kasinger, Graham, WA

Prep: 10 min. • **Cook:** 4 hours
Makes: 8 cups

- 2 **lbs. frozen fully cooked Italian meatballs, thawed**
- 1 **bottle (16 oz.) zesty Italian salad dressing**
- 1 **pkg. (14 oz.) miniature smoked sausages**
- 2 **cups medium fresh mushrooms, stems removed**
- 1 **can (2¼ oz.) sliced ripe olives, drained**

Combine all ingredients in a 4- or 5-qt. slow cooker. Cook, covered, on low until heated through, 4-6 hours, stirring every hour.
1 serving: 200 cal., 16g fat (6g sat. fat), 29mg chol., 663mg sod., 4g carb. (1g sugars, 1g fiber), 9g pro.

SOUPS & SANDWICHES

SPINACH BEAN SOUP

SPINACH BEAN SOUP

This navy bean soup is heartwarming comfort food at its best. It's my signature soup that I make for family and friends. The red and green of the peppers and spinach give it a bright look.
—Barbara Shay, Pasadena, CA

- -

Prep: 20 min. + soaking · **Cook:** 7 hours
Makes: 3 qt.

- 1 **lb. dried navy beans**
- 2 **cartons (32 oz. each) chicken broth**
- 2 **cups water**
- 1 **smoked turkey wing (about 7 oz.)**
- 1 **medium onion, chopped**
- 1 **jalapeno pepper, seeded and finely chopped**
- 1 **Tbsp. minced garlic**
- 3 **bay leaves**
- 1 **tsp. pepper**
- ½ **tsp. crushed red pepper flakes**
- 10 **cups chopped fresh spinach (about 8 oz.)**
- 1 **large sweet red pepper, chopped**
- ½ **tsp. kosher salt**
   Grated Parmesan cheese, optional

1. Rinse and sort beans; soak according to package directions.
2. In a 5- or 6-qt. slow cooker, combine beans, broth, water, turkey wing, onion, jalapeno, garlic, bay leaves, pepper and pepper flakes. Cook, covered, on low until beans are tender, 7-9 hours.
3. Remove turkey wing and bay leaves; discard. Stir in spinach, red pepper and salt; heat through. If desired, serve with grated Parmesan cheese.

Note: Wear disposable gloves when cutting hot peppers; the oils can burn skin. Avoid touching your face.

1½ cups: 230 cal., 2g fat (0 sat. fat), 5mg chol., 1171mg sod., 40g carb. (5g sugars, 10g fiber), 15g pro.

HONEY BUFFALO MEATBALL SLIDERS

These little sliders deliver big Buffalo chicken flavor without the messiness of wings. The spicy-sweet meatballs are a hit on game day with kids and adults alike.
—Julie Peterson, Crofton, MD

- -

Prep: 10 min. · **Cook:** 2 hours
Makes: 6 servings

- ¼ **cup packed brown sugar**
- ¼ **cup Louisiana-style hot sauce**
- ¼ **cup honey**
- ¼ **cup apricot preserves**
- 2 **Tbsp. cornstarch**
- 2 **Tbsp. reduced-sodium soy sauce**
- 1 **pkg. (24 oz.) frozen fully cooked Italian turkey meatballs, thawed Additional hot sauce, optional Bibb lettuce leaves**
- 12 **mini buns Crumbled blue cheese Ranch salad dressing, optional**

1. In a 3- or 4-qt. slow cooker, mix the first 6 ingredients until smooth. Stir in meatballs until coated. Cook, covered, on low 2-3 hours, until meatballs are heated through.
2. If desired, stir in additional hot sauce. Serve meatballs on lettuce-lined buns; top with cheese and, if desired, the ranch dressing.

2 sliders: 524 cal., 21g fat (6g sat. fat), 110mg chol., 1364mg sod., 61g carb. (29g sugars, 1g fiber), 28g pro.

HONEY BUFFALO MEATBALL SLIDERS

CHICKEN TOMATILLO SOUP

I had tomatillos to use and wanted to make something more exquisite than salsa verde. I combined two favorite recipes and added my own special touches to make this soup. Feel free to add cayenne pepper or Tabasco sauce to spice it up.
—Katrina Krumm, Apple Valley, MN

- -

Prep: 1 hour • **Cook:** 3¾ hours
Makes: 8 servings (3 qt.)

- 2 **Tbsp. olive oil**
- 1 **medium onion, chopped**
- 3 **garlic cloves, minced**
- 1 **carton (32 oz.) reduced-sodium chicken broth**
- 1 **lb. tomatillos, husked and chopped (about 2 cups)**
- 2 **medium tomatoes, chopped**
- 1 **medium sweet red pepper, chopped**
- 1 **lb. boneless skinless chicken breast halves**
- 2 **Tbsp. taco seasoning**
- 1 **can (15 oz.) garbanzo beans or chickpeas, rinsed and drained**
- 1 **can (15 oz.) Southwestern black beans, undrained**
- 3 **cups fresh or frozen corn, thawed**
Optional toppings: Shredded cheddar cheese, minced fresh cilantro, sour cream, cubed avocado, jalapeno and fresno peppers, fried tortilla strips, and lime wedges

1. In a Dutch oven, heat oil over medium-high heat. Add onion; cook and stir until tender, 6-8 minutes. Add garlic; cook 1 minute longer. Stir in the broth, tomatillos, tomatoes and red pepper. Bring to a boil; reduce heat. Simmer, covered, until vegetables are tender, about 15 minutes. Cool slightly and puree in batches in a blender.

2. Place chicken in a 5- or 6-qt. slow cooker; sprinkle with taco seasoning. Pour pureed tomatillo mixture over the top. Add garbanzo and black beans. Cook, covered, on low until a thermometer inserted in chicken reads 165°, 3½-4 hours.

3. Remove chicken; shred with 2 forks. Return to slow cooker. Add corn. Cook, covered, until heated through, 15-30 minutes longer. Serve with toppings of your choice.

Freeze option: Freeze cooled soup in freezer containers. To use, partially thaw in refrigerator overnight. Heat through in a saucepan, stirring occasionally; add a little broth if necessary.

1½ cups: 290 cal., 8g fat (1g sat. fat), 31mg chol., 722mg sod., 36g carb. (10g sugars, 8g fiber), 21g pro. **Diabetic exchanges:** 2 starch, 2 lean meat, 1 vegetable, 1 fat.

CHICKEN TOMATILLO SOUP

SLOW-COOKER SHREDDED TURKEY SANDWICHES

This easy slow-cooked sandwich gets its zesty flavor from onion soup mix and beer. In total, it takes only five ingredients to make the recipe!
—Werner Knuth, Owatonna, MN

Prep: 15 minutes • **Cook:** 7 hours
Makes: 24 sandwiches

- 2 boneless skinless turkey breast halves (2 to 3 lbs. each)
- 1 bottle (12 oz.) beer or nonalcoholic beer
- ½ cup butter, cubed
- 1 envelope onion soup mix
- 24 French rolls, split

1. Place turkey in a 5-qt. slow cooker. Combine the beer, butter and soup mix; pour over meat. Cover and cook on low for 7-9 hours or until meat is tender.
2. Shred meat and return to slow cooker; heat through. Serve on rolls.
1 sandwich: 294 cal., 7g fat (3g sat. fat), 57mg chol., 476mg sod., 31g carb. (2g sugars, 1g fiber), 24g pro. **Diabetic exchanges:** 3 lean meat, 2 starch, ½ fat.

GOURMET BARBECUE BEEF SANDWICHES

These beef sandwiches were a tradition in my family on vacations, but they're a hit anytime we make them. Serving the savory barbecue beef on croissants with melty provolone cheese makes the sandwiches a little more special.
—Katie Anderson, Vancouver, WA

Prep: 10 min. • **Cook:** 8 hours 5 min.
Makes: 12 sandwiches

- 1   beef rump roast or bottom round roast (3 to 4 lbs.)
- ½   tsp. salt
- ¼   tsp. pepper
- 1   cup barbecue sauce
- 12 croissants, split
- 12 slices provolone cheese
      Optional: Tomato slices, lettuce leaves and red onion slices

1. Rub roast with salt and pepper. Place in a 5- or 6-qt. slow cooker. Cook, covered, on low 8-10 hours or until meat is tender.
2. Remove roast; cool slightly. Skim fat from cooking juices. Slice beef; return beef and cooking juices to slow cooker. Add barbecue sauce; heat through. Place croissant bottoms on a baking sheet; top with cheese. Broil 4-6 in. from heat until cheese is melted, 1-2 minutes. Top with beef. If desired, serve with optional toppings. Replace croissant tops.
1 sandwich: 511 cal., 25g fat (13g sat. fat), 125mg chol., 805mg sod., 38g carb. (15g sugars, 2g fiber), 33g pro.

CHICKEN WILD RICE SOUP WITH SPINACH

I stir together this creamy chicken soup whenever we're craving something warm and comforting. Reduced-fat and reduced-sodium ingredients make it a healthier option.
—Deborah Williams, Peoria, AZ

Prep: 10 min. • **Cook:** 5¼ hours
Makes: 6 servings (about 2 qt.)

- 3   cups water
- 1   can (14½ oz.) reduced-sodium chicken broth
- 1   can (10¾ oz.) reduced-fat reduced-sodium condensed cream of chicken soup, undiluted
- ⅔   cup uncooked wild rice
- 1   garlic clove, minced
- ½   tsp. dried thyme
- ½   tsp. pepper
- ¼   tsp. salt
- 3   cups cubed cooked chicken breast
- 2   cups fresh baby spinach

1. In a 3-qt. slow cooker, mix the first 8 ingredients until blended. Cook, covered, on low 5-7 hours or until rice is tender.
2. Stir in chicken and spinach. Cook, covered, on low until heated through, about 15 minutes longer.
1¼ cups: 212 cal., 3g fat (1g sat. fat), 56mg chol., 523mg sod., 19g carb. (4g sugars, 2g fiber), 25g pro. **Diabetic exchanges:** 3 lean meat, 1 starch.

CHICKEN WILD RICE SOUP WITH SPINACH

**CUBAN PULLED
PORK SANDWICHES**

1. In a 6- or 7-qt. slow cooker, combine the first 9 ingredients. Add pork; cook, covered, on low until tender, 8-10 hours. Remove roast; shred with 2 forks. In a large skillet, heat oil over medium-high heat. Cook meat in batches until lightly browned and crisp in spots.

2. Cut each loaf of bread in half lengthwise. If desired, spread mustard over cut sides of bread. Layer bottom halves of bread with pickles, pork, ham and cheese. Replace tops. Cut each loaf into 8 slices.

1 sandwich: 619 cal., 31g fat (13g sat. fat), 143mg chol., 1257mg sod., 35g carb. (5g sugars, 2g fiber), 50g pro.

SLOW-COOKER SECRETS

You can use regular bread and toast the Cuban sandwiches as you would a grilled cheese. To make a Cuban wrap, place the meat and toppings in flour tortillas and roll up.

CUBAN PULLED PORK SANDWICHES

I lived in Florida for a while and loved the pork I had there, so I went about making it for myself. The flavorful meat makes amazing Cuban sandwiches, but you can also use it in traditional pulled pork sandwiches or tacos.
—Lacie Griffin, Austin, TX

Prep: 30 min. • **Cook:** 8 hours
Makes: 16 sandwiches

- 1 cup orange juice
- ½ cup lime juice
- 12 garlic cloves, minced
- 2 Tbsp. spiced rum, optional
- 2 Tbsp. ground coriander
- 2 tsp. salt
- 2 tsp. white pepper
- 2 tsp. pepper
- 1 tsp. cayenne pepper
- 5 to 6 lbs. boneless pork shoulder roast, cut into 4 pieces
- 1 Tbsp. olive oil

SANDWICHES
- 2 loaves (1 lb. each) French bread
  Yellow mustard, optional
- 16 dill pickle slices
- 1½ lbs. thinly sliced deli ham
- 1½ lbs. Swiss cheese, sliced

CHEESY HAM
& CORN CHOWDER

BUFFALO CHICKEN SLIDERS

I got the idea for these sliders from my mom and dad, who had made a similar recipe for a family get-together. To make it special, I sometimes use several different styles of hot sauce and let guests add their favorites.
—Christina Addison, Blanchester, OH

- -

Prep: 20 min. • **Cook:** 3 hours
Makes: 6 servings

- 1   **lb. boneless skinless chicken breasts**
- 2   **Tbsp. plus ⅓ cup Louisiana-style hot sauce, divided**
- ¼   **tsp. pepper**
- ¼   **cup butter, cubed**
- ¼   **cup honey**
- 12 **Hawaiian sweet rolls, warmed Optional: Lettuce leaves, sliced tomato, thinly sliced red onion and crumbled blue cheese**

1. Place chicken in a 3-qt. slow cooker. Toss with 2 Tbsp. hot sauce and pepper; cook, covered, on low for 3-4 hours or until tender.
2. Remove chicken; discard cooking juices. In a small saucepan, combine butter, honey and remaining hot sauce; cook and stir over medium heat until blended. Shred chicken with 2 forks; stir into sauce and heat through. Serve on rolls with desired optional ingredients.
Freeze option: Freeze cooled chicken mixture in freezer containers. To use, partially thaw in refrigerator overnight. Microwave, covered, on high in a microwave-safe dish until heated through, stirring occasionally; add water or broth if necessary.
2 sliders: 396 cal., 15g fat (8g sat. fat), 92mg chol., 873mg sod., 44g carb. (24g sugars, 2g fiber), 24g pro.

CHEESY HAM & CORN CHOWDER

When the day calls for a big bowl of chunky soup, we haul out the slow cooker and whip up a big batch of this satisfying favorite.
—Andrea Laidlaw, Shady Side, MD

- -

Prep: 25 min. • **Cook:** 8½ hours
Makes: 12 servings (3¾ qt.)

- 1½ **lbs. potatoes (about 3 medium), peeled and cut into ½-in. cubes**
- 4   **cups fresh or frozen corn, thawed (about 20 oz.)**
- 4   **cups cubed deli ham**
- 2   **small onions, chopped**
- 4   **celery ribs, chopped**
- 4   **garlic cloves, minced**
- ¼   **tsp. pepper**
- 3   **cups chicken broth**
- 2   **Tbsp. cornstarch**
- 2   **cups whole milk**
- 2   **cups shredded sharp cheddar cheese**
- 1   **cup sour cream**
- 3   **Tbsp. minced fresh parsley**

1. Place the first 8 ingredients in a 6-qt. slow cooker. Cook, covered, on low 8-10 hours or until potatoes are tender.
2. In a small bowl, mix cornstarch and milk until smooth; stir into soup. Cook, covered, on high 20-30 minutes or until thickened, stirring occasionally. Add cheese, sour cream and parsley. Stir until cheese is melted.
1¼ cups: 291 cal., 14g fat (8g sat. fat), 65mg chol., 974mg sod., 23g carb. (7g sugars, 2g fiber), 19g pro.

BUFFALO CHICKEN SLIDERS

SAUSAGE & KRAUT BUNS

This recipe has become a regular at our church potlucks. Let's just say I'm in trouble if I show up at a get-together and they don't appear! For a fun dinner spin, try the sausages and kraut over mashed potatoes.
—Patsy Unruh, Perryton, TX

Prep: 20 min. • **Cook:** 4 hours
Makes: 12 sandwiches

- 2 **cans (14½ oz. each) no-salt-added diced tomatoes, drained**
- 2 **cans (14 oz. each) sauerkraut, rinsed and drained**
- ½ **lb. sliced fresh mushrooms**
- 1 **large sweet pepper, thinly sliced**
- 1 **large onion, halved and thinly sliced**
- 2 **Tbsp. brown sugar**
- ½ **tsp. pepper**
- 2 **pkg. (14 oz. each) smoked sausage, sliced**
- 12 **pretzel sausage buns, warmed and split partway**

1. In a 5- or 6-qt. slow cooker, combine first 7 ingredients. In a large skillet, saute sausage over medium-high heat until lightly browned. Stir into tomato mixture.

2. Cook, covered, on low until vegetables are tender, 4-5 hours. Serve in buns.

1 sandwich: 468 cal., 23g fat (8g sat. fat), 44mg chol., 1491mg sod., 51g carb. (12g sugars, 4g fiber), 17g pro.

SOUTHWESTERN
BEEF TORTILLAS

SOUTHWESTERN BEEF TORTILLAS

Beef chuck roast makes a savory filling in satisfying tortillas. Cooked to tender perfection in the slow cooker, the beef is treated to an easy and delicious jalapeno-flavored sauce.
—Marie Rizzio, Interlochen, MI

Prep: 25 min. • **Cook:** 8½ hours
Makes: 8 servings

- 1 **boneless beef chuck roast (2 lbs.)**
- ½ **cup water**
- 4 **large tomatoes, peeled and chopped**
- 1 **large green pepper, thinly sliced**
- 1 **medium onion, chopped**
- 1 **garlic clove, minced**
- 1 **bay leaf**
- 2 **Tbsp. canola oil**
- ¾ **cup ketchup**
- ½ **cup pickled jalapeno slices**
- 1 **Tbsp. juice from pickled jalapeno slices**
- 1 **Tbsp. cider vinegar**
- 1 **tsp. salt**
- ⅛ **tsp. garlic salt**
- 8 **flour tortillas (8 in.), warmed**

1. Place roast and water in a 3-qt. slow cooker. Cover and cook on low for 8-9 hours or until meat is tender.
2. Remove meat. When cool enough to handle, shred meat with 2 forks. Skim fat from cooking juices; set aside ½ cup. Meanwhile, in a large skillet, cook the tomatoes, green pepper, onion, garlic and bay leaf in oil over low heat for 15-20 minutes or until the vegetables are softened.
3. Stir in ketchup, jalapeno slices and juice, vinegar, salt, garlic salt and reserved cooking juices. Bring to a boil. Stir in shredded beef; heat through. Discard bay leaf. Serve on tortillas.

1 filled tortilla: 425 cal., 17g fat (5g sat. fat), 74mg chol., 1135mg sod., 39g carb. (10g sugars, 2g fiber), 28g pro.

READER RAVE...

"A huge hit! Very flavorful and makes a large batch. I also seasoned it with about ½ packet of taco seasoning and it was awesome."

—AVACCA08, TASTEOFHOME.COM

COCONUT-LIME CHICKEN CURRY SOUP

I created this chicken recipe to replicate the flavors of my favorite curry dish—slightly sweet with just the right amount of spicy heat.
—Lisa Renshaw, Kansas City, MO

- -

Prep: 15 min. • **Cook:** 4¼ hours
Makes: 8 servings (2½ qt.)

- 2 **cans (13.66 oz. each) light coconut milk**
- 2 **cans (4 oz. each) chopped green chiles**
- 8 **green onions, sliced**
- 2 **tsp. grated lime zest**
- ½ **cup lime juice**
- ¼ **cup sweet chili sauce**
- 6 **garlic cloves, minced**
- 4 **tsp. curry powder**
- ½ **tsp. salt**
- 2 **lbs. boneless skinless chicken thighs, cut into ½-in. pieces**
- 3 **cups cooked basmati rice**
  Minced fresh cilantro

1. Place the first 9 ingredients in a 4- or 5-qt. slow cooker; stir in chicken. Cook, covered, on low 4-5 hours or until chicken is tender.
2. Skim off fat; stir in cooked rice. Cook, covered, on low 15-30 minutes or until heated through. Sprinkle servings with cilantro.

1¼ cups: 356 cal., 16g fat (7g sat. fat), 76mg chol., 455mg sod., 28g carb. (7g sugars, 2g fiber), 23g pro.

BEEF & VEGGIE SLOPPY JOES

BEEF & VEGGIE SLOPPY JOES

I'm always looking for ways to serve my family healthy and delicious food, so I started experimenting with my favorite veggies and ground beef. I came up with this favorite that my kids actually request!
—Megan Niebuhr, Yakima, WA

- -

Prep: 35 min. • **Cook:** 5 hours
Makes: 10 sandwiches

- 4 **medium carrots, shredded**
- 1 **medium yellow summer squash, shredded**
- 1 **medium zucchini, shredded**
- 1 **medium sweet red pepper, finely chopped**
- 2 **medium tomatoes, seeded and chopped**
- 1 **small red onion, finely chopped**
- ½ **cup ketchup**
- 3 **Tbsp. minced fresh basil or 3 tsp. dried basil**
- 3 **Tbsp. molasses**
- 2 **Tbsp. cider vinegar**
- 2 **garlic cloves, minced**
- ½ **tsp. salt**
- ½ **tsp. pepper**
- 2 **lbs. lean ground beef (90% lean)**
- 10 **whole wheat hamburger buns, split**

1. In a 5- or 6-qt. slow cooker, combine the first 13 ingredients. In a large skillet, cook beef over medium heat until no longer pink, 8-10 minutes; crumble meat; drain. Transfer beef to slow cooker. Stir to combine.
2. Cook, covered, on low 5-6 hours or until heated through and vegetables are tender. Use a slotted spoon to serve beef mixture on buns.

1 sandwich: 316 cal., 10g fat (3g sat. fat), 57mg chol., 565mg sod., 36g carb. (15g sugars, 5g fiber), 22g pro. **Diabetic exchanges:** 2 starch, 2 lean meat, 1 vegetable.

GREEN CHILE POSOLE

This recipe combines parts of my nanny's and my mother's recipes that were taught to me when I was young. An optional sprinkling of queso fresco on top is an absolute delight, in my opinion.
—Jaime Love, Las Vegas, NV

- -

Prep: 10 min. • **Cook:** 4 hours
Makes: 6 servings (2 qt.)

- 1 pork tenderloin (1 lb.), cut into 1-in. pieces
- 2 cans (15 oz. each) hominy, rinsed and drained
- 1 can (4 oz.) chopped green chiles
- ¼ tsp. salt
- ¼ tsp. pepper
- 4 cups chicken broth, divided
- 3 tomatillos, husked and chopped
  Optional: Sliced avocado, lime wedge, sliced jalapenos, sliced radishes, chopped cilantro and sour cream

1. Place first 5 ingredients and 3¾ cups broth in a 3- or 4-qt. slow cooker. Puree tomatillos with remaining ¼ cup broth in a blender; stir into pork mixture.
2. Cook, covered, on low until pork is tender, 4-5 hours. If desired, serve with avocado and other toppings.

1⅓ cups: 173 cal., 3g fat (1g sat. fat), 46mg chol., 1457mg sod., 17g carb. (1g sugars, 4g fiber), 17g pro.

GREEN CHILE POSOLE

CHICKEN & KALE TORTELLINI SOUP

With tender tortellini, chicken, spinach and lots of herbs, this comforting soup is so flavorful. The fact that it's easy to make is just a busy-day bonus.
—Emily Hobbs, Springfield, MO

- -

Prep: 15 min. • **Cook:** 2½ hours
Makes: 8 servings (3 qt.)

- 1 lb. boneless skinless chicken breasts, cut into 1¼-in. cubes
- 2 garlic cloves, minced
- 1½ tsp. Italian seasoning
- ¼ tsp. pepper
- 6 cups chicken broth
- 1 pkg. (20 oz.) refrigerated cheese tortellini
- 1 can (15 oz.) cannellini beans, rinsed and drained
- 1 jar (7½ oz.) marinated quartered artichoke hearts, drained and coarsely chopped
- 4 cups coarsely chopped fresh kale (about 2 oz.)
  Shaved Parmesan cheese, optional

1. Place the first 5 ingredients in a 5- or 6-qt. slow cooker. Cook, covered, on low 2-3 hours, until chicken is no longer pink.
2. Stir in tortellini, beans, artichoke hearts and kale. Cook, covered, on low about 30 minutes, until tortellini and kale are tender, stirring halfway through cook time. Serve immediately. If desired, top with cheese.

1½ cups: 386 cal., 12g fat (4g sat. fat), 66mg chol., 1185mg sod., 43g carb. (4g sugars, 4g fiber), 24g pro.

EASY POT STICKER SOUP

EASY POT STICKER SOUP

Because my husband and I have soup often, I'm always coming up with something new. I saw pot stickers in the freezer and decided to feature them in an Asian soup. The results were delicious. Rice vinegar adds just the right tang, and the green onions and carrots act as a garnish. Stir in chopped cabbage or bok choy if you'd like. A little sesame oil goes a long way, but you can always add a bit more.
—Darlene Brenden, Salem, OR

- -

Prep: 15 min. • **Cook:** 5¼ hours
Makes: 6 servings

- ½ **lb. Chinese or napa cabbage, thinly sliced**
- 2 **celery ribs, thinly sliced**
- 2 **medium carrots, cut into matchsticks**
- ⅓ **cup thinly sliced green onions**
- 2 **to 3 Tbsp. soy sauce**
- 2 **Tbsp. rice vinegar**
- 3 **garlic cloves, minced**
- 2 **tsp. minced fresh gingerroot or ½ tsp. ground ginger**
- ½ **tsp. sesame oil**
- 6 **cups reduced-sodium chicken broth**
- 1 **pkg. (16 oz.) frozen chicken pot stickers Crispy chow mein noodles, optional**

In a 4-qt. slow cooker, combine the first 9 ingredients. Stir in broth. Cook, covered, on low until vegetables are tender, 5-6 hours. Add pot stickers; cook, covered, on high until heated through, 15-20 minutes. If desired, sprinkle with chow mein noodles before serving.

CHIPOTLE BEEF SANDWICHES

1⅓ cups: 198 cal., 6g fat (2g sat. fat), 28mg chol., 1302mg sod., 23g carb. (5g sugars, 2g fiber), 13g pro.

CHIPOTLE BEEF SANDWICHES

A jar of chipotle salsa makes it easy to spice up beef sirloin for these mouthwatering sandwiches. Keep this no-stress recipe in mind the next time you have to feed a hungry crowd.
—Jessica Ring, Madison, WI

- -

Prep: 25 min. • **Cook:** 7 hours
Makes: 10 sandwiches

- 1 **large sweet onion, halved and thinly sliced**
- 1 **beef sirloin tip roast (3 lbs.)**
- 1 **jar (16 oz.) chipotle salsa**
- ½ **cup beer or nonalcoholic beer**
- 1 **envelope Lipton beefy onion soup mix**
- 10 **kaiser rolls, split**

1. Place onion in a 5-qt. slow cooker. Cut roast in half; place over onion. Combine the salsa, beer and soup mix. Pour over top. Cover and cook on low for 7-8 hours or until meat is tender.
2. Remove roast. Shred meat with 2 forks and return to the slow cooker; heat through. Using a slotted spoon, spoon shredded meat onto rolls.
1 sandwich: 362 cal., 9g fat (3g sat. fat), 72mg chol., 524mg sod., 37g carb. (6g sugars, 2g fiber), 31g pro. **Diabetic exchanges:** 3 lean meat, 2½ starch.

BLACKBERRY SRIRACHA CHICKEN SLIDERS

Dump everything in a slow cooker and then watch these spicy-sweet sliders become an instant party-time classic.
—Julie Peterson, Crofton, MD

Prep: 20 min. • **Cook:** 5 hours
Makes: 1 dozen

- 1   **jar (10 oz.) seedless blackberry spreadable fruit**
- ¼   **cup ketchup**
- ¼   **cup balsamic vinegar**
- ¼   **cup Sriracha chili sauce**
- 2   **Tbsp. molasses**
- 1   **Tbsp. Dijon mustard**
- ¼   **tsp. salt**
- 3½ **lbs. bone-in chicken thighs**
- 1   **large onion, thinly sliced**
- 4   **garlic cloves, minced**
- 12 **pretzel mini buns, split**
     Additional Sriracha chili sauce
     Leaf lettuce and tomato slices

1. In a 4- or 5-qt. slow cooker, stir together the first 7 ingredients. Add the chicken, onion and garlic. Toss to combine.

2. Cook, covered, on low until chicken is tender, 5-6 hours. Remove chicken. When cool enough to handle, remove bones and skin; discard. Shred meat with 2 forks. Reserve 3 cups cooking juices; discard remaining juices. Skim fat from reserved juices. Return chicken and reserved juices to slow cooker; heat through. Using slotted spoon, serve on pretzel buns. Drizzle with additional chili sauce; top with lettuce and tomato.

Freeze option: Freeze cooled chicken mixture in freezer containers. To use, partially thaw in refrigerator overnight. Heat through in a covered saucepan, stirring occasionally; add a little broth if necessary.

1 slider: 352 cal., 14g fat (3g sat. fat), 63mg chol., 413mg sod., 35g carb. (12g sugars, 1g fiber), 21g pro.

BLACKBERRY SRIRACHA CHICKEN SLIDERS

SLOW-COOKER CREAMY CAULIFLOWER SOUP

I love indulgent cream soups but not the fat that goes along with them. In this healthier version, the soup's velvety texture makes it feel rich, and the spicy kick is a perfect accent.
—Teri Rasey, Cadillac, MI

Prep: 20 min. • **Cook:** 6 hours
Makes: 14 servings (3½ qt.)

1¾ lbs. Yukon Gold potatoes (about 4 medium), peeled and cut into 1-in. cubes
1 medium head cauliflower (about 1½ lbs.), cut into 1-in. pieces
1 small onion, chopped
3 garlic cloves, minced
1 large bay leaf
3 tsp. dried celery flakes
1½ tsp. salt
1½ tsp. adobo seasoning
¾ tsp. ground mustard
¼ tsp. cayenne pepper
6 cups water
¾ cup nonfat dry milk powder
Optional toppings: Shredded cheddar cheese, sliced green onions and croutons

1. Place first 10 ingredients in a 6-qt. slow cooker. Add water; sprinkle milk powder over the top.
2. Cook, covered, on low until cauliflower is very tender, 6-8 hours. Remove bay leaf. Puree soup using an immersion blender. Or cool slightly and puree soup in batches in a blender; return to slow cooker and heat through. If desired, serve with toppings.

1 cup: 80 cal., 0 fat (0 sat. fat), 1mg chol., 434mg sod., 17g carb. (4g sugars, 2g fiber), 3g pro. **Diabetic exchanges:** 1 vegetable, ½ starch.

BOURBON BARBECUE
CHICKEN TACOS

BOURBON BARBECUE CHICKEN TACOS

I wanted to try a different take on taco night and decided on a barbecue theme. Even my father enjoyed this meal, and he doesn't usually care for tacos.
—LaDale Hymer, Cleveland, OK

- -

Prep: 30 min. • **Cook:** 3 hours
Makes: 8 servings

- 1   **cup ketchup**
- 1   **small red onion, finely chopped**
- ¼   **cup packed brown sugar**
- 2   **Tbsp. Worcestershire sauce**
- 2   **Tbsp. maple syrup**
- 2   **Tbsp. cider vinegar**
- 1   **Tbsp. chopped fresh parsley**
- 2   **garlic cloves, minced**
- ¼   **tsp. pepper**
- 3   **Tbsp. bourbon, divided**
- 1½ **lbs. boneless skinless chicken breasts**

SALSA

- 2   **cups fresh or thawed frozen corn**
- 1   **cup chopped sweet red pepper**
- ½   **cup finely chopped red onion**
- 2   **medium limes, zested and juiced**
- ⅛   **tsp. hot pepper sauce**
- ½   **tsp. salt**
- ¼   **tsp. pepper**
- 8   **flour tortillas (8 in.)**
      Minced cilantro, optional

1. In a 3-qt. slow cooker, combine the first 9 ingredients and 2 Tbsp. bourbon. Add chicken; turn to coat. Cook, covered, on low until a thermometer reads 165°, 3-4 hours. Remove chicken; shred with 2 forks. Return to slow cooker; stir in remaining bourbon. Heat through.
2. For the salsa, combine corn, pepper, onion, lime juice and zest, hot sauce, salt and pepper. Serve chicken in tortillas with salsa. If desired, top with cilantro.

GREEN CHILE RIBS

1 taco: 387 cal., 6g fat (2g sat. fat), 47mg chol., 855mg sod., 58g carb. (22g sugars, 4g fiber), 23g pro.

GREEN CHILE RIBS

I like my food with a spicy kick; my wife does not. These ribs with green chiles suit her taste. For more firepower, add cayenne or jalapenos.
—Guy Newton, Nederland, CO

- -

Prep: 20 min. • **Cook:** 5 hours
Makes: 8 servings

- 4   **lbs. pork baby back ribs**
- 2   **Tbsp. ground cumin, divided**
- 2   **Tbsp. olive oil**
- 1   **small onion, finely chopped**
- 1   **jar (16 oz.) salsa verde**
- 3   **cans (4 oz. each) chopped green chiles**
- 2   **cups beef broth**
- ¼   **cup minced fresh cilantro**
- 1   **Tbsp. all-purpose flour**
- 3   **garlic cloves, minced**
- ¼   **tsp. cayenne pepper**
      Additional minced fresh cilantro

1. Cut ribs into serving-size pieces; rub with 1 Tbsp. cumin. In a large skillet, heat oil over medium-high heat. Brown ribs in batches. Place ribs in a 6-qt. slow cooker.
2. Add onion to same pan; cook and stir 2-3 minutes or until onion is tender. Add salsa verde, green chiles, broth, ¼ cup cilantro, flour, garlic, cayenne and remaining cumin to slow cooker. Cook, covered, on low 5-6 hours or until the meat is tender. Sprinkle with additional cilantro.

1 serving: 349 cal., 25g fat (8g sat. fat), 81mg chol., 797mg sod., 8g carb. (2g sugars, 1g fiber), 24g pro.

FARM-STYLE BBQ RIBS

Inspiration struck when I saw a recipe similar to this one in a newspaper. My version was an instant hit with my husband and our friends. It got even better when I discovered how easy it is to make in the slow cooker.
—Bette Jo Welton, Eugene, OR

Prep: 20 min. • **Cook:** 6 hours
Makes: 4 servings

- 4 lbs. bone-in beef short ribs
- 1 can (15 oz.) thick and zesty tomato sauce
- 1½ cups water
- 1 medium onion, chopped
- 1 can (6 oz.) tomato paste
- ⅓ cup packed brown sugar
- 3 Tbsp. cider vinegar
- 3 Tbsp. Worcestershire sauce
- 2 Tbsp. chili powder
- 4 garlic cloves, minced
- 2 tsp. ground mustard
- 1½ tsp. salt

Place ribs in a 5- or 6-qt. slow cooker. In a large saucepan, combine the remaining ingredients. Bring to a boil. Reduce heat; simmer, uncovered, 5 minutes or until slightly thickened. Pour over ribs; cook, covered, on low 6-8 hours or until tender.

1 serving: 578 cal., 24g fat (9g sat. fat), 110mg chol., 2503mg sod., 46g carb. (32g sugars, 7g fiber), 44g pro.

SIMPLE POACHED SALMON

I love this recipe because it's healthy and almost effortless. The salmon always cooks to perfection!
—Erin Chilcoat, Central Islip, NY

Prep: 10 min. • **Cook:** 1½ hours
Makes: 4 servings

- 2 cups water
- 1 cup white wine
- 1 medium onion, sliced
- 1 celery rib, sliced
- 1 medium carrot, sliced
- 2 Tbsp. lemon juice
- 3 fresh thyme sprigs
- 1 fresh rosemary sprig
- 1 bay leaf
- ½ tsp. salt
- ¼ tsp. pepper
- 4 salmon fillets (1¼ in. thick and 6 oz. each)
  Lemon wedges

1. In a 3-qt. slow cooker, combine the first 11 ingredients. Cook, covered, on low 45 minutes.
2. Carefully place fillets in liquid; add additional warm water (120° to 130°) to cover if needed. Cook, covered, just until fish flakes easily with a fork (a thermometer inserted in fish should read at least 145°), 45-55 minutes. Remove the fish from cooking liquid. Serve warm or cold with lemon wedges.

1 salmon fillet: 272 cal., 16g fat (3g sat. fat), 85mg chol., 115mg sod., 1g carb. (0 sugars, 0 fiber), 29g pro. **Diabetic exchanges:** 4 lean meat.

COCONUT CHICKEN & SWEET POTATO STEW

COCONUT CHICKEN & SWEET POTATO STEW

This stew tastes as if you spent hours in the kitchen. The flavors of coconut milk, sweet potato and coriander nicely complement the chicken. A garnish of cilantro and toasted coconut adds a bit of sophistication.
—Nicole Filizetti, Stevens Point, WI

Prep: 20 min. • **Cook:** 6 hours
Makes: 8 servings (2½ qt.)

- 1½ **lbs. boneless skinless chicken breasts, cubed**
- 2 **lbs. sweet potatoes (about 3 medium), peeled and cubed**
- 3 **cups canned coconut milk, divided**
- 1 **can (8 oz.) unsweetened pineapple tidbits, drained**
- 1 **small onion, chopped**
- 1 **tsp. ground coriander**
- ½ **tsp. salt**
- ½ **tsp. crushed red pepper flakes**
- ¼ **tsp. pepper**
  Optional: Hot cooked basmati rice, toasted unsweetened shredded coconut, minced fresh cilantro and lime wedges

1. Combine chicken, sweet potatoes, 2 cups coconut milk, pineapple, onion and seasonings in a 4- or 5-qt. slow cooker. Cook, covered, on low until chicken and sweet potatoes are tender, 6-8 hours.
2. Stir in remaining 1 cup coconut milk. If desired, serve with optional ingredients.

1¼ cups: 365 cal., 16g fat (14g sat. fat), 47mg chol., 223mg sod., 34g carb. (17g sugars, 4g fiber), 21g pro.

HULI HULI CHICKEN THIGHS

I'm allergic to store-bought barbecue sauces, so when I found a marinade recipe I could use, I tweaked it a little and began using it with chicken thighs. My fiance especially loves this over Parmesan couscous.

—Erin Rockwell, Lowell, MA

Prep: 10 min. • **Cook:** 4 hours
Makes: 8 servings

- 1   **cup crushed pineapple, drained**
- ¾   **cup ketchup**
- ⅓   **cup reduced-sodium soy sauce**
- 3   **Tbsp. brown sugar**
- 3   **Tbsp. lime juice**
- 1   **garlic clove, minced**
- 8   **boneless skinless chicken thighs (about 2 lbs.)**
     Hot cooked rice
     Sliced green onions, optional

1. Mix the first 6 ingredients. Place chicken in a 3-qt. slow cooker; top with pineapple mixture.
2. Cook, covered, on low until chicken is tender, 4-5 hours. Serve with rice. If desired, top with green onions.
1 serving: 239 cal., 8g fat (2g sat. fat), 76mg chol., 733mg sod., 19g carb. (16g sugars, 0 fiber), 22g pro. **Diabetic exchanges:** 3 lean meat, 1 starch.

SMOTHERED ROUND STEAK

SMOTHERED ROUND STEAK

Try affordable round steak and gravy served over egg noodles for a hearty meal. Meaty and packed with veggies, this slow-cooker creation will take the worry out of wondering what's for dinner.

—Kathy Garrett, Camden, WV

Prep: 15 min. • **Cook:** 6 hours
Makes: 4 servings

- 1½ **lbs. beef top round steak, cut into strips**
- ⅓   **cup all-purpose flour**
- ½   **tsp. salt**
- ¼   **tsp. pepper**
- 1   **large onion, sliced**
- 1   **large green pepper, sliced**
- 1   **can (14½ oz.) diced tomatoes, undrained**
- 1   **jar (4 oz.) sliced mushrooms, drained**
- 3   **Tbsp. reduced-sodium soy sauce**
- 2   **Tbsp. molasses**
     Hot cooked egg noodles, optional

1. In a 3-qt. slow cooker, toss beef with flour, salt and pepper. Stir in all remaining ingredients except noodles.
2. Cook, covered, on low until meat is tender, 6-8 hours. If desired, serve with noodles.
1¼ cups beef mixture: 335 cal., 6g fat (2g sat. fat), 95mg chol., 1064mg sod., 28g carb. (14g sugars, 4g fiber), 42g pro.

KOREAN PULLED PORK TACOS

I created this unique pulled pork recipe so we could replicate our favorite food truck tacos at home. They're a little sweet, a little spicy and totally delicious any time of year.
—Julie Orr, Fullerton, CA

Prep: 25 min. • **Cook:** 8 hours
Makes: 10 servings

½ cup reduced-sodium soy sauce
½ cup water
3 Tbsp. brown sugar
2 Tbsp. sesame oil
1 Tbsp. baking cocoa
3 tsp. chili powder
1 garlic clove, minced
¼ tsp. ground ginger
1 boneless pork shoulder butt roast (4-5 lbs.)

SLAW
3 Tbsp. sugar
2 Tbsp. reduced-sodium soy sauce
1 Tbsp. Sriracha chili sauce
2 tsp. sesame oil
1 tsp. rice vinegar
1 pkg. (14 oz.) coleslaw mix
1 Tbsp. toasted sesame seeds, optional

ASSEMBLY
20 flour tortillas (6 in.), warmed
Optional: Thinly sliced green onions and additional Sriracha chili sauce

KOREAN
PULLED PORK TACOS

1. Whisk together first 8 ingredients. Place roast in a 6-qt. slow cooker. Pour the soy sauce mixture over top. Cook, covered, on low until pork is tender, 8-10 hours.

2. About 1 hour before serving, mix first 5 slaw ingredients until blended. Place coleslaw mix in a large bowl; toss with dressing and, if desired, sesame seeds. Refrigerate, covered, until serving.

3. Remove roast; skim fat from cooking juices. Shred pork with 2 forks; return to slow cooker and heat through. Serve in tortillas with slaw. If desired, serve with sliced green onions and additional chili sauce.

Freeze option: Freeze cooled pork mixture in freezer containers. To use, partially thaw in refrigerator overnight. Heat through in a saucepan, stirring occasionally; add a little water or broth if necessary.

2 tacos: 603 cal., 29g fat (10g sat. fat), 108mg chol., 1177mg sod., 46g carb. (11g sugars, 4g fiber), 37g pro.

MOROCCAN LAMB
LETTUCE WRAPS

2 filled lettuce wraps: 221 cal., 8g fat
(2g sat. fat), 74mg chol., 257mg sod.,
13g carb. (8g sugars, 1g fiber), 24g
pro. **Diabetic exchanges:** 3 lean meat,
1 starch.

SPICED LIME & CILANTRO CHICKEN

As a working mom and a home cook,
I strive to have fabulous, flavor-packed
dinners that make my family smile.
Nothing is more awesome than a
slow-cooker recipe that makes it
seem as though you've been cooking
in the kitchen all day!
—Mari Smith, Ashburn, VA

Prep: 15 min. • **Cook:** 3 hours
Makes: 6 servings

- 2 tsp. chili powder
- 1 tsp. sea salt
- 1 tsp. ground cumin
- 1 tsp. pepper
- ¼ tsp. cayenne pepper
- 6 bone-in chicken thighs
  (about 2¼ lbs.)
- ⅓ cup lime juice (about 3 limes)
- 1 Tbsp. olive oil
- ½ cup fresh cilantro leaves
- 5 garlic cloves, halved

1. Combine the first 5 ingredients;
rub over the chicken. Place in a 4- or
5-qt. slow cooker. Combine remaining
ingredients in a blender; cover and
process until pureed. Pour over
the chicken.
2. Cook, covered, on low until a
thermometer inserted in chicken
reads 170°-175°, 3-4 hours.

1 chicken thigh: 253 cal., 17g fat
(4g sat. fat), 81mg chol., 390mg sod.,
2g carb. (0 sugars, 0 fiber), 23g pro.

MOROCCAN LAMB LETTUCE WRAPS

I am a huge fan of both lamb and
lettuce wraps. This combination—
with the creamy dressing and crunchy
cucumber—makes a tasty slow-cooked
dish. The wine and chili powder add
even more flavor elements.
—Arlene Erlbach, Morton Grove, IL

Prep: 25 min. • **Cook:** 5 hours
Makes: 8 servings

- 2 lbs. lamb stew meat
- 1 cup chunky salsa
- ⅓ cup apricot preserves
- 6 Tbsp. dry red wine, divided
- 1 to 2 Tbsp. Moroccan seasoning
  (ras el hanout)
- 2 tsp. chili powder
- ½ tsp. garlic powder
- 1 English cucumber,
  very thinly sliced
- 2 Tbsp. prepared ranch
  salad dressing
- 16 Bibb or Boston lettuce leaves

1. Combine lamb, salsa, preserves,
4 Tbsp. wine, Moroccan seasoning,
chili powder and garlic powder. Transfer
to a 3-qt. slow cooker. Cook, covered,
on low 5-6 hours, until lamb is tender.
Remove the lamb; shred with 2 forks.
Strain cooking juices and skim fat.
Return lamb and cooking juices to
the slow cooker; heat through. Stir in
remaining 2 Tbsp. wine; heat through.
2. Combine cucumber and ranch
dressing; toss to coat. Serve lamb
mixture in lettuce leaves; top with
cucumber mixture.

SPICED LIME &
CILANTRO CHICKEN

BBQ BRATS

In Wisconsin, brats are a food group! We are always looking for new ways to cook them. This recipe is easy and a hit at any tailgate party or cookout, any time of year.
—Jessica Abnet, DePere, WI

- -

Prep: 20 min. • **Cook:** 3 hours
Makes: 10 servings

- 10 **uncooked bratwurst links**
- 1 **bottle (12 oz.) beer or**
  1½ cups chicken broth
- 1 **cup ketchup**
- 1 **cup honey barbecue sauce**
- 10 **hot dog buns, split**
  Spicy brown mustard

1. Grill the bratwursts, covered, on an oiled rack over medium heat or broil 4 in. from heat for 10 minutes, turning frequently. Transfer to a 5-qt. slow cooker.

2. In a large bowl, mix beer, ketchup and barbecue sauce; pour over the bratwursts. Cook, covered, on low until cooked through, 3-4 hours. Place the bratwursts on buns. Serve with mustard and, if desired, cooking liquid.

1 serving: 480 cal., 27g fat (9g sat. fat), 64mg chol., 1659mg sod., 41g carb. (20g sugars, 1g fiber), 16g pro.

BBQ BRATS

FRESH SPINACH TAMALE PIE

I got this recipe from my mother, who loved quick and easy meals for dinner. I made a few variations by adding spinach, bell peppers and fresh corn. The changes were well worth it— my family and friends love this dish!
—Nancy Heishman, Las Vegas, NV

Prep: 20 min. • **Cook:** 3 hours
Makes: 10 servings

- 8 frozen beef tamales, thawed
- 2 cans (15 oz. each) pinto beans, rinsed and drained
- 2 cups fresh or frozen corn
- 4 green onions, chopped
- 1 can (2¼ oz.) sliced ripe olives, drained
- ½ tsp. garlic powder
- ¾ cup chopped sweet red pepper
- ¾ cup sour cream
- 1 can (4 oz.) whole green chiles, drained and chopped
- 3 cups chopped fresh spinach
- 12 bacon strips, cooked and crumbled
- 2 cups shredded cheddar cheese
   Additional green onions, chopped

1. Place tamales in a single layer in a greased 6-qt. slow cooker. In a large bowl, combine beans, corn, onions, olives and garlic powder; spoon over tamales. In same bowl, combine pepper, sour cream and chiles; spoon over bean mixture. Top with spinach.
2. Cook, covered, on low until heated through, 3-4 hours. Sprinkle with bacon, cheese and additional green onions.
1 serving: 459 cal., 24g fat (9g sat. fat), 49mg chol., 1013mg sod., 40g carb. (4g sugars, 7g fiber), 23g pro.

GREEK SAUSAGE & PEPPERS

This recipe is an old family favorite. My grandmother, mother and I make this. Just toss all the ingredients in your slow cooker and let the meal cook all day on low. It makes the house smell amazing and is wonderful comfort food. You can double the recipe and freeze the other portion for a hot meal in a pinch.
—Debbie Vair, Wake Forest, NC

Prep: 30 min. • **Cook:** 5½ hours
Makes: 12 servings

- 4 lbs. loukaniko or other smoked sausage, cut into ½-in. slices
- 1 each large sweet yellow, orange and red peppers, chopped
- 1 large sweet onion, chopped
- 2 cups beef stock
- 1 whole garlic bulb, minced
- 1 Tbsp. minced fresh oregano or 1 tsp. dried oregano
- 1 tsp. coarse sea salt
- 1 tsp. coarsely ground pepper
- 3 to 3½ cups cherry tomatoes
   Hot cooked rice, optional

In a 7- or 8-qt. slow cooker, combine sausage, sweet peppers, onion, stock, garlic, oregano, salt and pepper. Cook, covered, on low until vegetables are tender, 5-6 hours. Add tomatoes; cook until wilted, about 30 minutes longer. If desired, serve with rice.
1¼ cups: 504 cal., 41g fat (17g sat. fat), 101mg chol., 1958mg sod., 10g carb. (7g sugars, 2g fiber), 23g pro.

BBQ CHICKEN & SMOKED SAUSAGE

My party-ready barbecue recipe works like a dream for weeknights, too. With just a few minutes of prep time, you still get that low-and-slow flavor everybody craves (thanks, slow cooker!). Throw in minced jalapenos for extra oomph.
—Kimberly Young, Mesquite, TX

Prep: 30 min. • **Cook:** 4 hours
Makes: 8 servings

- 1 **medium onion, chopped**
- 1 **large sweet red pepper, cut into 1-in. pieces**
- 4 **bone-in chicken thighs, skin removed**
- 4 **chicken drumsticks, skin removed**
- 1 **pkg. (12 oz.) smoked sausage links, cut into 1-in. pieces**
- 1 **cup barbecue sauce**
   Sliced seeded jalapeno pepper, optional

1. Place first 5 ingredients in a 4- or 5-qt. slow cooker; top with barbecue sauce. Cook, covered, on low 4-5 hours or until the chicken is tender and a thermometer inserted in chicken reads at least 170°-175°.
2. Remove chicken, sausage and vegetables from slow cooker; keep warm. Transfer cooking juices to a saucepan; bring to a boil. Reduce heat; simmer, uncovered, until thickened, 15-20 minutes, stirring occasionally.
3. Serve the chicken, sausage and vegetables with sauce. If desired, top with jalapeno.
1 serving: 331 cal., 18g fat (6g sat. fat), 91mg chol., 840mg sod., 17g carb. (13g sugars, 1g fiber), 24g pro.

SLOW-COOKER SALSA CHICKEN

This is a go-to recipe when I know I'll be having a busy day. My family loves salsa, so I came up with this recipe for something to throw into a slow cooker and simmer on low. We love it served over rice or noodles, and then top it with tortilla chips and sour cream.
—Deborah Pennington, Falkville, AL

Prep: 15 min. • **Cook:** 3 hours
Makes: 4 servings

- 4 **boneless skinless chicken breast halves (6 oz. each)**
- 1 **jar (16 oz.) salsa**
- 1¾ **cups frozen corn, thawed**
- 1 **can (15 oz.) pinto beans, rinsed and drained**
- 1 **can (15 oz.) no-salt-added black beans, rinsed and drained**
- 1 **can (10 oz.) diced tomatoes and green chiles, undrained**
- 1 **tsp. sugar**
- ½ **tsp. salt**
- ¼ **tsp. pepper**
   Optional: Hot cooked rice, cubed avocado, chopped fresh tomato, sliced green onions and lime wedges

Place chicken in a 4- or 5-qt. slow cooker. Top with salsa, corn, beans, diced tomatoes and chiles, sugar, salt and pepper. Cook, covered, on low until a thermometer inserted in the chicken reads 165°, 3-4 hours. If desired, serve with optional ingredients.
1 chicken breast half with 1½ cups bean mixture: 470 cal., 6g fat (1g sat. fat), 94mg chol., 1270mg sod., 55g carb. (8g sugars, 11g fiber), 47g pro.

SLOW-COOKER SALSA CHICKEN

BEEF BRISKET IN BEER

One bite of this super tender brisket and your family will be hooked! The rich gravy is perfect for spooning over a side of creamy mashed potatoes.
—Eunice Stoen, Decorah, IA

- -

Prep: 15 min. • **Cook:** 8 hours
Makes: 6 servings

1   **fresh beef brisket (2½ to 3 lbs.)**
2   **tsp. liquid smoke, optional**
1   **tsp. celery salt**
½   **tsp. pepper**
¼   **tsp. salt**
1   **large onion, sliced**
1   **can (12 oz.) beer or nonalcoholic beer**
2   **tsp. Worcestershire sauce**
2   **Tbsp. cornstarch**
¼   **cup cold water**

1. Cut brisket in half; rub with liquid smoke, if desired, and celery salt, pepper and salt. Place in a 3-qt. slow cooker. Top with onion. Combine beer and Worcestershire sauce; pour over the meat. Cover and cook on low for 8-9 hours or until tender.

2. Remove brisket and keep warm. Strain cooking juices; transfer to a small saucepan. In a small bowl, combine cornstarch and water until smooth; stir into juices. Bring to a boil; cook and stir until thickened, about 2 minutes. Serve beef with gravy.

Note: This is a fresh beef brisket, not corned beef.

5 oz. cooked brisket with about ⅓ cup sauce: 285 cal., 8g fat (3g sat. fat), 80mg chol., 430mg sod., 7g carb. (3g sugars, 0 fiber), 39g pro. **Diabetic exchanges:** 5 lean meat, ½ starch.

SLOW-COOKER SECRETS

Liquid smoke is a fabulous addition to slow-cooked dishes because it adds depth of flavor. Be careful not to overdo it; a small amount goes a long way. Look for liquid smoke in your grocery store near the spices and marinades.

BEEF BRISKET IN BEER

SLOW-COOKER
MALAYSIAN CHICKEN

SLOW-COOKER MALAYSIAN CHICKEN

Malaysian food has influences from the Malays, Chinese, Indians, Thai, British and Portuguese. In this dish, Asian ingredients combine for maximum flavor and sweet potatoes thicken the sauce as the meal slowly cooks.
—Suzanne Banfield, Basking Ridge, NJ

Prep: 20 min. • **Cook:** 5 hours
Makes: 6 servings

- 1 **cup coconut milk**
- 2 **Tbsp. brown sugar**
- 2 **Tbsp. soy sauce**
- 2 **Tbsp. creamy peanut butter**
- 1 **Tbsp. fish sauce**
- 2 **tsp. curry powder**
- 2 **garlic cloves, minced**
- ½ **tsp. salt**
- ½ **tsp. pepper**
- 1 **can (14½ oz.) diced tomatoes, undrained**
- 2 **medium sweet potatoes, peeled and cut into ½-in.-thick slices**
- 2 **lbs. boneless skinless chicken thighs**
- 2 **Tbsp. cornstarch**
- 2 **Tbsp. water**

1. In a bowl, whisk together the first 9 ingredients; stir in tomatoes. Place sweet potatoes in a 5- or 6-qt. slow cooker; top with chicken. Pour tomato mixture over top. Cook, covered, on low until chicken is tender and a thermometer reads 170°, 5-6 hours.
2. Remove chicken and sweet potatoes; keep warm. Transfer the cooking juices to a saucepan. In a small bowl, mix the cornstarch and water until smooth; stir into cooking juices. Bring to a boil; cook and stir 1-2 minutes or until thickened. Serve sauce with chicken and potatoes.

BEST ITALIAN SAUSAGE SANDWICHES

1 serving: 425 cal., 20g fat (10g sat. fat), 101mg chol., 964mg sod., 28g carb. (14g sugars, 4g fiber), 33g pro.

BEST ITALIAN SAUSAGE SANDWICHES

Need a different type of Italian dinner? This rich tomato sauce simmers all afternoon in the slow cooker, ready to top freshly grilled Italian sausages. It's a fantastic combination with lots of crowd appeal!
—*Taste of Home* Test Kitchen

Prep: 10 min. • **Cook:** 4 hours
Makes: 10 servings

- 2 **jars (24 oz. each) pasta sauce**
- 2 **medium green peppers, cut into strips**
- 2 **medium onions, thinly sliced**
- ½ **tsp. garlic powder**
- ½ **tsp. fennel seed, crushed**
- 2 **pkg. (20 oz. each) Italian turkey sausage links**
- 10 **hoagie buns, split**

1. In a 3-qt. slow cooker, combine the first 5 ingredients. Cook, covered, on low until vegetables are tender, about 4 hours.
2. Grill sausages according to package directions. Serve on buns with sauce.
Freeze option: Freeze cooled sauce in freezer containers. To use, partially thaw in refrigerator overnight. Heat through in a saucepan, stirring occasionally; add water if necessary.
1 sandwich: 454 cal., 15g fat (3g sat. fat), 68mg chol., 1716mg sod., 52g carb. (17g sugars, 4g fiber), 29g pro.

COUNTRY BACON-BEEF MAC & CHEESE

This extra-meaty mac and cheese is easy to make in the slow cooker. Kids love it, and I like that I can sneak in some veggies.
—Nancy Heishman, Las Vegas, NV

- -

Prep: 35 min. • **Cook:** 1 hour
Makes: 8 servings

  5 **bacon strips, chopped**
1½ **lbs. ground beef**
  1 **medium onion, chopped**
  3 **garlic cloves, minced**
  1 **medium sweet red pepper, chopped**
  1 **large carrot, coarsely grated**
  1 **Tbsp. dried parsley flakes**
 ¼ **tsp. salt**
  1 **tsp. pepper**
  3 **cups uncooked protein-enriched or whole wheat elbow macaroni**
  1 **can (14½ oz.) reduced-sodium beef broth**
  1 **cup sour cream**
  2 **cups shredded sharp cheddar cheese**
  2 **cups shredded part-skim mozzarella cheese**

1. In a large skillet, cook the bacon over medium heat until crisp, stirring occasionally, 5-6 minutes. Remove with a slotted spoon; drain on paper towels. Discard all but 1 Tbsp. drippings. Brown the ground beef in drippings, breaking it into crumbles; remove from pan. Add onion to skillet; cook and stir until translucent, 2-3 minutes. Add garlic; cook 1 minute longer.

2. Combine the red pepper, carrot, seasonings and pasta in a 4-qt. slow cooker. Layer with ground beef, bacon and onion mixture (do not stir). Pour in broth.

3. Cook, covered, on low for about 1 hour or until meat and vegetables are tender. Thirty minutes before serving, stir in sour cream and cheeses.

1½ cups: 591 cal., 36g fat (17g sat. fat), 113mg chol., 719mg sod., 29g carb. (5g sugars, 3g fiber), 38g pro.

SLOW-COOKER SECRETS
If the mixture becomes too dry, stir in milk or broth to desired consistency. If you'd like a creamier macaroni, stir in more sour cream.

COUNTRY BACON-BEEF MAC & CHEESE

SECRET'S IN THE SAUCE BBQ RIBS

A sweet, rich sauce makes these ribs so tender that the meat literally falls off the bones. And the aroma is wonderful. Yum!
—Tanya Reid, Winston-Salem, NC

- -

Prep: 10 min. • **Cook:** 6 hours
Makes: 5 servings

4½ lbs. pork baby back ribs
1½ tsp. pepper
2½ cups barbecue sauce
¾ cup cherry preserves
1 Tbsp. Dijon mustard
1 garlic clove, minced

Cut ribs into serving-size pieces; sprinkle with the pepper. Place in a 5- or 6-qt. slow cooker. Combine the remaining ingredients; pour over ribs. Cook, covered, on low until meat is tender, 6-8 hours. Serve with sauce.
1 serving: 921 cal., 58g fat (21g sat. fat), 220mg chol., 1402mg sod., 50g carb. (45g sugars, 2g fiber), 48g pro.

CARIBBEAN CHICKEN STEW

I lived with a West Indian family for a while and enjoyed watching them cook. I lightened this recipe by leaving out the oil and sugar, removing the skin from the chicken and using chicken sausage.
—Joanne Iovino, Kings Park, NY

Prep: 25 min. + marinating
Cook: 6 hours • **Makes:** 8 servings

- ¼ cup ketchup
- 3 garlic cloves, minced
- 1 Tbsp. sugar
- 1 Tbsp. hot pepper sauce
- 1 tsp. browning sauce, optional
- 1 tsp. dried basil
- 1 tsp. dried thyme
- 1 tsp. paprika
- ½ tsp. salt
- ½ tsp. dried oregano
- ½ tsp. ground allspice
- ½ tsp. pepper
- 8 bone-in chicken thighs (about 3 lbs.), skin removed
- 1 lb. fully cooked andouille chicken sausage links, sliced
- 1 medium onion, finely chopped
- 2 medium carrots, finely chopped
- 2 celery ribs, finely chopped

1. In a bowl, combine ketchup, garlic, sugar, pepper sauce and, if desired, browning sauce; stir in seasonings. Add chicken thighs, sausage and vegetables. Cover; refrigerate 8 hours or overnight.
2. Transfer chicken mixture to a 4- or 5-qt. slow cooker. Cook, covered, on low 6-8 hours or until chicken is tender.
1 serving: 309 cal., 14g fat (4g sat. fat), 131mg chol., 666mg sod., 9g carb. (6g sugars, 1g fiber), 35g pro. **Diabetic exchanges:** 5 lean meat, ½ starch.

SLOW-COOKER
JAMBALAYA RISOTTO

SLOW-COOKER JAMBALAYA RISOTTO

I love risotto, but I don't always love the time and stirring it takes to get the creamy goodness. I found a slow-cooker risotto recipe and thought it was too good to be true. I decided to adapt a jambalaya recipe for this dish.
—Angela Westra, Cambridge, MA

Prep: 20 min. • **Cook:** 2 hours
Makes: 6 servings

- 2½ cups chicken broth
- 1 can (14½ oz.) diced tomatoes, undrained
- 1½ cups tomato sauce
- 1¼ cups uncooked arborio rice
- 3 Tbsp. finely chopped onion
- 1 Tbsp. dried parsley flakes
- 1 Tbsp. olive oil
- ½ tsp. garlic powder
- ½ tsp. dried thyme
- ½ tsp. pepper
- ¼ tsp. salt
- ¼ tsp. cayenne pepper
- 1 bay leaf
- ½ lb. uncooked shrimp (31-40 per lb.), peeled, deveined and tails removed
- ½ lb. fully cooked andouille sausage links, sliced
- ⅔ cup shredded Parmesan cheese, optional

In a 4- or 5-qt. slow cooker, combine the first 13 ingredients. Cook, covered, on high for 1¾ hours. Stir in shrimp, sausage and, if desired, cheese. Cook until shrimp turn pink and rice is tender, 10-15 minutes longer. Remove bay leaf.
1½ cups: 335 cal., 11g fat (3g sat. fat), 97mg chol., 1276mg sod., 42g carb. (4g sugars, 3g fiber), 19g pro.

SLOW-COOKER CHICKEN ENCHILADA STUFFED PEPPERS

Utilize leftovers and clean out the fridge by making these super simple and tasty stuffed peppers! This is an ideal weekend meal or a dish that you can put together quickly and let cook while you run errands.
—Katie Jasiewicz, Belle Isle, FL

- -

Prep: 20 min. • **Cook:** 3 hours
Makes: 6 servings

2 cups shredded cooked chicken
1 pkg. (8.8 oz.) ready-to-serve long grain rice
1 cup enchilada sauce
¾ cup shredded cheddar cheese, divided
3 Tbsp. minced red onion
½ tsp. ground cumin
⅓ cup water
6 medium bell peppers
Minced fresh cilantro, green onions and sour cream

1. In a bowl, combine chicken, rice, enchilada sauce, ½ cup cheese, red onion and cumin.
2. Pour water into a 6-qt. slow cooker. Cut and discard tops from peppers; remove seeds. Fill with chicken mixture; place in slow cooker. Cover slow cooker with a double layer of white paper towels; place lid securely over towels. Cook on low until tender, 3-4 hours. During the last 20 minutes, remove and discard paper towels; add remaining cheese and cook, covered, until melted. Serve with cilantro, green onions and sour cream.

1 stuffed pepper: 267 cal., 10g fat (4g sat. fat), 56mg chol., 364mg sod., 23g carb. (6g sugars, 3g fiber), 20g pro. **Diabetic exchanges:** 3 lean meat, 1 starch, 1 vegetable, ½ fat.

SLOW-COOKER SECRETS
To make these peppers even healthier, consider switching to ready-to-serve brown rice. It has nearly 6 times the fiber as white rice.

SLOW-COOKER CHICKEN ENCHILADA STUFFED PEPPERS

**GULF COAST
JAMBALAYA RICE**

GULF COAST
JAMBALAYA RICE

As the stew of the South, jambalaya is a definite staple. For ages, home cooks have been making their own versions of the traditional recipe. This slow-cooked rendition is my personal favorite.
—Judy Batson, Tampa, FL

Prep: 20 min. • **Cook:** 3¼ hours
Makes: 8 servings

- 1 **lb. boneless skinless chicken breasts, cut into 1-in. cubes**
- 1 **lb. smoked kielbasa, cut into ¼-in. slices**
- 2 **cups chicken stock**
- 1 **large green pepper, chopped**
- 1 **cup chopped sweet onion**
- 2 **celery ribs, chopped**
- 2 **garlic cloves, minced**
- 2 **tsp. Creole seasoning**
- 1 **tsp. seafood seasoning**
- 1 **tsp. pepper**
- 1 **lb. uncooked medium shrimp, peeled and deveined**
- 2 **cups uncooked instant rice**

1. Place the first 10 ingredients in a 5-qt. slow cooker. Cook, covered, on low 3-4 hours, until chicken is tender.
2. Stir in shrimp and rice. Cook, covered, 15-20 minutes longer, until shrimp turn pink and rice is tender.
Note: If you don't have Creole seasoning in your cupboard, you can make your own using ½ tsp. each salt, garlic powder and paprika, and a pinch each dried thyme, ground cumin and cayenne pepper.
1⅓ cups: 395 cal., 18g fat (6g sat. fat), 138mg chol., 861mg sod., 25g carb. (3g sugars, 1g fiber), 31g pro.

GREEK-STYLE CHICKEN
WITH GREEN BEANS

My Greek grandmother used to make the most delicious, melt-in-your-mouth Greek-style green beans with a lemon-tomato flavor. Whenever I make this slow-cooker recipe, I think of her. The chicken juices help flavor the green beans, but the beans can be prepared alone as a side dish without the chicken.
—Elizabeth Lindemann, Driftwood, TX

Prep: 20 min. • **Cook:** 4 hours
Makes: 4 servings

- 1 **lb. fresh green beans, trimmed**
- 2 **large tomatoes, chopped**
- 1 **medium onion, chopped**
- 1 **cup chicken broth**
- ¼ **cup snipped fresh dill**
- 2 **to 3 Tbsp. lemon juice**
- 2 **garlic cloves, minced**
- 4 **bone-in chicken thighs (about 1½ lbs.)**
- 1 **Tbsp. olive oil**
- ¾ **tsp. salt**
- ¼ **tsp. pepper**
  Optional: Lemon wedges and additional snipped fresh dill

1. Combine the first 7 ingredients in a 5- or 6-qt. slow cooker. Top with chicken. Drizzle with oil; sprinkle with salt and pepper. Cook, covered, on low until a thermometer inserted in chicken reads 170°-175°, 4-6 hours.
2. Preheat broiler. Place chicken on a greased rack in a broiler pan. Broil 4-6 in. from heat until golden brown, 3-4 minutes. Serve with bean mixture and, if desired, lemon wedges and additional fresh dill.
1 serving: 324 cal., 18g fat (5g sat. fat), 82mg chol., 769mg sod., 16g carb. (7g sugars, 6g fiber), 26g pro.

GREEK-STYLE CHICKEN
WITH GREEN BEANS

SIDES

MOIST CORN SPOON BREAD

MOIST CORN SPOON BREAD

Enjoy this easy take on a southern specialty that utilizes the convenience of a slow cooker. Here's an excellent side dish for your next summer party or any special feast.
—*Taste of Home* Test Kitchen

Prep: 20 min. • **Cook:** 4 hours
Makes: 8 servings

- 1 pkg. (8 oz.) cream cheese, softened
- 2 Tbsp. sugar
- 2 large eggs, beaten
- 1 cup 2% milk
- 2 Tbsp. butter, melted
- ½ tsp. salt
- ¼ tsp. cayenne pepper
- ⅛ tsp. pepper
- 2 cups frozen corn
- 1 can (14¾ oz.) cream-style corn
- 1 cup yellow cornmeal
- 1 cup shredded Monterey Jack cheese
- 3 green onions, thinly sliced
  Optional: Coarsely ground pepper and thinly sliced green onions

1. In a large bowl, beat cream cheese and sugar until smooth. Gradually beat in eggs. Beat in the milk, butter, salt, cayenne and pepper until blended. Stir in the next 5 ingredients.
2. Pour into a greased 3-qt. slow cooker. Cover and cook on low for 4-5 hours, until a toothpick inserted in the center comes out clean. If desired, top with additional pepper and green onions.
1 serving: 350 cal., 18g fat (11g sat. fat), 54mg chol., 525mg sod., 38g carb. (8g sugars, 3g fiber), 12g pro.

SLOW-COOKER SAUERKRAUT

SLOW-COOKER SAUERKRAUT

This recipe was made by a special someone in my life. I was never a fan of sauerkraut until I tried this and fell in love. It's terrific as a side dish or on Reuben sandwiches.
—Karen Tringali, Minooka, IL

Prep: 20 min. • **Cook:** 1 hour
Makes: 10 servings

- ½ lb. bacon strips, chopped
- 1 medium onion, chopped
- ¾ cup white vinegar
- ¾ cup sugar
- 2 cans (14 oz. each) sauerkraut, rinsed and well drained
- ½ tsp. caraway seeds

In a large skillet, cook bacon and onions over medium heat until bacon is crisp and onions are just tender, 5-7 minutes. Add vinegar and sugar to skillet; cook and stir 5 minutes. Add sauerkraut and caraway seeds to skillet; stir to combine. Transfer mixture to a 4-qt. slow cooker. Cover and cook on low to allow flavors to blend, 1-2 hours.
½ cup: 173 cal., 9g fat (3g sat. fat), 15mg chol., 675mg sod., 20g carb. (17g sugars, 2g fiber), 4g pro.

SLOW-COOKER SECRETS
If the sauerkraut gets too dry, add a little water or apple juice.

SLOW-COOKER BBQ BAKED BEANS

I was under a doctor's orders to reduce the amount of sodium I was eating, but I just couldn't part with some of my favorite foods. After many experiments, I came up with this potluck favorite—now everyone's happy!
—Sherrel Hendrix, Arkadelphia, AR

Prep: 10 min. + soaking • **Cook:** 8½ hours
Makes: 12 servings

- 1 **pkg. (16 oz.) dried great northern beans**
- 2 **smoked ham hocks (about ½ lb. each)**
- 2 **cups water**
- 1 **medium onion, chopped**
- 2 **tsp. garlic powder, divided**
- 2 **tsp. onion powder, divided**
- 1 **cup barbecue sauce**
- ¾ **cup packed brown sugar**
- ½ **tsp. ground nutmeg**
- ¼ **tsp. ground cloves**
- 2 **tsp. hot pepper sauce, optional**

1. Rinse and sort beans; soak according to package directions. Drain and rinse beans, discarding liquid.
2. In a 4-qt. slow cooker, combine beans, ham hocks, water, onion, 1 tsp. garlic powder and 1 tsp. onion powder. Cook, covered, on low 8-10 hours until beans are tender.
3. Remove ham hocks; cool slightly. Cut meat into small cubes, discarding bones; return meat to slow cooker. Stir in barbecue sauce, brown sugar, nutmeg, cloves, remaining garlic powder, remaining onion powder and, if desired, pepper sauce. Cook, covered, on high about 30 minutes or until heated through.

½ cup: 238 cal., 1g fat (0 sat. fat), 4mg chol., 347mg sod., 48g carb. (22g sugars, 8g fiber), 10g pro.

SLOW-COOKER SECRETS
Using hot sauce to flavor your food can be a smart alternative to salt, but make sure you check nutrition labels. We like to use Tabasco sauce, which has only 26 mg of sodium per 5-7 drops.

SLOW-COOKER BBQ BAKED BEANS

MIXED VEGGIES & RICE

To add variety to sides for those who don't care for potatoes, I came up with this colorful dish. It's an easy slow-cooker recipe that you can put right onto the buffet table.
—Judy Batson, Tampa, FL

Prep: 5 min. • **Cook:** 3 hours
Makes: 8 servings

    4 pkg. (10 oz. each) frozen long grain white rice with mixed vegetables
   12 oz. frozen mixed vegetables
   ½   cup vegetable broth or light beer
    1 tsp. onion powder
    1 tsp. garlic powder
    1 tsp. seasoned salt
       Butter, optional

In a 5-qt. slow cooker, combine first 6 ingredients. Cook, covered, on low until heated through, 3-4 hours. If desired, serve with butter.
¾ cup: 120 cal., 0 fat (0 sat. fat), 0 chol., 254mg sod., 26g carb. (3g sugars, 3g fiber), 3g pro. **Diabetic exchanges:** 1½ starch.

CREAMED CORN WITH BACON

Every time I take this rich corn to a potluck or work party, I leave with an empty slow cooker. It's decadent, homey and so worth the splurge.
—Melissa Pelkey Hass, Waleska, GA

Prep: 10 min. • **Cook:** 4 hours
Makes: 20 servings

- 10 cups frozen corn (about 50 oz.), thawed
- 3 pkg. (8 oz. each) cream cheese, cubed
- ½ cup 2% milk
- ½ cup heavy whipping cream
- ½ cup butter, melted
- ¼ cup sugar
- 2 tsp. salt
- ¼ tsp. pepper
- 4 bacon strips, cooked and crumbled Chopped green onions

In a 5-qt. slow cooker, combine the first 8 ingredients. Cook, covered, on low 4-5 hours or until heated through. Stir just before serving. Sprinkle with bacon and onions.

½ cup: 259 cal., 20g fat (11g sat. fat), 60mg chol., 433mg sod., 18g carb. (6g sugars, 1g fiber), 5g pro.

SLOW-COOKER
CITRUS CARROTS

SLOW-COOKER CITRUS CARROTS

These carrots are yummy and so simple. The recipe is from my mom, who tweaked it a bit to suit her tastes. You can make this dish a day in advance and refrigerate it until needed. Then just reheat it before the party!
—Julie Puderbaugh, Berwick, PA

Prep: 10 min. • **Cook:** 4¼ hours
Makes: 12 servings

- 12 cups frozen sliced carrots (about 48 oz.), thawed
- 1¾ cups orange juice
- ½ cup sugar
- 3 Tbsp. butter, cubed
- ½ tsp. salt
- 3 Tbsp. cornstarch
- ¼ cup cold water Minced fresh parsley, optional

1. In a 3- or 4-qt. slow cooker, combine the first 5 ingredients. Cook, covered, on low 4-5 hours or until the carrots are tender.

2. In a small bowl, mix cornstarch and water until smooth; gradually stir into slow cooker. Cook, covered, on high until sauce is thickened, 15-30 minutes. Garnish with fresh parsley if desired.

¾ cup: 136 cal., 4g fat (2g sat. fat), 8mg chol., 208mg sod., 25g carb. (18g sugars, 5g fiber), 1g pro.

SIMPLE VEGETARIAN SLOW-COOKED BEANS

When I have a hungry family to feed, these tasty beans with spinach, tomatoes and carrots are a go-to dish. This veggie delight is frequently on our menu.
—Jennifer Reid, Farmington, ME

Prep: 15 min. • **Cook:** 4 hours
Makes: 8 servings

4   cans (15½ oz. each) great northern beans, rinsed and drained
4   medium carrots, finely chopped (about 2 cups)
1   cup vegetable stock
6   garlic cloves, minced
2   tsp. ground cumin
¾   tsp. salt
⅛   tsp. chili powder
4   cups fresh baby spinach, coarsely chopped
1   cup oil-packed sun-dried tomatoes, patted dry and chopped
⅓   cup minced fresh cilantro
⅓   cup minced fresh parsley

In a 3-qt. slow cooker, combine the first 7 ingredients. Cook, covered, on low 4-5 hours or until carrots are tender, adding spinach and tomatoes during the last 10 minutes of cooking. Stir in cilantro and parsley.
¾ cup: 229 cal., 3g fat (0 sat. fat), 0 chol., 672mg sod., 40g carb. (2g sugars, 13g fiber), 12g pro.

READER RAVE...
"These were creamy with a burst of flavor from the sun-dried tomatoes—an amazing, healthy side dish that's high in protein."
—RWIPPEL, TASTEOFHOME.COM

SIMPLE VEGETARIAN
SLOW-COOKED BEANS

SLOW-COOKED
SUMMER SQUASH

SLOW-COOKED SUMMER SQUASH

We love squash, but I got tired of fixing just plain squash and cheese. I decided to jazz up the dish a bit. This was a huge hit with my family.
—Joan Hallford,
North Richland Hills, TX

Prep: 15 min. • **Cook:** 2½ hours
Makes: 8 servings

- 1 lb. medium yellow summer squash
- 1 lb. medium zucchini
- 2 medium tomatoes, chopped
- ¼ cup thinly sliced green onions
- ½ tsp. salt
- ¼ tsp. pepper
- 1 cup vegetable broth
- 1½ cups Caesar salad croutons, coarsely crushed
- ½ cup shredded cheddar cheese
- 4 bacon strips, cooked and crumbled

1. Cut squash and zucchini into ¼-in.-thick slices. In a 3- or 4-qt. slow cooker, combine squash, zucchini, tomatoes and green onions. Add salt, pepper and broth. Cook, covered, on low until tender, 2½-3½ hours. Remove with a slotted spoon.
2. To serve, top with croutons, cheese and bacon.

¾ cup: 111 cal., 6g fat (2g sat. fat), 12mg chol., 442mg sod., 10g carb. (4g sugars, 2g fiber), 6g pro. **Diabetic exchanges:** 1 vegetable, 1 fat.

SLOW-COOKED BAKED BEANS

SLOW-COOKED BAKED BEANS

My friend suggested this recipe when I needed a new dish to bring to a barbecue. It was an incredible success, and I've been making it ever since.
—Jodi Caple, Cortez, CO

Prep: 25 min. + soaking • **Cook:** 9 hours
Makes: 8 servings

- 1 lb. dried navy beans
- 2 cups water
- ½ cup dark molasses
- 5 slices salt pork belly (about 3 oz.), cut into ½-in. pieces
- 1 small onion, finely chopped
- 3 Tbsp. brown sugar
- 2 garlic cloves, minced
- 1 tsp. ground ginger
- ½ tsp. salt
- ½ tsp. ground mustard
- ½ tsp. pepper

1. Rinse and sort beans; soak according to package directions.
2. Drain and rinse beans, discarding liquid. Transfer beans to a 4-qt. slow cooker. Stir in remaining ingredients. Cook, covered, on low until beans are tender, 9-11 hours.

¾ cup: 463 cal., 20g fat (7g sat. fat), 19mg chol., 1429mg sod., 56g carb. (23g sugars, 9g fiber), 15g pro.

SPICE TRADE BEANS & BULGUR

A rich blend of spices adds flavor to tender, nutritious bulgur and garbanzo beans in this tangy dish that has just the right amount of heat. A hint of sweetness from golden raisins is the perfect accent.

—Faith Cromwell, San Francisco, CA

Prep: 30 min. • **Cook:** 3½ hours
Makes: 10 servings

- 3   **Tbsp. canola oil, divided**
- 2   **medium onions, chopped**
- 1   **medium sweet red pepper, chopped**
- 5   **garlic cloves, minced**
- 1   **Tbsp. ground cumin**
- 1   **Tbsp. paprika**
- 2   **tsp. ground ginger**
- 1   **tsp. pepper**
- ½   **tsp. ground cinnamon**
- ½   **tsp. cayenne pepper**
- 1½ **cups bulgur**
- 1   **can (28 oz.) crushed tomatoes**
- 1   **can (14½ oz.) diced tomatoes, undrained**
- 1   **carton (32 oz.) vegetable broth**
- 2   **Tbsp. brown sugar**
- 2   **Tbsp. soy sauce**
- 1   **can (15 oz.) garbanzo beans or chickpeas, rinsed and drained**
- ½   **cup golden raisins**
     Minced fresh cilantro, optional

1. In a large skillet, heat 2 Tbsp. oil over medium-high heat. Add onions and pepper; cook and stir until tender, 3-4 minutes. Add garlic and seasonings; cook 1 minute longer. Transfer to a 5-qt. slow cooker.

2. In same skillet, heat remaining oil over medium-high heat. Add bulgur; cook and stir until lightly browned, 2-3 minutes.

3. Add bulgur, tomatoes, broth, brown sugar and soy sauce to slow cooker. Cook, covered, on low 3-4 hours or until bulgur is tender. Stir in beans and raisins; cook 30 minutes longer. If desired, sprinkle with cilantro.

1¼ cups: 245 cal., 6g fat (0 sat. fat), 0 chol., 752mg sod., 45g carb. (15g sugars, 8g fiber), 8g pro.

READER RAVE...

"If you like international food, you will love this dish! It's easy to make and very flavorful."

—COOKING919, TASTEOFHOME.COM

CHEDDAR CREAMED CORN

I took this super easy recipe to a school potluck once and it was gone in no time. I've been asked to bring it to every function since.
—Jessica Maxwell, Englewood, NJ

Prep: 10 min. • **Cook:** 3 hours
Makes: 9 servings

- 2 pkg. (one 16 oz., one 12 oz.) frozen corn, thawed
- 1 pkg. (8 oz.) cream cheese, cubed
- ¾ cup shredded cheddar cheese
- ¼ cup butter, melted
- ¼ cup heavy whipping cream
- ½ tsp. salt
- ¼ tsp. pepper

In a 3- or 4-qt. slow cooker, combine all ingredients. Cook, covered, on low 3-3½ hours or until cheese is melted and corn is tender. Stir just before serving.
½ cup: 272 cal., 20g fat (12g sat. fat), 56mg chol., 317mg sod., 20g carb. (3g sugars, 2g fiber), 7g pro.

SPICE TRADE
BEANS & BULGUR

SLOW-COOKER SRIRACHA CORN

A restaurant here advertised Sriracha corn on the cob, but I knew I could make my own. The golden ears cooked up a little sweet, a little smoky and a little hot—perfect, if you ask my three teenage boys!
—Julie Peterson, Crofton, MD

- -

Prep: 15 min. • **Cook:** 3 hours
Makes: 8 servings

- ½ cup butter, softened
- 2 Tbsp. honey
- 1 Tbsp. Sriracha chili sauce
- 1 tsp. smoked paprika
- ½ tsp. kosher salt
- 8 small ears sweet corn, husked
- ¼ cup water
  Additional smoked paprika, optional

1. Mix first 5 ingredients. Place each ear of corn on a 12x12-in. piece of heavy-duty foil and spread with 1 Tbsp. butter mixture. Wrap foil around corn, sealing tightly. Place in a 6-qt. slow cooker.
2. Add water; cook, covered, on low 3-4 hours or until the corn is tender. If desired, sprinkle corn with additional paprika before serving.
1 ear of corn: 209 cal., 13g fat (8g sat. fat), 31mg chol., 287mg sod., 24g carb. (11g sugars, 2g fiber), 4g pro.

PINEAPPLE BAKED BEANS

Tangy pineapple dresses up these hearty baked beans. Brown the beef while you open the cans and chop the vegetables—it doesn't take long to get this side dish ready for the slow cooker.
—Gladys De Boer, Castleford, ID

- -

Prep: 15 min. • **Cook:** 6 hours
Makes: 8 servings

- 1 lb. ground beef
- 1 can (28 oz.) baked beans
- ¾ cup pineapple tidbits, drained
- 1 jar (4½ oz.) sliced mushrooms, drained
- 1 large onion, chopped
- 1 large green pepper, chopped
- ½ cup barbecue sauce
- 2 Tbsp. reduced-sodium soy sauce
- 1 garlic clove, minced
- ½ tsp. salt
- ¼ tsp. pepper

1. In a large skillet, cook beef over medium heat until no longer pink, breaking it into crumbles; drain. Transfer to a 5-qt. slow cooker. Add remaining ingredients and mix well.
2. Cover and cook on low 6-8 hours or until bubbly.
¾ cup: 249 cal., 9g fat (3g sat. fat), 42mg chol., 1032mg sod., 28g carb. (6g sugars, 7g fiber), 17g pro.

PINEAPPLE BAKED BEANS

SLOW-COOKED RATATOUILLE

thaw in refrigerator overnight. Microwave, covered, on high in a microwave-safe dish until heated through, stirring gently.

¾ cup: 102 cal., 5g fat (1g sat. fat), 0 chol., 380mg sod., 13g carb. (7g sugars, 4g fiber), 3g pro. **Diabetic exchanges:** 2 vegetable, 1 fat.

SLOW-COOKER POTLUCK BEANS

It was the morning of our family potluck and I still needed something to take. I threw together this recipe while drinking my morning coffee. By the end of the gathering, the beans were all gone and someone had even washed the slow cooker for me!
—Mary Anne Thygesen, Portland, OR

Prep: 10 min. • **Cook:** 4 hours
Makes: 12 servings

- 1 cup brewed coffee
- ½ cup packed brown sugar
- ¼ cup spicy brown mustard
- 2 Tbsp. molasses
- 2 cans (16 oz. each) butter beans
- 2 cans (16 oz. each) kidney beans
- 2 cans (16 oz. each) navy beans

In a greased 3- or 4-qt. slow cooker, mix first 4 ingredients. Rinse and drain beans; stir into coffee mixture. Cook, covered, on low until flavors are blended, 4-5 hours.

Freeze option: Freeze cooled beans in freezer containers. To use, partially thaw in refrigerator overnight. Heat through in a covered saucepan, stirring occasionally; add water if necessary.

½ cup: 243 cal., 0 fat (0 sat. fat), 0 chol., 538mg sod., 50g carb. (13g sugars, 10g fiber), 14g pro.

SLOW-COOKED RATATOUILLE

I get my son to eat eggplant by cooking it low and slow in this classic French veggie dish.
—Diane Goedde, Red Lodge, MT

Prep: 25 min. + standing • **Cook:** 5 hours
Makes: 10 servings

- 1 medium eggplant, peeled and cut into 1-in. cubes
- 1 Tbsp. plus 1 tsp. salt, divided
- 2 medium onions, halved and thinly sliced
- 4 medium tomatoes, chopped
- 3 medium zucchini, cut into ¾-in. slices
- 2 celery ribs, chopped
- 3 Tbsp. olive oil
- 2 tsp. dried basil or 2 Tbsp. minced fresh basil
- 4 garlic cloves, minced
- ½ tsp. pepper
- 1 can (6 oz.) tomato paste
- 1 can (2¼ oz.) sliced ripe olives, drained
- ⅓ cup coarsely chopped fresh basil

1. Place eggplant in a strainer over a plate; sprinkle with 1 Tbsp. salt and toss. Let stand 45 minutes. Rinse and drain well; blot dry with paper towels.
2. Place eggplant and the remaining vegetables in a 5- or 6-qt. slow cooker. Add oil, dried basil, garlic, pepper and remaining salt; toss to combine.
3. Cook, covered, on low 5-6 hours or until onions are tender. Stir in the tomato paste, olives and fresh basil; heat through.

Freeze option: Freeze cooled ratatouille in freezer containers. To use, partially

SLOW-COOKED
CAJUN CORN

Mexican Street Corn: Substitute mayonnaise and chili powder for butter and Cajun seasoning. Cook as directed; serve with queso fresco and lime wedges.

Garlic Parmesan Corn: Substitute 1 clove minced garlic for the Cajun seasoning; sprinkle corn with Parmesan cheese. Cook as directed.

SIMPLE SAUCY POTATOES

These rich and creamy potatoes are simple to prepare for potlucks. The saucy side dish always gets rave reviews wherever I take it.
—Gloria Schroeder, Ottawa Lake, MI

- -

Prep: 10 min. • **Cook:** 4 hours
Makes: 12 servings

- 4 cans (14½ oz. each) sliced potatoes, drained
- 2 cans (10¾ oz. each) condensed cream of celery soup, undiluted
- 2 cups sour cream
- 10 bacon strips, cooked and crumbled, divided
- 6 green onions, thinly sliced
  Optional: Chopped chives and coarse cracked pepper

Place potatoes in a 3-qt. slow cooker. Combine next 4 ingredients, reserving ⅓ cup bacon crumbles; pour mixture over potatoes and mix well. Cover and cook on high for 4-5 hours. Top with reserved bacon and, if desired, chopped chives and coarse cracked pepper.
¾ cup: 144 cal., 10g fat (6g sat. fat), 32mg chol., 369mg sod., 7g carb. (2g sugars, 1g fiber), 4g pro.

SLOW-COOKED CAJUN CORN

My husband loves corn on the cob, and I love this slow-cooker recipe because I don't have to stand at a hot stove. We like a little spice, so the Cajun seasoning works well for us, but any spice blend works.
—Audra Rorick, Lyons, KS

- -

Prep: 15 min. • **Cook:** 4 hours
Makes: 4 servings

- 4 Tbsp. butter, softened
- 2 tsp. Cajun seasoning, or more to taste
- 4 medium ears sweet corn, husked
- ¾ cup water

1. Combine butter and Cajun seasoning until well blended. Place each ear of corn on a double thickness of heavy-duty foil. Spread butter mixture over each ear. Wrap foil tightly around corn.
2. Place ears in a 6-qt. slow cooker; add water. Cook, covered, on high until corn is tender, 4-6 hours.
1 ear of corn: 190 cal., 13g fat (8g sat. fat), 31mg chol., 307mg sod., 19g carb. (6g sugars, 2g fiber), 3g pro.

SIMPLE SAUCY POTATOES

COMFORTING CHEESY POTATOES

As a four-generation Idaho family, we love our potatoes and cook with them in every way possible. I have served this dish for weddings, family dinners and special occasions. It has become a favorite of many.
—Karla Kimball, Emmett, ID

- -

Prep: 10 min. • **Cook:** 4 hours
Makes: 8 servings

- 1 **can (10¾ oz.) condensed cream of chicken soup, undiluted**
- 1 **cup sour cream**
- 1 **small onion, finely chopped**
- ¼ **cup butter, melted**
- ¾ **tsp. salt**
- ¼ **tsp. pepper**
- 1 **pkg. (32 oz.) frozen cubed hash brown potatoes, thawed**
- 2 **cups shredded cheddar cheese, divided**

In a 4-qt. slow cooker, combine the first 6 ingredients. Stir in hash browns and 1½ cups cheese. Cook, covered, on low until potatoes are tender, 4-5 hours, sprinkling with remaining cheese during the last 5 minutes.
¾ cup: 358 cal., 24g fat (13g sat. fat), 53mg chol., 764mg sod., 27g carb. (3g sugars, 2g fiber), 11g pro.

PIZZA BEANS

PIZZA BEANS

This dish is wonderful for parties or as a main dish. It can even be made the day before and reheated.
—*Taste of Home* Test Kitchen

Prep: 20 min. • **Cook:** 6 hours
Makes: 20 servings

- 1 **lb. bulk Italian sausage**
- 2 **cups chopped celery**
- 2 **cups chopped onion**
- 1 **can (14½ oz.) cut green beans, drained**
- 1 **can (14½ oz.) cut wax beans, drained**
- 1 **can (16 oz.) kidney beans, rinsed and drained**
- 1 **can (16 oz.) butter beans, drained**
- 1 **can (15 oz.) pork and beans**
- 3 **cans (8 oz. each) pizza sauce**
  Optional toppings: Grated Parmesan cheese, minced fresh oregano and crushed red pepper flakes

In a large skillet, brown the sausage over medium heat until no longer pink, breaking it into crumbles. Transfer to a 5-qt. slow cooker with a slotted spoon. Add celery and onion to skillet; cook until softened, about 5 minutes. Drain. Add vegetable mixture and the next 6 ingredients to slow cooker; mix well. Cover; cook on low 6-8 hours or until bubbly. If desired, serve with toppings.

Freeze option: Freeze cooled beans in freezer containers. To use, partially thaw in refrigerator overnight. Heat through in a saucepan, stirring occasionally; add a little water or broth if necessary.

¾ cup: 142 cal., 6g fat (2g sat. fat), 12mg chol., 542mg sod., 17g carb. (4g sugars, 5g fiber), 7g pro.

SLOW-COOKER SECRETS
To amp up the Italian flavor, saute 2-3 chopped bell peppers along with the Italian sausage.

DESSERTS

SLOW-COOKER LAVA CAKE

SLOW-COOKER LAVA CAKE

I love chocolate. Perhaps that's why this decadent slow-cooker cake has long been a family favorite. The cake can also be served cold.
—Elizabeth Farrell, Hamilton, MT

- -

Prep: 15 min. • **Cook:** 2 hours + standing
Makes: 8 servings

- 1 cup all-purpose flour
- 1 cup packed brown sugar, divided
- 5 Tbsp. baking cocoa, divided
- 2 tsp. baking powder
- ¼ tsp. salt
- ½ cup fat-free milk
- 2 Tbsp. canola oil
- ½ tsp. vanilla extract
- ⅛ tsp. ground cinnamon
- 1¼ cups hot water

1. In a large bowl, whisk flour, ½ cup brown sugar, 3 Tbsp. cocoa, baking powder and salt. In another bowl, whisk milk, oil and vanilla until blended. Add to flour mixture; stir just until moistened.
2. Spread into a 3-qt. slow cooker coated with cooking spray. In a small bowl, mix cinnamon and the remaining brown sugar and cocoa; stir in hot water. Pour over batter (do not stir).
3. Cook, covered, on high 2-2½ hours or until a toothpick inserted in cake portion comes out clean. Turn off slow cooker; let the cake stand at least 15 minutes before serving.
1 serving: 207 cal., 4g fat (0 sat. fat), 0 chol., 191mg sod., 41g carb. (28g sugars, 1g fiber), 3g pro.

STRAWBERRY-BANANA PUDDING CAKE

STRAWBERRY-BANANA PUDDING CAKE

This luscious pink pudding cake is so easy to put together. Top it with ice cream and fresh fruit, and you'll have one very happy family.
—Nadine Mesch, Mount Healthy, OH

- -

Prep: 15 min. • **Cook:** 3½ hours + standing
Makes: 10 servings

- 1 pkg. strawberry cake mix (regular size)
- 1 pkg. (3.4 oz.) instant banana cream pudding mix
- 2 cups plain Greek yogurt
- 4 large eggs, room temperature
- 1 cup water
- ¾ cup canola oil
- 2 Tbsp. minced fresh basil
- 1 cup white baking chips
  Optional toppings: Vanilla ice cream, sliced bananas, sliced strawberries and fresh basil

1. In a large bowl, combine the first 6 ingredients; beat on low speed for 30 seconds. Beat on medium for 2 minutes; stir in basil. Transfer to a greased 5-qt. slow cooker. Cook, covered, on low until edges of cake are golden brown (center will be moist), 3½-4 hours.
2. Remove slow-cooker insert; sprinkle cake with baking chips. Let cake stand, uncovered, 10 minutes before serving. Serve with toppings as desired.
1 serving: 373 cal., 29g fat (8g sat. fat), 90mg chol., 239mg sod., 23g carb. (21g sugars, 0 fiber), 5g pro.

CHOCOLATE PUDDING CAKE

Try this recipe if you want a rich, fudgy dessert that's a cross between pudding and cake. I like to serve it warm with a scoop of vanilla ice cream.
—Paige Arnette, Lawrenceville, GA

Prep: 10 min. • **Cook:** 6 hours
Makes: 12 servings

- 1 pkg. chocolate cake mix (regular size)
- 1 pkg. (3.9 oz.) instant chocolate pudding mix
- 2 cups sour cream
- 4 large eggs, room temperature
- 1 cup water
- ¾ cup canola oil
- 1 cup semisweet chocolate chips
   Optional: Whipped cream or ice cream

1. In a large bowl, combine the first 6 ingredients; beat on low speed for 30 seconds. Beat on medium for 2 minutes. Stir in chocolate chips. Pour into a greased 5-qt. slow cooker.
2. Cover and cook on low until a toothpick inserted in the center comes out with moist crumbs, 6-8 hours. Serve in bowls, with whipped cream or ice cream if desired.
1 serving: 505 cal., 30g fat (11g sat. fat), 98mg chol., 449mg sod., 54g carb. (36g sugars, 2g fiber), 6g pro.

CHERRY PEAR BUCKLE

I added pears to my classic cherry cobbler recipe to create this delightful slow-cooked buckle. You could also add fresh summer plums and berries to the sweet cherries. You'll love this old-fashioned and pretty dessert.
—Mary Anne Thygesen, Portland, OR

Prep: 20 min. • **Cook:** 4½ hours
Makes: 8 servings

- 6 medium pears, peeled and sliced
- 4 cups fresh or frozen pitted dark sweet cherries, thawed
- 1 cup sugar
- ¼ cup tapioca flour
- 1¾ cups all-purpose flour
- ¼ cup old-fashioned oats
- 3 tsp. baking powder
- ½ tsp. salt
- ¼ cup cold butter
- ¾ cup 2% milk
- 2 tsp. cinnamon sugar
   Sweetened whipped cream

1. Line inside of a 5-qt. slow cooker with a double thickness of heavy-duty foil; spray foil with cooking spray. In a large bowl, combine pears, cherries, sugar and tapioca flour; spoon into the slow cooker. Cook, covered, on high 4-5 hours or until bubbly.
2. Meanwhile, combine flour, oats, baking powder and salt. Cut in butter until crumbly. Stir in milk. Drop by tablespoonfuls over pear mixture; sprinkle with cinnamon sugar. Cover and cook until a toothpick inserted in center of topping comes out clean, 30-45 minutes longer. Serve with whipped cream.
1 serving: 411 cal., 7g fat (4g sat. fat), 17mg chol., 386mg sod., 86g carb. (48g sugars, 6g fiber), 5g pro.

PINA COLADA BANANAS FOSTER

I took bananas Foster one step further and combined it with the flavors of my favorite tropical drink—a pina colada. Make sure your bananas are not super ripe. You will want to choose ones that are still nice and firm, as they'll work best in this recipe.
—Trisha Kruse, Eagle, ID

Prep: 10 min. • **Cook:** 2 hours
Makes: 3 cups

- 4   medium firm bananas
- 1   can (8 oz.) pineapple tidbits, drained
- ¼   cup butter, melted
- 1   cup packed brown sugar
- ¼   cup rum
- ½   tsp. coconut extract
- ½   cup sweetened shredded coconut, toasted
  Optional: Coconut ice cream, vanilla wafers and cream-filled wafer cookies

Cut bananas in half lengthwise, then widthwise. Layer sliced bananas and pineapple in bottom of a 1½-qt. slow cooker. Combine butter, brown sugar, rum and coconut extract in small bowl; pour over fruit. Cover and cook on low until heated through, 2 hours. Sprinkle with toasted coconut. If desired, serve with coconut ice cream, vanilla wafers or cream-filled wafer cookies.

½ cup: 358 cal., 11g fat (7g sat. fat), 20mg chol., 95mg sod., 63g carb. (53g sugars, 3g fiber), 1g pro.

PINA COLADA
BANANAS FOSTER

CHERRY BUCKLE

I saw this recipe on a cooking show and came up with my own version. When the comforting aroma of this homey dessert drifts through the house, it's hard not to take a quick peek inside the slow cooker.
—Sherri Melotik, Oak Creek, WI

- -

Prep: 10 min. • **Cook:** 3 hours
Makes: 8 servings

- 2 cans (15 oz. each) sliced pears, drained
- 1 can (21 oz.) cherry pie filling
- ¼ tsp. almond extract
- 1 pkg. yellow cake mix (regular size)
- ¼ cup old-fashioned oats
- ¼ cup sliced almonds
- 1 Tbsp. brown sugar
- ½ cup butter, melted
  Vanilla ice cream, optional

1. In a greased 5-qt. slow cooker, combine pears and pie filling; stir in extract. In a large bowl, combine cake mix, oats, almonds and brown sugar; stir in melted butter. Sprinkle over fruit.
2. Cook, covered, on low until topping is golden brown, 3-4 hours. If desired, serve with ice cream.
1 serving: 324 cal., 13g fat (8g sat. fat), 31mg chol., 152mg sod., 49g carb. (24g sugars, 2g fiber), 1g pro.

PEACH COBBLER

PEACH COBBLER

Unlike conventional cobblers, the topping of this simple dessert is on the bottom. Placing the batter underneath the peaches helps it cook through evenly in the slow cooker.
—*Taste of Home* Test Kitchen

- -

Prep: 15 min. • **Cook:** 2 hours
Makes: 8 servings

- 1¼ cups all-purpose flour, divided
- 2 Tbsp. sugar
- 1 tsp. baking powder
- ¼ tsp. ground cinnamon
- ⅛ tsp. salt
- 1 large egg, room temperature
- ¼ cup 2% milk, warmed
- 2 Tbsp. butter, melted
- 6 cups sliced peeled fresh peaches (about 6 large)
- 2 Tbsp. brown sugar
- 1 Tbsp. lemon juice
- 1 Tbsp. vanilla extract
  Vanilla ice cream, optional

1. Whisk together 1 cup flour, sugar, baking powder, cinnamon and salt. In another bowl, whisk together the egg, milk and melted butter. Add to dry ingredients; stir just until moistened (batter will be thick). Spread onto bottom of a greased 5-qt. slow cooker.
2. Combine peaches, the remaining ¼ cup flour, brown sugar, lemon juice and vanilla; spoon over batter. Cook, covered, on high until peach mixture is bubbly, 1¾-2 hours. If desired, serve with vanilla ice cream.
1 serving: 198 cal., 6g fat (3g sat. fat), 35mg chol., 145mg sod., 33g carb. (17g sugars, 2g fiber), 4g pro.

PINEAPPLE RUMCHATA SHORTCAKES

This deliciously different dessert is made in the slow cooker in jars instead of in the oven. After they are cooked, add final touches to the cooled shortcake jars and serve.
—Joan Hallford,
North Richland Hills, TX

Prep: 20 min. • **Cook:** 1½ hours + cooling
Makes: 6 cakes

1½ cups all-purpose flour
¼ cup sugar
1 tsp. baking powder
½ tsp. salt
¼ tsp. baking soda
⅓ cup cold butter
1 large egg, room temperature
¾ cup sour cream
3 Tbsp. RumChata liqueur

TOPPING
1½ cups fresh pineapple, cut into ½-in. pieces

3 Tbsp. sugar, divided
1 to 2 Tbsp. RumChata liqueur
1 tsp. grated lime zest
½ cup heavy whipping cream
1 medium lime, thinly sliced, optional

1. In a large bowl, whisk flour, sugar, baking powder, salt and baking soda. Cut in butter until mixture resembles coarse crumbs. In another bowl, whisk egg, sour cream and RumChata. Add to flour mixture; stir just until moistened.

2. Spoon the mixture into 6 greased half-pint jars. Center lids on jars and screw on bands until fingertip tight. Place jars in a 6- or 7-qt. oval slow cooker; add enough hot water to reach halfway up the jars, about 5 cups. Cook, covered, on high 1½-2 hours or until a toothpick inserted in center of shortcake comes out clean.

3. Meanwhile, combine the pineapple, 2 Tbsp. sugar, RumChata and lime zest. Refrigerate, covered, at least 1 hour. Remove jars from slow cooker to wire racks to cool completely. In a large bowl, beat cream until it begins to thicken. Add remaining 1 Tbsp. sugar; beat until soft peaks form.

4. Top shortcakes with the pineapple mixture, whipped cream and, if desired, lime slices.

1 cake: 463 cal., 28g fat (17g sat. fat), 101mg chol., 442mg sod., 47g carb. (20g sugars, 1g fiber), 6g pro.

PINEAPPLE RUMCHATA
SHORTCAKES

BLUEBERRY COBBLER

BLUEBERRY COBBLER

I love blueberries, and this easy cake mix cobbler showcases them deliciously. Serve the treat warm with a big scoop of French vanilla ice cream or a dollop of whipped cream.
—Teri Rasey, Cadillac, MI

Prep: 15 min. • **Cook:** 3 hours
Makes: 12 servings

4   cups fresh or frozen blueberries
1   cup sugar
1   Tbsp. cornstarch
2   tsp. vanilla extract
1   pkg. French vanilla cake mix (regular size)
½   cup butter, melted
⅓   cup chopped pecans
    Vanilla ice cream, optional

In a greased 5-qt. slow cooker, combine blueberries, sugar and cornstarch; stir in vanilla. In a large bowl, combine cake mix and melted butter. Crumble over blueberries. Top with pecans. Cover slow cooker insert with a double layer of white paper towels; place lid securely over towels. Cook, covered, on low until topping is set, 3-4 hours. If desired, serve with ice cream.

½ cup: 331 cal., 11g fat (6g sat. fat), 20mg chol., 343mg sod., 58g carb. (39g sugars, 2g fiber), 2g pro.

SLOW-COOKER SECRETS
Using paper towels under the lid will catch condensation and keep it from dripping on the cobbler topping.

SPUMONI CAKE

SPUMONI CAKE

I created this cake for a potluck and it has since become one of my most requested desserts. If you prefer, you can use all semisweet chips instead of a mix.
—Lisa Renshaw, Kansas City, MO

Prep: 10 min. • **Cook:** 4 hours + standing
Makes: 10 servings

3   cups cold 2% milk
1   pkg. (3.4 oz.) instant pistachio pudding mix
1   pkg. white cake mix (regular size)
¾   cup chopped maraschino cherries
1   cup white baking chips
1   cup semisweet chocolate chips
1   cup pistachios, chopped

1. In a large bowl, whisk milk and pudding mix for 2 minutes. Transfer to a greased 5-qt. slow cooker. Prepare cake mix batter according to package directions, folding cherries into batter. Pour into slow cooker.
2. Cook, covered, on low about 4 hours, until edges of cake are golden brown.
3. Remove slow-cooker insert; sprinkle cake with baking chips and chocolate chips. Let the cake stand, uncovered, 10 minutes. Sprinkle with pistachios before serving.

1 serving: 588 cal., 27g fat (9g sat. fat), 9mg chol., 594mg sod., 79g carb. (54g sugars, 3g fiber), 10g pro.

SHREDDED LAMB
SLIDERS, PAGE 161

AUTUMN

SNACKS & APPETIZERS

SPICY HONEY SRIRACHA GAME DAY DIP

SPICY HONEY SRIRACHA GAME DAY DIP

You can easily whip up this creamy, spicy, salty dip. For parties, I love dips in the slow cooker—just turn it to low once the dip is cooked and let your guests help themselves. No need to worry about the dip getting cold and having to reheat it.
—Julie Peterson, Crofton, MD

Prep: 20 min. • **Cook:** 3 hours
Makes: 3 cups

- 1　lb. ground chicken
- 1　pkg. (8 oz.) cream cheese, cubed
- 1　cup shredded white cheddar cheese
- ¼　cup chicken broth
- 2　to 4 Tbsp. Sriracha chili sauce
- 2　Tbsp. honey
- 　　Tortilla chips
- 　　Chopped green onions, optional

1. In a large skillet, cook the chicken over medium heat until no longer pink, 6-8 minutes, breaking it into crumbles; drain. Transfer to a greased 3-qt. slow cooker. Stir in cream cheese, cheddar cheese, broth, chili sauce and honey.
2. Cook, covered, on low until cheese is melted, 3-4 hours, stirring every 30 minutes. Serve with tortilla chips. If desired, sprinkle with green onions.
¼ cup: 168 cal., 13g fat (6g sat. fat), 54mg chol., 243mg sod., 5g carb. (4g sugars, 0 fiber), 9g pro.

HARVEST APPLE CIDER

HARVEST APPLE CIDER

I simmer this comforting cider in my slow cooker every fall.
—Lesley Geisel, Severna Park, MD

Prep: 5 min. • **Cook:** 2 hours
Makes: 2 qt.

- 8　whole cloves
- 4　cups apple cider or juice
- 4　cups pineapple juice
- ½　cup water
- 1　cinnamon stick (3 in.)
- 1　tea bag

1. Place cloves on a double thickness of cheesecloth; bring up corners of cloth and tie with kitchen string to form a bag. Place bag and remaining ingredients in a 3-qt. slow cooker.
2. Cover and cook on low until cider reaches desired temperature, about 2 hours. Discard spice bag, cinnamon stick and tea bag before serving.
1 cup: 130 cal., 0 fat (0 sat. fat), 0 chol., 14mg sod., 32g carb. (30g sugars, 0 fiber), 0 pro.

MAPLE PULLED PORK BUNS

Maple syrup is the sweet secret to these irresistible buns. Slow-cooking the flavorful pork couldn't be easier, and the buns are quick to roll up. We love them for parties because they serve a packed house.
—Rashanda Cobbins, Milwaukee, WI

- -

Prep: 25 min. + rising • **Cook:** 5½ hours
Makes: 16 servings

- 1 **boneless pork shoulder butt roast (2½ lbs.)**
- 1½ **tsp. ground mustard**
- 1 **tsp. salt**
- ½ **tsp. cayenne pepper**
- ½ **tsp. ground ginger**
- 1 **cup thinly sliced onion**
- 2 **garlic cloves, peeled**
- 1 **cup maple syrup, divided**
- ½ **cup water**
- 3 **Tbsp. cider vinegar**
- 2 **loaves (1 lb. each) frozen bread dough, thawed**
- 1 **cup barbecue sauce**
- 1 **cup shredded pepper jack cheese**
  Chopped green onions and crushed red pepper flakes

1. Season pork with mustard, salt, cayenne pepper and ginger; place in a 4-qt. slow cooker. Top with the onion and garlic; pour in ½ cup maple syrup, water and cider vinegar. Cook, covered, on low 5-7 hours or until meat is tender. Shred meat with 2 forks; discard the cooking liquid and vegetables.
2. On a lightly floured surface, roll 1 loaf dough into a 16x10-in. rectangle. Combine barbecue sauce with the remaining syrup; brush ¼ cup sauce mixture to within ½ in. of dough edges. Top with half the pork. Roll up jelly-roll style, starting with a long side; pinch seam to seal. Cut crosswise into 8 slices. Place in a 9-in. pie plate, cut sides down. Repeat with remaining dough and additional pie plate. Cover with kitchen towels; let rise in a warm place until doubled, about 1 hour. Reserve remaining sauce mixture. Preheat oven to 400°.
3. Bake until golden brown, 20 minutes. Sprinkle with cheese and bake until melted, 5-10 minutes longer. Serve with reserved sauce mixture; sprinkle with green onions and red pepper flakes.
1 roll: 358 cal., 12g fat (4g sat. fat), 50mg chol., 727mg sod., 41g carb. (14g sugars, 2g fiber), 20g pro.

SLOW-COOKER SECRETS

Want to prepare the pork faster? Use your pressure cooker instead of a slow cooker. Adjust to pressure-cook on high for 75 minutes. Allow pressure to naturally release for 10 minutes, then quick-release any remaining pressure. Once the pork is prepared, continue with the recipe as directed.

MAPLE
PULLED PORK
BUNS

TOMATO APPLE CHUTNEY

During the fall and winter, I love to make different kinds of chutney to give as hostess gifts. Cook this chutney in a slow cooker, and you don't have to fuss with it until you are ready to serve it.
—Nancy Heishman, Las Vegas, NV

Prep: 15 min. • **Cook:** 5 hours
Makes: 30 servings

3   cans (14½ oz. each)
    fire-roasted diced tomatoes
    with garlic, undrained
2   medium red onions, chopped
1   large apple, peeled and chopped
1   cup golden raisins
¾   cup cider vinegar
½   cup packed brown sugar
1   Tbsp. chopped seeded
    jalapeno pepper
1   Tbsp. minced fresh cilantro
2   tsp. curry powder
½   tsp. salt
¼   tsp. ground allspice
    Baked pita chips

Combine the first 11 ingredients in a greased 3-qt. slow cooker. Cook, uncovered, on high 5-6 hours or until thickened. Serve warm with pita chips.
Note: Wear disposable gloves when cutting hot peppers; the oils can burn skin. Avoid touching your face.
¼ cup: 48 cal., 0 fat (0 sat. fat), 0 chol., 152mg sod., 11g carb. (8g sugars, 1g fiber), 1g pro.

PARTY SAUSAGES

Don't want any leftovers from your party? Serve these tempting sausages in this sweet and savory sauce. I've never had even one piece go uneaten.
—Jo Ann Renner, Xenia, OH

Prep: 15 min. • **Cook:** 1 hour
Makes: 16 servings

2   lbs. smoked sausage links
1   bottle (8 oz.) Catalina
    salad dressing
1   bottle (8 oz.) Russian
    salad dressing
½   cup packed brown sugar
½   cup pineapple juice
    Sliced green onions, optional

1. Cut sausages diagonally into ½-in. slices; cook in a skillet over medium heat until lightly browned. Transfer sausages to a 3-qt. slow cooker; discard drippings.

2. Add dressings, brown sugar and juice to skillet; cook and stir over medium-low heat until sugar is dissolved. Pour over sausages. Cover and cook on low for 1-2 hours or until heated through. If desired, sprinkle with green onions.

2 sausage pieces: 306 cal., 22g fat (7g sat. fat), 38mg chol., 1008mg sod., 18g carb. (16g sugars, 0 fiber), 8g pro.

Zesty Smoked Links: Omit dressings and pineapple juice. Increase brown sugar to 1 cup; add ½ cup ketchup and ¼ cup prepared horseradish. Cook as directed.

MARINARA-MOZZARELLA DIP

Talk about easy! With just three ingredients and two loaves of baguette-style French bread, you'll have an appetizer that will please family and guests. For a tasty variation, try using goat cheese instead of mozzarella.
—Janie Colle, Hutchinson, KS

Prep: 10 min. • **Cook:** 2½ hours
Makes: 12 servings (3 cups)

2   cups marinara sauce
1   carton (8 oz.) fresh mozzarella
    cheese pearls, drained
2   Tbsp. minced fresh basil
    French bread baguette,
    thinly sliced and toasted

Optional: Crushed
red pepper flakes and
additional minced fresh basil

Pour marinara into a 1½-qt. slow cooker. Cook, covered, on low about 2 hours, until hot. Stir in mozzarella and basil. Cook until the cheese is melted, about 30 minutes longer. Serve with toasted baguette slices and, if desired, top with crushed red pepper flakes and additional basil.

¼ cup: 76 cal., 5g fat (3g sat. fat), 16mg chol., 219mg sod., 4g carb. (3g sugars, 1g fiber), 4g pro.

MARINARA-MOZZARELLA D

to a 6- or 7-qt. slow cooker. In the same skillet, cook and stir carrots, shallots and garlic until crisp-tender, about 4 minutes. Add stock, stirring to loosen browned bits from pan. Pour over lamb. Cook, covered, on low until the lamb is tender, 6-8 hours.

2. Meanwhile, for pesto, place mint, basil, pine nuts and salt in a food processor; pulse until chopped. Continue processing while gradually adding oil in a steady stream. Add the Parmesan and Asiago cheeses; pulse just until blended.

3. When cool enough to handle, remove meat from bones; discard bones. Shred meat with 2 forks. Strain cooking juices, adding vegetables to shredded meat; skim the fat. Return the cooking juices and meat to slow cooker. Heat through. Serve on buns with pesto and feta.

1 slider: 339 cal., 22g fat (7g sat. fat), 56mg chol., 459mg sod., 16g carb. (2g sugars, 1g fiber), 18g pro.

SHREDDED LAMB SLIDERS

SHREDDED LAMB SLIDERS

I made about 1,500 of these easy, tasty sliders for the Great American Beer Fest. Everyone—right down to the last customer—thought the bites were delish.
—Craig Kuczek, Aurora, CO

Prep: 45 min. • **Cook:** 6 hours
Makes: 2 dozen

- 1   boneless lamb shoulder roast (3½ to 4¼ lbs.)
- 1½ tsp. salt
- ½   tsp. pepper
- 1   Tbsp. olive oil
- 2   medium carrots, chopped
- 4   shallots, chopped
- 6   garlic cloves
- 2   cups beef stock

PESTO
- ¾   cup fresh mint leaves
- ¾   cup loosely packed basil leaves
- ⅓   cup pine nuts
- ¼   tsp. salt
- ¾   cup olive oil
- ¾   cup shredded Parmesan cheese
- ⅓   cup shredded Asiago cheese
- 24 slider buns
- 1   pkg. (4 oz.) crumbled feta cheese

1. Sprinkle roast with salt and pepper. In a large skillet, heat oil over medium-high heat; brown meat. Transfer meat

RANCH MUSHROOMS

RANCH MUSHROOMS

I got this recipe from my sister-in-law, and it is adored by my family. The mushrooms don't last long once people know I made them.
—Jackie McGee, Byron, MN

Prep: 10 min. • **Cook:** 3 hours
Makes: 4 cups

1½ lbs. whole fresh mushrooms
1   cup butter, melted
1   envelope ranch
    salad dressing mix
    **Optional: Chopped fresh
    dill weed or parsley**

Place mushrooms in a 4- or 5-qt. slow cooker. In a small bowl, whisk the butter and ranch mix; pour over mushrooms. Cook, covered, on low until mushrooms are tender, about 3 hours. Serve with a slotted spoon. If desired, sprinkle with dill or parsley.
Freeze option: Freeze mushrooms and juices in freezer containers. To use, partially thaw in the refrigerator overnight. Microwave, covered, on high in a microwave-safe dish until heated through, stirring occasionally; add a little broth or water if necessary.
¼ cup: 21 cal., 1g fat (1g sat. fat), 3mg chol., 47mg sod., 2g carb. (1g sugars, 0 fiber), 1g pro.

WARM SPICED CIDER PUNCH

WARM SPICED CIDER PUNCH

This is a nice warm-up punch. I like to serve it when there is a nip in the air. The aroma of the apple cider, orange juice and spices as the punch simmers in the slow cooker is wonderful.
—Susan Smith, Forest, VA

Prep: 5 min. • **Cook:** 4 hours
Makes: 8 servings

4   cups apple cider or
    unsweetened apple juice
2¼ cups water
1   can (6 oz.) frozen orange juice
    concentrate, thawed
¾   tsp. ground nutmeg
¾   tsp. ground ginger
3   whole cloves
2   cinnamon sticks
    **Optional: Orange slices and
    additional cinnamon sticks**

1. In a 3-qt. slow cooker, combine apple cider, water, orange juice concentrate, nutmeg and ginger. Place cloves and cinnamon sticks on a double thickness of cheesecloth; bring up corners of cloth and tie with string to form a bag. Place bag in slow cooker.
2. Cover and cook on low for 4-5 hours or until heated through. Remove and discard spice bag. Garnish with orange slices and additional cinnamon sticks if desired.
¾ cup: 94 cal., 0 fat (0 sat. fat), 0 chol., 14mg sod., 23g carb. (19g sugars, 0 fiber), 1g pro.

CREAMY ARTICHOKE DIP

This creamy dip is a family favorite.
My sister Teresa got this recipe from
a friend and passed it along to me.
It's loaded with four types of cheese,
artichoke hearts and just the right
amount of spice.
—Mary Spencer, Greendale, WI

- -

Prep: 20 min. • **Cook:** 1 hour
Makes: 5 cups

- 2   cans (14 oz. each) water-packed
    artichoke hearts, rinsed,
    drained and coarsely chopped
- 2   cups shredded part-skim
    mozzarella cheese
- 1   pkg. (8 oz.) cream cheese, cubed
- 1   cup shredded Parmesan cheese
- ½   cup mayonnaise
- ½   cup shredded Swiss cheese
- 2   Tbsp. lemon juice
- 2   Tbsp. plain yogurt
- 1   Tbsp. seasoned salt
- 1   Tbsp. chopped seeded
    jalapeno pepper
- 1   tsp. garlic powder
    Tortilla chips

In a 3-qt. slow cooker, combine the
first 11 ingredients. Cover and cook on
low for 1 hour or until heated through.
Serve with tortilla chips.
Note: Wear disposable gloves when
cutting hot peppers; the oils can burn
skin. Avoid touching your face.
¼ cup: 152 cal., 12g fat (5g sat. fat),
27mg chol., 519mg sod., 4g carb.
(1g sugars, 0 fiber), 7g pro.

SLOW-COOKED
CRANBERRY HOT WINGS

SLOW-COOKED CRANBERRY HOT WINGS

Cranberry wings remind me of all the fantastic celebrations and parties we have had through the years. My daughter's friends can't get enough of these wings.
—Noreen McCormick Danek, Cromwell, CT

Prep: 45 min. • **Cook:** 3 hours
Makes: 4 dozen

- 1   **can (14 oz.) jellied cranberry sauce**
- ½   **cup orange juice**
- ¼   **cup Louisiana-style hot sauce**
- 2   **Tbsp. soy sauce**
- 2   **Tbsp. honey**
- 1   **Tbsp. packed brown sugar**
- 1   **Tbsp. Dijon mustard**
- 2   **tsp. garlic powder**
- 1   **tsp. dried minced onion**
- 1   **garlic clove, minced**
- 5   **lbs. chicken wings (about 24 wings)**
- 1   **tsp. salt**
- 4   **tsp. cornstarch**
- 2   **Tbsp. cold water**

1. Whisk together first 10 ingredients. For chicken, use a sharp knife to cut through 2 wing joints; discard the wing tips. Place wings in a 6-qt. slow cooker; sprinkle with salt. Pour the cranberry mixture over top. Cook, covered, on low until tender, 3-4 hours.

2. Remove wings to a 15x10x1-in. pan; arrange the wings in a single layer. Preheat broiler.

3. Carefully transfer cooking juices to a skillet; skim fat. Bring juices to a boil; cook until mixture is reduced by half, 15-20 minutes, stirring occasionally. Mix cornstarch and water until smooth; stir into juices. Return to a boil, stirring constantly; cook and stir until thickened, 1-2 minutes.

4. Meanwhile, broil wings 3-4 in. from heat until lightly browned, 2-3 minutes. Brush with glaze before serving. Serve with remaining glaze.

Note: Uncooked chicken wing sections (wingettes) may be substituted for whole chicken wings.

1 serving: 71 cal., 4g fat (1g sat. fat), 15mg chol., 122mg sod., 5g carb. (3g sugars, 0g fiber), 5g pro.

SLOW-COOKER SECRETS
You can substitute Sriracha for the hot sauce to switch it up.

SOUPS, STEWS & SANDWICHE

BEEF TACO CHILI

BEEF TACO CHILI

This is one of my husband's absolute favorite dishes. It was voted Best Chili at our county's autumn harvest festival. If you like less broth, use just 1¾ cups water and 1½ teaspoons beef bouillon.
—Dana Beery, Lone, WA

Prep: 25 min. • **Cook:** 7 hours
Makes: 6 servings (2¼ qt.)

- 1 lb. ground beef
- 1 medium onion, chopped
- 2½ cups water
- 2 cans (15 oz. each) pinto beans, rinsed and drained
- 1 can (14½ oz.) diced tomatoes, undrained
- 2 cans (8 oz. each) tomato sauce
- 2½ tsp. beef bouillon granules
- 2 garlic cloves, minced
- 1 envelope taco seasoning
- 2 Tbsp. chili powder
- 2 tsp. dried oregano
- 2 tsp. baking cocoa
- 1½ tsp. ground cumin
- 1 tsp. Louisiana-style hot sauce
- ½ tsp. pepper
  Optional toppings: Sour cream, tortilla strips and sliced jalapenos

1. Cook beef and onion in a large skillet over medium heat until meat is no longer pink, 5-7 minutes, breaking beef into crumbles; drain. Transfer to a 4-qt. slow cooker. Stir in the next 13 ingredients.
2. Cover and cook on low for 7-9 hours or until heated through. Serve with toppings if desired.
1½ cups: 337 cal., 11g fat (3g sat. fat), 47mg chol., 1657mg sod., 39g carb. (7g sugars, 10g fiber), 23g pro.

SLOW-COOKED TURKEY SANDWICHES

SLOW-COOKED TURKEY SANDWICHES

These sandwiches have been such a hit at office potlucks that I keep copies of the recipe in my desk to hand out.
—Diane Twait Nelsen, Ringsted, IA

Prep: 15 min.
Cook: 3 hours
Makes: 18 servings

- 6 cups cubed cooked turkey
- 2 cups cubed Velveeta
- 1 can (10¾ oz.) condensed cream of chicken soup, undiluted
- 1 can (10¾ oz.) condensed cream of mushroom soup, undiluted
- ½ cup finely chopped onion
- ½ cup chopped celery
- 18 wheat sandwich buns, split

In a 4-qt. slow cooker, combine the first 6 ingredients. Cover and cook on low until vegetables are tender and cheese is melted, 3-4 hours. Stir mixture; spoon ½ cup onto each bun.
1 sandwich: 263 cal., 9g fat (3g sat. fat), 62mg chol., 680mg sod., 26g carb. (5g sugars, 4g fiber), 20g pro.

SWEET POTATO CHOCOLATE MOLE SOUP

This recipe is perfect for those days when you're craving something just a little bit different. It's spicy, flavorful and a delightful excuse to open up a bar of chocolate—if you're the type of person who needs an excuse!
—Colleen Delawder, Herndon, VA

- -

Prep: 30 min. • **Cook:** 6 hours
Makes: 8 servings (2½ qt.)

- 2 **Tbsp. olive oil**
- 1 **large sweet onion, finely chopped**
- 2 **Tbsp. chili powder**
- 1 **tsp. dried oregano**
- 1 **tsp. dried tarragon**
- 1 **tsp. ground cumin**
- ¾ **tsp. salt**
- ½ **tsp. ground cinnamon**
- ½ **tsp. pepper**
- 3 **garlic cloves, minced**
- 2 **Tbsp. tequila, optional**
- 1 **carton (32 oz.) reduced-sodium vegetable broth**
- 1 **can (14½ oz.) reduced-sodium chicken broth**
- 4 **medium sweet potatoes, peeled and cubed**
- 2 **oz. bittersweet chocolate, finely chopped**
  Optional: Cubed avocado, Cotija cheese, chopped onion, corn and cilantro leaves

1. In a large skillet, heat the oil over medium-high heat. Add onion and seasonings; cook and stir until onion is tender, 5-7 minutes. Add the garlic; cook 1 minute longer. If desired, add in tequila, stirring constantly.

2. Transfer to a 4- or 5-qt. slow cooker. Add broths and sweet potatoes. Cook, covered, on low until the potatoes are tender, 6-8 hours. Stir in the chocolate until melted. Cool soup slightly. Process in batches in a blender until smooth. Serve with toppings as desired.

Freeze option: Freeze cooled soup in freezer containers. To use, partially thaw in the refrigerator overnight. Heat through in a saucepan, stirring occasionally; add broth if necessary.

1¼ cups: 203 cal., 6g fat (2g sat. fat), 0 chol., 511mg sod., 31g carb. (14g sugars, 5g fiber), 4g pro. **Diabetic exchanges:** 2 starch, 1 fat.

SLOW-COOKER SECRETS
Make this soup vegan by replacing the chicken broth with more vegetable broth and omitting the cheese.

SWEET POTATO CHOCOLATE MOLE SOUP

BEER BRAT CHILI

My husband and I love this chili because it smells so good as it simmers in the slow cooker all day. I can't think of a better way to use up leftover brats. He can't think of a better way to eat them!
—Katrina Krumm, Apple Valley, MN

Prep: 10 min. • **Cook:** 5 hours
Makes: 8 servings (2½ qt.)

- 1 **can (15 oz.) cannellini beans, rinsed and drained**
- 1 **can (15 oz.) pinto beans, rinsed and drained**
- 1 **can (15 oz.) southwestern black beans, undrained**
- 1 **can (14½ oz.) Italian diced tomatoes, undrained**
- 1 **can (10 oz.) diced tomatoes and green chiles, undrained**
- 1 **pkg. (14 oz.) fully cooked beer bratwurst links, sliced**
- 1½ **cups frozen corn**
- 1 **medium sweet red pepper, chopped**
- 1 **medium onion, finely chopped**
- ¼ **cup chili seasoning mix**
- 1 **garlic clove, minced**

In a 5-qt. slow cooker, combine all ingredients. Cook, covered, on low 5-6 hours.
1¼ cups: 383 cal., 16g fat (5g sat. fat), 34mg chol., 1256mg sod., 42g carb. (7g sugars, 10g fiber), 17g pro.

VEGETABLE WILD RICE SOUP

This thick and hearty soup is packed with colorful vegetables.
—Thomas Faglon, Somerset, NJ

Prep: 25 min. • **Cook:** 5 hours
Makes: 12 servings (3 qt.)

- 6 cups reduced-sodium vegetable broth
- 2 cans (14½ oz. each) fire-roasted diced tomatoes
- 2 celery ribs, sliced
- 2 medium carrots, chopped
- 1¾ cups sliced baby portobello mushrooms
- 1 medium onion, chopped
- 1 medium parsnip, peeled and chopped
- 1 medium sweet potato, peeled and cubed
- 1 medium green pepper, chopped
- 1 cup uncooked wild rice
- 2 garlic cloves, minced
- ¾ tsp. salt
- ¼ tsp. pepper
- 2 bay leaves
- 2 fresh thyme sprigs, plus more for optional topping

Combine all ingredients in a 6- or 7-qt. slow cooker. Cover and cook on high until rice and vegetables are tender, 5-6 hours. Discard bay leaves and thyme sprigs before serving. If desired, remove leaves from remaining thyme sprigs and sprinkle over each serving.
1 cup: 117 cal., 0 fat (0 sat. fat), 0 chol., 419mg sod., 25g carb. (7g sugars, 4g fiber), 4g pro. **Diabetic exchanges:** 2 vegetable, 1 starch.

PARSNIP & APPLE SOUP

Here's a light, lovely soup ideal for the first course at your next special dinner. You'll love the harmony of fall flavors.
—Shelly Bevington, Hermiston, OR

Prep: 15 min. • **Cook:** 3 hours
Makes: 8 servings (2 qt.)

- 2 medium tart apples, chopped
- 2 cups chopped parsnips
- 1 cup thinly sliced fresh carrots
- ½ cup chopped onion
- 2 cans (14½ oz. each) vegetable broth
- 2 cups water
- 2 tsp. cider vinegar
- 1½ tsp. minced fresh rosemary, plus more for optional topping
- ½ tsp. salt
- ¼ tsp. pepper
  Fresh cracked pepper, optional

Combine all ingredients in a 4- or 5-qt. slow cooker. Cook, covered, until parsnips are tender, 3 hours. If desired, top with additional minced rosemary and cracked pepper.
1 cup: 61 cal., 0 fat (0 sat. fat), 0 chol., 454mg sod., 15g carb. (7g sugars, 3g fiber), 1g pro. **Diabetic exchanges:** 1 starch.

PARSNIP & APPLE SOUP

FALL VEGETABLE
SLOPPY JOES

1¼ tsp. salt
1 tsp. ground allspice
½ tsp. pepper
18 hamburger buns, split

1. In a large skillet, cook bacon over medium heat until crisp, stirring occasionally. Remove with a slotted spoon; drain on paper towels. Discard drippings. In the same skillet, cook beef, onion and garlic over medium heat until beef is no longer pink and onion is tender, 10-12 minutes, breaking beef into crumbles; drain.

2. Transfer to a 5- or 6-qt. slow cooker. Stir in squash, parsnips, carrots, cola, tomato paste, water, mustard and seasonings. Cook, covered, on low until vegetables are tender, 4-5 hours. Stir in bacon. Serve on buns.

Freeze option: Freeze cooled meat mixture in freezer containers. To use, partially thaw in refrigerator overnight. Heat through in a saucepan, stirring occasionally; add water if necessary.

1 sandwich: 275 cal., 8g fat (3g sat. fat), 35mg chol., 526mg sod., 35g carb. (9g sugars, 3g fiber), 17g pro. **Diabetic exchanges:** 2 starch, 2 lean meat.

FALL VEGETABLE SLOPPY JOES

I make this dish in the fall and sneak grated vegetables into the sloppy joe mixture, which is especially good for children who don't like to eat their vegetables! Just walk away and let the slow cooker do all the work. Top the filling with a little shredded cheese before serving.
—Nancy Heishman, Las Vegas, NV

Prep: 30 min. • **Cook:** 4 hours
Makes: 18 servings

8 bacon strips, cut into 1-in. pieces
2 lbs. lean ground beef (90% lean)
1 medium onion, chopped
2 garlic cloves, minced
2 cups shredded peeled butternut squash
2 medium parsnips, peeled and shredded
2 medium carrots, peeled and shredded
1 can (12 oz.) cola
1 can (8 oz.) tomato paste
1 cup water
⅓ cup honey mustard
1½ tsp. ground cumin

CRANBERRY TURKEY
SLOPPY JOES

CABBAGE BARLEY SOUP

My neighbor had an abundance of cabbage, so a group of us had a contest to see who could come up with the best cabbage dish. My vegetarian soup was the clear winner.
—Lorraine Caland, Shuniah, ON

Prep: 15 min. • **Cook:** 6¼ hours
Makes: 8 servings (3 qt.)

- **1** cup dried brown lentils, rinsed
- **½** cup medium pearl barley
- **3** medium carrots, chopped
- **2** celery ribs, chopped
- **½** tsp. poultry seasoning
- **¼** tsp. pepper
- **1** bottle (46 oz.) V8 juice
- **4** cups water
- **8** cups shredded cabbage (about 16 oz.)
- **½** lb. sliced fresh mushrooms
- **¾** tsp. salt

1. Place the first 8 ingredients in a 5- or 6-qt. slow cooker. Add cabbage. Cook, covered, on low until lentils are tender, 6-8 hours.
2. Stir in mushrooms and salt. Cook, covered, on low until mushrooms are tender, 15-20 minutes.
Freeze option: Freeze cooled soup in freezer containers. To use, partially thaw in the refrigerator overnight. Heat through in a saucepan, stirring occasionally; add water if necessary.
1½ cups: 197 cal., 1g fat (0 sat. fat), 0 chol., 678mg sod., 39g carb. (7g sugars, 9g fiber), 11g pro. **Diabetic exchanges:** 2½ starch, 1 lean meat.

CRANBERRY TURKEY SLOPPY JOES

Want a seasonal spin on classic sloppy joes? This combination of turkey and cranberries is a hit with everyone! The flavor has a touch of sweet and a touch of salt—just right for any cold-weather get-together. A slow cooker easily keeps the mixture warm on a buffet.
—Christine Grimm, Mount Wolf, PA

Prep: 30 min. • **Cook:** 5 hours
Makes: 20 servings

- **4** lbs. lean ground turkey
- **2½** cups ketchup
- **1¾** cups reduced-sodium beef broth
- **1½** cups dried cranberries
- **2** envelopes onion soup mix
- **¼** cup packed brown sugar
- **3** Tbsp. cider vinegar
- **20** hamburger buns, split

In a Dutch oven, cook turkey in batches over medium heat until no longer pink, 6-8 minutes, breaking it into crumbles; drain. Transfer to a 5- or 6-qt. slow cooker. Stir in the ketchup, broth, cranberries, soup mixes, brown sugar and vinegar. Cook, covered, on low until flavors are blended, 5-6 hours. Serve on buns.
1 sandwich: 344 cal., 9g fat (2g sat. fat), 63mg chol., 934mg sod., 45g carb. (23g sugars, 2g fiber), 23g pro.

CABBAGE BARLEY SOUP

CONTEST-WINNING BAVARIAN MEATBALL HOAGIES

When my husband is not manning the grill, I count on my slow cooker. These mouthwatering meatballs are just one reason why. They're a guaranteed crowd pleaser when I serve them as a party appetizer or spooned over crusty rolls and topped with cheese for irresistible sandwiches.
—Peggy Rios, Mechanicsville, VA

Prep: 15 min. • **Cook:** 3 hours
Makes: 12 sandwiches

- 1 **pkg. (32 oz.) frozen fully cooked Italian meatballs**
- ½ **cup chopped onion**
- ¼ **cup packed brown sugar**
- 1 **envelope onion soup mix**
- 1 **can (12 oz.) beer or nonalcoholic beer**
- 12 **hoagie buns, split**
- 3 **cups shredded Swiss cheese**

1. In a 3-qt. slow cooker, combine meatballs, onion, brown sugar, soup mix and beer. Cook, covered, on low until meatballs are heated through, 3-4 hours.
2. Place 5-6 meatballs on each bun bottom. Sprinkle each sandwich with ¼ cup cheese. Place on baking sheets. Broil 4-6 in. from the heat until cheese is melted, 2-3 minutes. Replace bun tops.

1 sandwich: 643 cal., 36g fat (18g sat. fat), 95mg chol., 1302mg sod., 49g carb. (13g sugars, 4g fiber), 29g pro.

SLOW-COOKER BUTTERNUT SQUASH SOUP

Much of the work for this soup can be done in advance, and it keeps all day in the slow cooker. The recipe can easily be doubled if you're feeding a crowd. Once you've tried it, try mixing it up—add sage or savory with the thyme, or replace the thyme with nutmeg. For a vegan version, replace the chicken broth with vegetable broth.
—Jennifer Machado, Alta, CA

- -

Prep: 30 min. • **Cook:** 6 hours
Makes: 12 servings (3 qt.)

- 1 Tbsp. olive oil
- 1 large onion, chopped
- 2 garlic cloves, minced
- 1 medium butternut squash (about 4 lbs.), peeled and cut into 1-in. pieces
- 1 lb. Yukon Gold potatoes (about 2 medium), cut into ¾-in. pieces
- 2 tsp. minced fresh thyme or ¾ tsp. dried thyme
- 1 tsp. salt
- ¼ tsp. pepper
- 5 to 6 cups chicken or vegetable broth
  Sour cream, optional

1. In a large skillet, heat oil over medium heat. Add onion; saute until tender, 4-5 minutes. Add garlic; cook 1 minute longer. Transfer to a 6-qt. slow cooker. Add the next 5 ingredients and 5 cups broth to slow cooker. Cook, covered, on low until vegetables are soft, 6-8 hours.

2. Puree soup using an immersion blender. Or cool slightly and puree soup in batches in a blender; return to slow cooker. Stir in additional broth to reach desired consistency; heat through. If desired, top servings with sour cream.

Freeze option: Freeze cooled soup in freezer containers. To use, partially thaw in the refrigerator overnight. Heat through in a saucepan, stirring occasionally; add a little broth if necessary.

1 cup: 124 cal., 2g fat (0 sat. fat), 2mg chol., 616mg sod., 27g carb. (6g sugars, 6g fiber), 3g pro. **Diabetic exchanges:** 2 starch.

SLOW-COOKER
BUTTERNUT SQUASH SOUP

ITALIAN SHREDDED PORK STEW

Need a warm meal for a chilly night? Throw together this slow-cooked stew that's brightened with fresh sweet potatoes, kale and Italian seasoning. The shredded pork is so tender, you're going to want to make this dish all season long.
—Robin Jungers, Campbellsport, WI

Prep: 20 min. • **Cook:** 8 hours
Makes: 9 servings (3½ qt.)

- 2 **medium sweet potatoes, peeled and cubed**
- 2 **cups chopped fresh kale**
- 1 **large onion, chopped**
- 3 **garlic cloves, minced**
- 1 **boneless pork shoulder butt roast (2½ to 3½ lbs.)**
- 1 **can (14 oz.) cannellini beans, rinsed and drained**
- 1½ **tsp. Italian seasoning**
- ½ **tsp. salt**
- ½ **tsp. pepper**
- 3 **cans (14½ oz. each) chicken broth**
  Sour cream, optional

1. Place the sweet potatoes, kale, onion and garlic in a 5-qt. slow cooker. Place roast on vegetables. Add the beans and seasonings. Pour broth over top. Cook, covered, on low until meat is tender, 8-10 hours.
2. Carefully remove the meat; cool slightly. Skim fat from cooking juices. Shred pork with 2 forks and return to slow cooker; heat through. If desired, garnish with sour cream.

1½ cups: 283 cal., 13g fat (5g sat. fat), 78mg chol., 860mg sod., 15g carb. (4g sugars, 3g fiber), 24g pro.

SLOW-COOKED BLACK BEAN SOUP

SLOW-COOKED BLACK BEAN SOUP

Life can get really crazy with young children, but I don't compromise when it comes to cooking. This recipe is healthy and so easy thanks to the slow cooker!
—Angela Lemoine, Howell, NJ

Prep: 15 min. • **Cook:** 6 hours
Makes: 8 servings (1½ qt.)

- 2 **cans (15 oz. each) black beans, rinsed and drained**
- 1 **medium onion, finely chopped**
- 1 **medium sweet red pepper, finely chopped**
- 4 **garlic cloves, minced**
- 2 **tsp. ground cumin**
- 2 **cans (14½ oz. each) vegetable broth**
- 1 **tsp. olive oil**
- 1 **cup fresh or frozen corn**
  Dash pepper
  Minced fresh cilantro

1. In a 3-qt. slow cooker, combine the first 6 ingredients. Cook, covered, on low until vegetables are softened, 6-8 hours.
2. Puree soup using an immersion blender, or cool soup slightly and puree in batches in a blender. Return to slow cooker and heat through.
3. In a small skillet, heat oil over medium heat. Add corn; cook and stir until golden brown, 4-6 minutes. Sprinkle soup with pepper. Garnish with corn and cilantro.

¾ cup: 117 cal., 1g fat (0 sat. fat), 0 chol., 616mg sod., 21g carb. (3g sugars, 5g fiber), 6g pro. **Diabetic exchanges:** 1½ starch.

FIRE-ROASTED TOMATO MINESTRONE

This soup was created to accommodate a few of my dinner guests who were vegetarians. It was so good, we all enjoyed it. This can also be cooked on the stove for two hours at a low simmer.
—Donna-Marie Ryan, Topsfield, MA

Prep: 20 min. • **Cook:** 4½ hours
Makes: 8 servings (about 3 qt.)

1   medium sweet onion, chopped
1   cup cut fresh green beans
1   small zucchini, cubed
1   medium carrot, chopped
1   celery rib, chopped
2   garlic cloves, minced
2   Tbsp. olive oil
¼   tsp. salt
¼   tsp. pepper
2   cans (14½ oz. each) fire-roasted diced tomatoes
1   can (15 oz.) cannellini beans, rinsed and drained
1   carton (32 oz.) vegetable broth
1   cup uncooked small pasta shells
1   cup chopped fresh spinach
    Shredded Parmesan cheese, optional

1. In a 5-qt. slow cooker, combine the first 9 ingredients. Add tomatoes and beans; pour in broth. Cook, covered, on low until vegetables are tender, 4-6 hours.
2. Stir in pasta; cook, covered, on low until pasta is tender, 30-40 minutes. Stir in the spinach before serving. If desired, top with shredded Parmesan.

1⅓ cups: 175 cal., 4g fat (1g sat. fat), 0 chol., 767mg sod., 29g carb. (7g sugars, 5g fiber), 6g pro.

SLOW-COOKER SECRETS
Fresh garlic is a fantastic ingredient to use when flavoring slow-cooked foods. To quickly peel fresh garlic, gently crush the clove with the flat side of a large knife blade to loosen the peel. If you don't have a large knife, you can also crush the garlic with a small can.

FIRE-ROASTED TOMATO MINESTRONE

POT ROAST SLIDERS

POT ROAST SLIDERS

This recipe reminds me of my mom's famous pot roast. Best of all, these sandwiches are simple to make with only a few ingredients. I love that I can enjoy the flavors of Mom's roast with the delicious portability of a slider.
—Lauren Drafke, Cape Coral, FL

- -

Prep: 20 min. • **Cook:** 5 hours
Makes: 2 dozen

- 1 boneless beef chuck roast (3 lbs.)
- 1½ cups water
- 1 envelope (1 oz.) onion soup mix
- 1 envelope (1 oz.) au jus gravy mix
- 2 pkg. (12 oz. each) Hawaiian sweet rolls, halved
- 12 slices Swiss cheese (¾ oz. each), cut in half
  Optional: Horseradish sauce, sliced tomato and baby arugula

1. Place roast in a 4-qt. slow cooker. In a small bowl, whisk together water and the soup and gravy mixes. Pour seasoning mixture over roast. Cook, covered, on low until tender, 5-6 hours. Remove from cooker. Cool slightly; shred meat with 2 forks.
2. Preheat broiler. Place halved rolls on a baking sheet. On each bottom half, place a cheese piece. Broil buns 4-6 in. from heat until cheese is melted and rolls start to brown, 1-2 minutes. Remove from broiler. Using tongs, place meat mixture on roll bottoms. If desired, layer with horseradish sauce, tomato and baby arugula. Replace roll tops.
2 sliders: 487 cal., 22g fat (11g sat. fat), 124mg chol., 721mg sod., 36g carb. (12g sugars, 2g fiber), 36g pro.

TOMATO BEEF BARLEY SOUP

TOMATO BEEF BARLEY SOUP

When my children were young, I needed a soup that everyone would eat—something filling but also something delicious. My sons really liked barley soup from a can, so I decided to try making it myself. My boys are now young adults, and this is one of the first things they ask me to make when they come to visit.
—Karla Johnson, Winter Haven, FL

- -

Prep: 20 min. • **Cook:** 7 hours
Makes: 8 servings (2½ qt.)

- 1 lb. ground beef
- 1 medium onion, finely chopped
- ½ medium head cabbage, coarsely shredded (about 5 cups)
- 1 large carrot, chopped
- 1¼ tsp. salt
- 1 tsp. pepper
- 1 carton (32 oz.) beef broth
- 2 cans (8 oz. each) roasted garlic tomato sauce
- 1 can (14½ oz.) diced tomatoes, undrained
- 2 cups fresh or frozen corn (about 10 oz.), thawed
- ½ cup medium pearl barley

1. In a large skillet, cook and crumble beef with onion over medium-high heat until no longer pink, 5-7 minutes. Using a slotted spoon, transfer beef mixture to a 5-qt. slow cooker.
2. Stir in cabbage, carrot, salt, pepper, broth, tomato sauce and tomatoes. Cook, covered, on low 6 hours.
3. Stir in corn and barley; turn up to high and cook until barley is tender, about 1 hour.
1⅓ cups: 239 cal., 8g fat (3g sat. fat), 35mg chol., 1372mg sod., 28g carb. (9g sugars, 6g fiber), 16g pro.

MEXICAN PORK

The first time I made this dish, it was a hit with everyone in my family, both young and old. Serve with black beans and white rice, or use as meat for tacos, enchiladas or tamales!
—Amy Vazquez, Brandon, MS

- -

Prep: 20 min. • **Cook:** 8 hours
Makes: 18 servings

- 1 bone-in pork shoulder roast (4 to 5 lbs.)
- 1 can (28 oz.) enchilada sauce
- 1 large green pepper, chopped
- 1 medium onion, finely chopped
- 2 garlic cloves, minced
- ¼ cup minced fresh cilantro
- 1 Tbsp. lime juice
- 1½ tsp. grated lime zest
  Flour tortillas (8 in.), optional
  Toppings of your choice

1. Cut roast in half; place in a 4- or 5-qt. slow cooker. Top with enchilada sauce, green pepper, onion and garlic. Cover and cook on low for 8-10 hours or until meat is tender.
2. Remove roast; cool slightly. Skim fat from cooking juices. Remove meat from bone; discard bone. Shred pork with 2 forks and return to slow cooker.
3. Stir in the cilantro, lime juice and lime zest; heat through. Using a slotted spoon, serve on tortillas, if desired, with toppings of your choice.

½ cup pork: 162 cal., 9g fat (3g sat. fat), 51mg chol., 280mg sod., 4g carb. (1g sugars, 1g fiber), 17g pro.

BACON-BEEF SOUP

Here's a robust dish that's perfect for hungry teenagers! Served over creamy mashed potatoes, this quick, comforting soup really hits the spot.
—Cathy Peterson, Menominee, MI

- -

Prep: 40 min. • **Cook:** 7 hours
Makes: 7 servings

- 4 bacon strips, chopped
- 1½ lbs. beef stew meat, cut into ½-in. pieces
- 1 medium onion, chopped
- 4 medium red potatoes, cut into ½-in. cubes
- 1½ cups fresh baby carrots, cut in half lengthwise
- 1 cup frozen corn
- ¼ cup medium pearl barley
- 2 cans (14½ oz. each) beef broth
- 1 can (14½ oz.) diced tomatoes with basil, oregano and garlic, undrained
- 1 jar (12 oz.) home-style beef gravy
- ½ tsp. pepper
  Mashed potatoes, optional

1. In a large skillet, cook the bacon over medium heat until crisp. Using a slotted spoon, remove to paper towels to drain. In the drippings, cook and crumble beef with onion until meat is browned; drain.
2. In a 5-qt. slow cooker, layer potatoes, carrots, corn and barley. Top with beef mixture and bacon. Combine the broth, tomatoes, gravy and pepper; pour over top (do not stir).
3. Cover and cook on low for 7-9 hours or until meat and vegetables are tender. Stir before serving. Serve over mashed potatoes if desired.

1¼ cups: 319 cal., 10g fat (3g sat. fat), 68mg chol., 1218mg sod., 32g carb. (7g sugars, 4g fiber), 26g pro.

BACON-BEEF SOUP

LENTIL PUMPKIN SOUP

Plenty of herbs and spices brighten this hearty pumpkin soup. It's fantastic to enjoy on nippy days and nights.
—Laura Magee, Houlton, WI

Prep: 15 min. • **Cook:** 7 hours
Makes: 6 servings

- 1 lb. red potatoes (about 4 medium), cut into 1-in. pieces
- 1 can (15 oz.) pumpkin
- 1 cup dried lentils, rinsed
- 1 medium onion, chopped
- 3 garlic cloves, minced
- ½ tsp. ground ginger
- ½ tsp. pepper
- ⅛ tsp. salt
- 2 cans (14½ oz. each) vegetable broth
- 1½ cups water

In a 3- or 4-qt. slow cooker, combine all ingredients. Cook, covered, on low for 7-9 hours or until potatoes and lentils are tender.

1⅓ cups: 210 cal., 1g fat (0 sat. fat), 0 chol., 463mg sod., 42g carb. (5g sugars, 7g fiber), 11g pro. **Diabetic exchanges:** 3 starch, 1 lean meat.

LASAGNA SOUP

I modified one of my favorite soup recipes so I can prep it the night before and simply put it in the slow cooker in the morning. This dish makes a welcome contribution to work parties. My colleagues love it!
—Sharon Gerst, North Liberty, IA

Prep: 35 min. • **Cook:** 5 hours + standing
Makes: 8 servings (2½ qt.)

- 1 **pkg. (19½ oz.) Italian turkey sausage links, casings removed**
- 1 **large onion, chopped**
- 2 **medium carrots, chopped**
- 2 **cups sliced fresh mushrooms**
- 3 **garlic cloves, minced**
- 1 **carton (32 oz.) reduced-sodium chicken broth**
- 2 **cans (14½ oz. each) no-salt-added stewed tomatoes**
- 2 **cans (8 oz. each) no-salt-added tomato sauce**
- 2 **tsp. Italian seasoning**
- 6 **lasagna noodles, broken into 1-in. pieces**
- 2 **cups coarsely chopped fresh spinach**
- 1 **cup cubed or shredded part-skim mozzarella cheese**
  Optional: Shredded Parmesan cheese and minced fresh basil

1. In a large skillet, cook the sausage over medium-high heat until no longer pink, 8-10 minutes, breaking it into crumbles; drain. Transfer to a 5- or 6-qt. slow cooker.
2. Add onion and carrots to the same skillet; cook and stir until softened, 2-4 minutes. Stir in mushrooms and garlic; cook and stir until mushrooms are softened, 2-4 minutes. Transfer to slow cooker. Stir in broth, tomatoes, tomato sauce and Italian seasoning. Cook, covered, on low 4-6 hours, until vegetables are tender.
3. Add noodles; cook 1 hour longer or until tender. Stir in spinach. Remove insert; let stand 10 minutes. Divide mozzarella cheese among serving bowls; ladle soup over cheese. If desired, sprinkle with Parmesan cheese and basil.

1⅓ cups: 266 cal., 8g fat (3g sat. fat), 36mg chol., 725mg sod., 30g carb. (11g sugars, 5g fiber), 18g pro. **Diabetic exchanges:** 2 vegetable, 2 lean meat, 1½ starch.

LASAGNA SOUP

SHREDDED PORK BURRITOS

SHREDDED PORK BURRITOS

This pork roast is slow-cooked with savory and sweet ingredients, including a can of cola, to create tender shredded pork burritos. A tomatillo sauce, made easy with a dressing mix, tops the pork for an out-of-this-world entree.
—Katherine Nelson, Centerville, UT

- -

Prep: 25 min. • **Cook:** 9 hours
Makes: 16 servings (2⅓ cups sauce)

- 1 bone-in pork shoulder roast (5 lbs.)
- 2 Tbsp. plus ½ cup packed brown sugar, divided
- 4 tsp. paprika, divided
- 2 tsp. crushed red pepper flakes
- 2 tsp. ground cumin
- 1 tsp. salt
- 1 can (12 oz.) cola
- 1 cup chicken broth
- 1 large sweet onion, thinly sliced
- 2 garlic cloves, minced

TOMATILLO SAUCE
- 1 cup mayonnaise
- ½ cup 2% milk
- 2 tomatillos, husked
- ¾ cup fresh cilantro leaves
- 1 jalapeno pepper, seeded and cut into chunks
- 1 envelope ranch salad dressing mix
- 1 Tbsp. lime juice
- 1 garlic clove, peeled
- ⅛ tsp. cayenne pepper
- 16 flour tortillas (8 in.), room temperature

1. Cut roast in half. Combine 2 Tbsp. brown sugar, 2 tsp. paprika, pepper flakes, cumin and salt; rub over meat. Place in a 4-qt. slow cooker. Add the cola, broth, onion and garlic. Cover and cook on low for 8-10 hours or until meat is tender.

2. Set meat aside until cool enough to handle. Remove meat from bones; discard bones. Shred meat with 2 forks. Skim fat from cooking juices and return meat to slow cooker. Stir in remaining brown sugar and paprika. Cover and cook on low for 1 hour or until heated through.

3. Meanwhile, in a blender, combine the mayonnaise, milk, tomatillos, cilantro, jalapeno, dressing mix, lime juice, garlic and cayenne. Cover and process until blended. Pour into a small bowl. Chill until serving.

4. Using a slotted spoon, spoon ½ cup filling off center on each tortilla. Drizzle with some of the tomatillo sauce. Fold sides and ends over filling and roll up. Serve with remaining sauce.

Note: Wear disposable gloves when cutting hot peppers; the oils can burn skin. Avoid touching your face.

1 burrito: 370 cal., 24g fat (6g sat. fat), 77mg chol., 451mg sod., 14g carb. (12g sugars, 1g fiber), 24g pro.

SLOW-COOKER THAI BUTTERNUT SQUASH PEANUT SOUP

This seemingly exotic dish is simple, vegan, healthy and hearty. The peanut butter blends beautifully with the sweetness of the squash and Thai seasonings. You can also serve this soup without pureeing it first.
—Kayla Capper, Ojai, CA

Prep: 25 min. • **Cook:** 5 hours
Makes: 8 servings (1½ qt.)

> 3 cups cubed peeled butternut squash
> 1 can (13.66 oz.) light coconut milk
> 1 medium sweet red pepper, finely chopped
> 1 medium onion, finely chopped
> 1 cup vegetable stock
> ½ cup chunky peanut butter
> 3 Tbsp. lime juice
> 2 Tbsp. red curry paste
> 4 garlic cloves, minced
> 1 Tbsp. reduced-sodium soy sauce
> 1 tsp. minced fresh gingerroot
> ½ tsp. salt
> ¼ tsp. pepper
> Optional: Chopped fresh cilantro and chopped salted peanuts

1. In a 4- or 5-qt. slow cooker, combine the first 13 ingredients. Cook, covered, on low until squash is tender, 5-6 hours.
2. Puree the soup using an immersion blender, or cool slightly and puree soup in batches in a blender. Return to slow cooker and heat through. If desired, garnish with cilantro and peanuts.
¾ cup: 181 cal., 12g fat (4g sat. fat), 0 chol., 470mg sod.,16g carb. (5g sugars, 3g fiber), 5g pro. **Diabetic exchanges:** 1 starch, 1 high-fat meat, 1 fat.

APPLE CIDER PULLED PORK

For potlucks and tailgates, we slow-cook pork with cider, onions and spices. These tangy sliders make a winning barbecue plate with sweet potato fries.
—Rachel Lewis, Danville, VA

Prep: 15 min. • **Cook:** 6¼ hours
Makes: 12 servings

> 2 tsp. seasoned salt
> ½ tsp. ground mustard
> ½ tsp. paprika
> ¼ tsp. ground coriander
> ¼ tsp. pepper
> 2 medium Granny Smith apples, peeled and coarsely chopped
> 1 medium onion, chopped
> 1 celery rib, chopped
> 1½ cups apple cider or juice
> 1 boneless pork shoulder butt roast (3 lbs.)
> 2 Tbsp. cornstarch
> 2 Tbsp. water
> 24 mini buns, warmed
> Additional apple slices, optional

1. Mix first 5 ingredients. Place apples, onion, celery and cider in a 5-qt. slow cooker; top with roast. Sprinkle roast with seasoning mixture. Cook, covered, on low until tender, 6-8 hours.
2. Remove roast; shred with 2 forks. Skim fat from cooking juices. Mix cornstarch and water; stir into cooking juices. Cook, covered, on high until thickened, 10-15 minutes; stir in pork. Serve on buns. If desired, top with apple slices.
Freeze option: Freeze cooled meat mixture in freezer containers. To use, partially thaw in refrigerator overnight. Heat through in a saucepan, stirring occasionally; add a little broth or water if necessary.
2 sliders: 375 cal., 15g fat (5g sat. fat), 69mg chol., 563mg sod., 35g carb. (9g sugars, 2g fiber), 25g pro.

SLOW-COOKER THAI
BUTTERNUT SQUASH
PEANUT SOUP

ENTREES

GARLIC BEEF STROGANOFF

GARLIC BEEF STROGANOFF

I am a mom and work full time, so I use my slow cooker whenever possible. This stroganoff is perfect because I can get it ready in the morning before the kids get up and I head out the door for work.
—Erika Anderson, Wausau, WI

- -

Prep: 20 min. • **Cook:** 7 hours
Makes: 6 servings

2 tsp. beef bouillon granules
1 cup boiling water
1 can (10¾ oz.) condensed cream of mushroom soup, undiluted
2 jars (4½ oz. each) sliced mushrooms, drained
1 large onion, chopped
3 garlic cloves, minced
1 Tbsp. Worcestershire sauce
1½ lbs. beef top round steak, cut into thin strips
2 Tbsp. canola oil
1 pkg. (8 oz.) cream cheese, cubed
Hot cooked noodles
Minced fresh parsley, optional

1. In a 3-qt. slow cooker, dissolve bouillon in water. Add the soup, mushrooms, onion, garlic and Worcestershire sauce. In a skillet, brown beef in oil.

2. Transfer to the slow cooker. Cover and cook on low until meat is tender, 7-8 hours. Stir in cream cheese until smooth. Serve with noodles and, if desired, minced parsley.

1 serving: 383 cal., 24g fat (10g sat. fat), 104mg chol., 991mg sod., 12g carb. (4g sugars, 2g fiber), 29g pro.

PORK CHOP DINNER

PORK CHOP DINNER

Family and friends like to call me the slow-cooker queen. Of my many slow-cooked specialties, this is my husband's favorite.
—Janet Phillips, Meadville, PA

- -

Prep: 15 min. • **Cook:** 4 hours
Makes: 6 servings

6 bone-in pork loin chops (7 oz. each)
1 Tbsp. canola oil
1 large onion, sliced
1 medium green pepper, chopped
1 can (4 oz.) mushroom stems and pieces, drained
1 can (8 oz.) tomato sauce
1 Tbsp. brown sugar
2 tsp. Worcestershire sauce
1½ tsp. cider vinegar
½ tsp. salt
Optional: Baked potatoes or hot cooked rice

In a skillet, brown pork chops on both sides in oil; drain. Place the chops in a 3-qt. slow cooker. Add onion, green pepper and mushrooms. In a bowl, combine tomato sauce, brown sugar, Worcestershire sauce, vinegar and salt. Pour over meat and vegetables. Cover and cook on low for 4-5 hours or until meat is tender. If desired, serve with baked potatoes or hot cooked rice.

1 serving: 338 cal., 19g fat (6g sat. fat), 97mg chol., 527mg sod., 8g carb. (5g sugars, 2g fiber), 33g pro. **Diabetic exchanges:** 4 lean meat, ½ fat.

HARVESTTIME CHICKEN WITH COUSCOUS

Even on busy days, I can start this chicken in the slow cooker and still get to work on time. When I come home, I whip up a spinach salad and crescent rolls to round out the menu.
—Heidi Rudolph, Oregon, IL

- -

Prep: 30 min. • **Cook:** 3 hours
Makes: 6 servings

- 2 **medium sweet potatoes (about 1¼ lbs.), peeled and cut into ½-in. pieces**
- 1 **medium sweet red pepper, coarsely chopped**
- 1½ **lbs. boneless skinless chicken breasts**
- 1 **can (14½ oz.) stewed tomatoes, undrained**
- ½ **cup peach or mango salsa**
- ¼ **cup golden raisins**
- ½ **tsp. salt**
- ¼ **tsp. ground cumin**
- ¼ **tsp. ground cinnamon**
- ¼ **tsp. pepper**

COUSCOUS

- 1 **cup water**
- ½ **tsp. salt**
- 1 **cup uncooked whole wheat couscous**

1. In a 4-qt. slow cooker, layer sweet potatoes, red pepper and chicken breasts. In a small bowl, mix tomatoes, salsa, raisins and seasonings; pour over chicken. Cook, covered, on low 3-4 hours or until sweet potatoes and chicken are tender.

2. About 10 minutes before serving, prepare couscous. In a small saucepan, bring water and salt to a boil. Stir in couscous. Remove from heat; let stand, covered, 5 minutes or until water is absorbed. Fluff with a fork.

3. Remove chicken from slow cooker; coarsely shred with 2 forks. Return chicken to slow cooker, stirring gently to combine. Serve with couscous.

Freeze option: Place cooled chicken mixture in freezer containers. To use, partially thaw in refrigerator overnight. Microwave, covered, on high in a microwave-safe dish until heated through, stirring gently; add a little broth or water if necessary.

1⅓ cups chicken mixture with ½ cup couscous: 351 cal., 3g fat (1g sat. fat), 63mg chol., 699mg sod., 52g carb. (15g sugars, 7g fiber), 30g pro.

HARVESTTIME CHICKEN
WITH COUSCOUS

HERBED SLOW-COOKER TURKEY BREAST

A holiday meal warrants an elegant, satisfying entree. This one promises to deliver. The turkey comes out of the slow cooker moist and tender, and the herbs make a flavorful gravy.
—Lorie Miner, Kamas, UT

Prep: 15 min. • **Cook:** 5 hours + standing
Makes: 12 servings

- 1 **bone-in turkey breast (6 to 7 lbs.), thawed and skin removed**
- ½ **cup water**
- ⅔ **cup spreadable garden vegetable cream cheese**
- ¼ **cup butter, softened**
- ¼ **cup soy sauce**
- 2 **Tbsp. minced fresh parsley**
- 1 **tsp. dried basil**
- 1 **tsp. rubbed sage**
- 1 **tsp. dried thyme**
- ½ **tsp. pepper**

1. Place turkey breast and water in a 6-qt. slow cooker. In a small bowl, mix remaining ingredients; rub over turkey. Cook, covered, on low 5-6 hours or until turkey is tender.
2. Carefully remove the turkey from slow cooker; tent with foil. Let stand 15 minutes before slicing.

6 oz. cooked turkey: 264 cal., 8g fat (5g sat. fat), 130mg chol., 486mg sod., 1g carb. (0 sugars, 0 fiber), 44g pro.
Diabetic exchanges: 6 lean meat.

TACO BOWLS

We love this dish because of its super simple prep. And each serving is so easy to customize with toppings.
—Hope Wasylenki, Gahanna, OH

- -

Prep: 15 min. • **Cook:** 7 hours
Makes: 10 servings

- 1 **boneless beef chuck roast (2½ lbs.), cut in half**
- ¼ **cup beef broth**
- 1 **Tbsp. canola oil**
- 1 **small onion, finely chopped**
- 1 **jalapeno pepper, seeded and finely chopped**
- 1 **garlic clove, minced**
- 3 **tsp. chili powder**
- 1½ **tsp. ground cumin**
  Dash salt
- 2 **cups canned crushed tomatoes in puree**
- 1 **cup salsa verde**
- 5 **cups hot cooked brown rice**
- 1 **can (15 oz.) black beans, rinsed, drained and warmed**
- 1 **cup pico de gallo**
  Optional: Shredded cheddar cheese, reduced-fat sour cream, sliced avocado, lime wedges and warmed corn tortillas

1. Place beef and broth in a 5-qt. slow cooker. Cook, covered, on low 6-8 hours or until meat is tender.
2. Remove beef; discard juices. Return beef to slow cooker; shred with 2 forks.
3. In a large skillet, heat oil over medium heat; saute onion and jalapeno until softened, 3-4 minutes. Add garlic and seasonings; cook and stir 1 minute. Stir in tomatoes and salsa; bring to a boil. Add to beef, stirring to combine. Cook, covered, on high 1 hour or until flavors are blended.

4. For each serving, place ½ cup rice in a soup bowl. Top with beef mixture, beans and pico de gallo. Serve with optional ingredients as desired.
Freeze option: Freeze cooled meat mixture in freezer containers. To use, partially thaw in refrigerator overnight. Heat through in a saucepan, stirring occasionally.

Note: Wear disposable gloves when cutting hot peppers; the oils can burn skin. Avoid touching your face.
1 serving: 389 cal., 13g fat (5g sat. fat), 74mg chol., 550mg sod., 38g carb. (4g sugars, 5g fiber), 28g pro.
Diabetic exchanges: 3 lean meat, 2½ starch, ½ fat.

TACO BOWLS

HEARTY
CHICKEN
CACCIATORE

1. Place chicken in a 4- or 5-qt. slow cooker. In a medium bowl, combine the green peppers, tomatoes, tomato paste, onion, broth, wine, garlic, salt and pepper; pour over chicken. Cook, covered, on low 8-10 hours or until chicken is tender.

2. In a small bowl, mix the cornstarch and water until smooth; gradually stir into slow cooker. Cook, covered, on high 30 minutes or until sauce is thickened. If desired, sprinkle with minced parsley before serving.

Freeze option: In an airtight freezer container, layer chopped green peppers, onions, garlic, salt, pepper and chicken. Seal. Freeze up to 6 months. Thaw chicken overnight in refrigerator before use.

 To prepare freezer meal in a slow cooker, empty the thawed contents of container into slow cooker. Add tomatoes, tomato paste, broth and red wine. Cook as directed.

To prepare freezer meal in an electric pressure cooker, empty thawed contents of container into a 6-qt. electric pressure cooker. Add tomatoes, tomato paste, broth and red wine. Lock lid; close pressure-release valve. Adjust to pressure-cook on high for 10 minutes. Allow pressure to naturally release for 10 minutes, then quick-release any remaining pressure. (A thermometer inserted in chicken should read at least 165°.) Thicken sauce as directed.

3 oz. cooked chicken with about ½ cup sauce: 207 cal., 9g fat (2g sat. fat), 76mg chol., 410mg sod., 8g carb. (4g sugars, 1g fiber), 23g pro. **Diabetic exchanges:** 3 lean meat, 1 vegetable, ½ fat.

HEARTY CHICKEN CACCIATORE

Treat company to this perfect Italian meal. You'll have time to visit with your guests while it simmers, and it often earns rave reviews. I like to serve it with couscous, green beans and a dry red wine. Mangia!
—Martha Schirmacher, Sterling Heights, MI

- -

Prep: 15 min. • **Cook:** 8½ hours
Makes: 12 servings

- 12 boneless skinless chicken thighs (about 3 lbs.)
- 2 medium green peppers, chopped
- 1 can (14½ oz.) diced tomatoes with basil, oregano and garlic, undrained
- 1 can (6 oz.) tomato paste
- 1 medium onion, chopped
- ½ cup reduced-sodium chicken broth
- ¼ cup dry red wine or additional reduced-sodium chicken broth
- 3 garlic cloves, minced
- ¾ tsp. salt
- ⅛ tsp. pepper
- 2 Tbsp. cornstarch
- 2 Tbsp. cold water
   Minced fresh parsley, optional

ROOT BEER BRATS

SLOW-COOKER BOURBON PORK CHOPS

My dad created a baked version of this recipe years ago. Delicious as it was, when I updated his recipe, I decided to try it in the slow cooker for even more moist and tender results. Bingo! Juicy, tasty and no fuss.
—Judy Batson, Tampa, FL

- -

Prep: 20 min. • **Cook:** 3 hours
Makes: 4 servings

- ¾ cup packed dark brown sugar
- ⅓ cup apple jelly
- 3 Tbsp. bourbon
- 3 Tbsp. reduced-sodium soy sauce
- 3 Tbsp. stone-ground mustard
- ½ tsp. coarsely ground pepper
- 1 Tbsp. olive oil
- 4 pork rib chops (1 in. thick and 8 oz. each)
- 2 Tbsp. water
- 1½ tsp. cornstarch

1. For sauce, whisk together the first 6 ingredients. In a large skillet, heat oil over high heat. Brown the pork chops; 2-3 minutes per side. Transfer to a 5-qt. slow cooker. Pour sauce over top.
2. Cook chops, covered, on low until a thermometer inserted in pork reads at least 145°, 3-4 hours.
3. Remove chops from the slow cooker; keep warm. Skim fat from the cooking juices; transfer half the cooking juices to a saucepan. Mix water and cornstarch until smooth; stir into saucepan. Bring to a boil; cook and stir until thickened, 1-2 minutes. Serve over chops.
1 pork chop with 3 Tbsp. sauce: 491 cal., 14g fat (4g sat. fat), 72mg chol., 715mg sod., 62g carb. (57g sugars, 1g fiber), 30g pro.

ROOT BEER BRATS

Here's an easy recipe that's versatile, too. Serve the saucy brats over rice for one meal and have them on buns the next. For extra punch, add a splash of root beer concentrate to the sauce.
—Pamela Thompson, Girard, IL

- -

Prep: 15 min. • **Cook:** 6 hours
Makes: 10 servings

- 1 can (12 oz.) root beer
- 3 Tbsp. cornstarch
- 3 tsp. ground mustard
- 3 tsp. caraway seeds
- 10 uncooked bratwurst links
- 1 large onion, coarsely chopped
- 1 bottle (12 oz.) chili sauce
- 10 hoagie buns, toasted

Optional: Thinly sliced red onion and prepared mustard

1. Whisk the first 4 ingredients until blended. In a large nonstick skillet, brown bratwursts over medium-high heat. Transfer to a 4- or 5-qt. slow cooker. Add onion, chili sauce and root beer mixture.
2. Cook, covered, on low 6-8 hours or until a thermometer inserted in sausage reads at least 160°. Serve in buns. If desired, top with onion and mustard.
1 serving: 563 cal., 30g fat (10g sat. fat), 63mg chol., 1575mg sod., 54g carb. (16g sugars, 2g fiber), 20g pro.

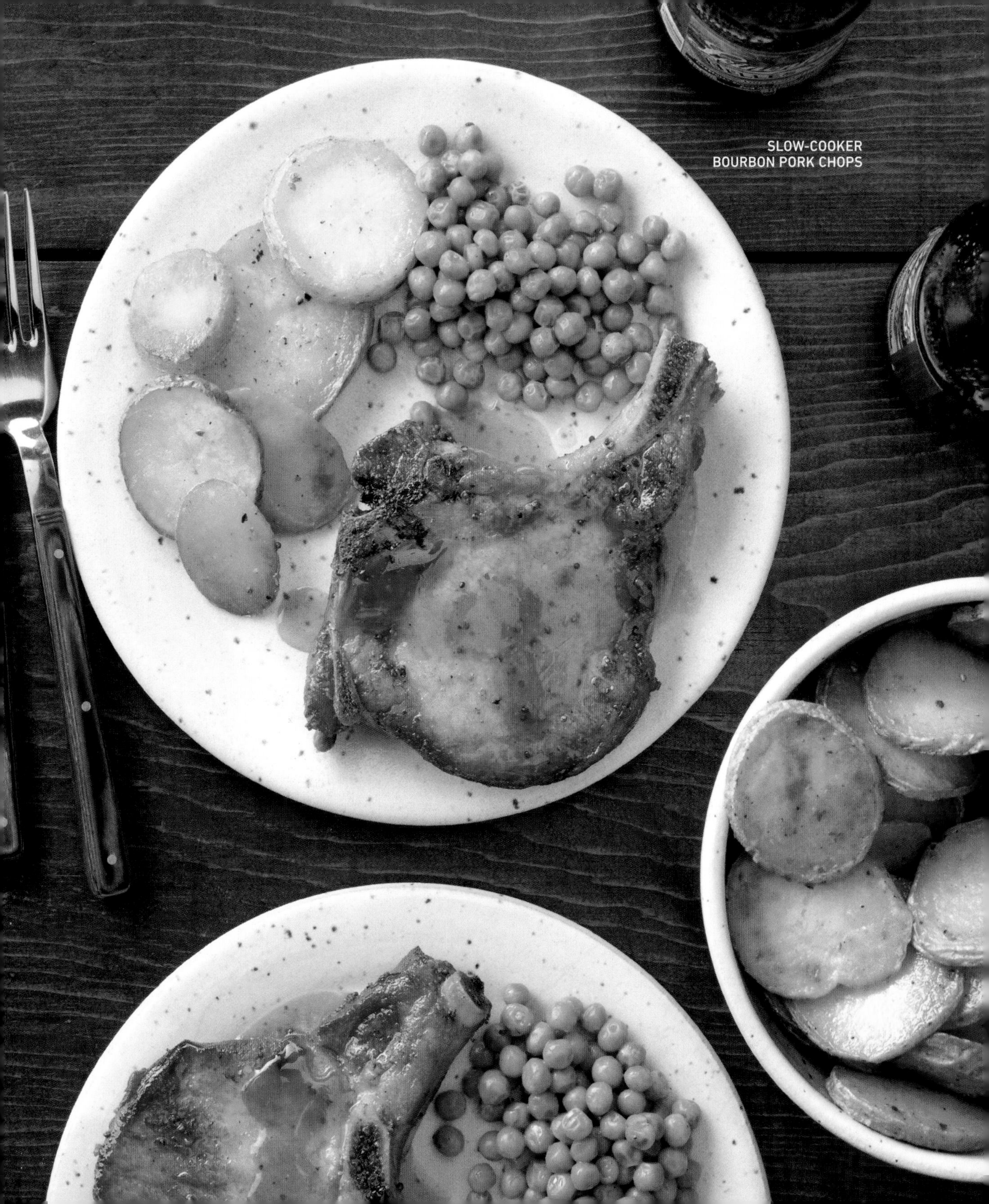

SLOW-COOKER
BOURBON PORK CHOPS

SAUSAGE SAUERKRAUT SUPPER

With big tender chunks of sausage, red potatoes and carrots, this lovely old-fashioned dinner will satisfy even the heartiest of appetites. It always disappears in a hurry whenever served at a family gathering or office potluck.
—Joalyce Graham, St. Petersburg, FL

- -

Prep: 25 min. • **Cook:** 8 hours
Makes: 10 servings

- 4 **cups carrot chunks (2-in. pieces)**
- 4 **cups red potato chunks**
- 2 **cans (14 oz. each) sauerkraut, rinsed and drained**
- 2½ **lbs. fresh Polish sausage links**
- 1 **medium onion, thinly sliced**
- 3 **garlic cloves, minced**
- 1½ **cups dry white wine or chicken broth**
- 1 **tsp. pepper**
- ½ **tsp. caraway seeds**

1. In a 5-qt. slow cooker, layer the carrots, potatoes and sauerkraut. In a large skillet, brown sausages. When cool enough to handle, cut into 3-in. pieces; transfer to slow cooker (slow cooker will be full). Reserve 1 Tbsp. drippings; saute onion and garlic in reserved drippings until tender.
2. Gradually add wine. Bring to a boil; stir to loosen browned bits. Stir in the pepper and caraway. Pour over sausage. Cover and cook on low for 8-10 hours or until a thermometer inserted in the sausage reads 160°.
1 cup: 517 cal., 37g fat (12g sat. fat), 72mg chol., 1442mg sod., 24g carb. (6g sugars, 5g fiber), 16g pro.

SLOW-COOKED ROPA VIEJA

SLOW-COOKED ROPA VIEJA

I traveled to Cuba a few years back and experienced some of the best food imaginable. One staple dish stuck out more than the rest, and that was ropa vieja. I had multiple variations, and when I returned home, I began to experiment. I went through roughly 5 trials before coming to this recipe.
—Joshua Boyer, Traverse City, MI

Prep: 35 min. • **Cook:** 8 hours
Makes: 6 servings

- 1 beef flank steak (2 lbs.)
- ½ tsp. salt
- ½ tsp. pepper
- 2 cups beef broth
- ½ cup dry vermouth
- ½ cup dry red wine or additional beef broth
- 1 can (6 oz.) tomato paste
- 1 large onion, thinly sliced
- 1 large carrot, sliced
- 1 small sweet red pepper, thinly sliced
- 1 Cubanelle or mild banana pepper, thinly sliced
- 3 sprigs fresh oregano
  Hot cooked rice
  Optional: Additional fresh oregano, lime wedges and sliced green olives with pimientos

1. Cut steak into 6 pieces; sprinkle with salt and pepper. Heat a large skillet over medium-high heat; brown meat in batches. Transfer meat to a 5- or 6-qt. slow cooker. Add broth, vermouth, wine and tomato paste to the pan. Cook 2-3 minutes, stirring to loosen browned bits from pan. Pour over meat.
2. Top with onion, carrot, red pepper, Cubanelle pepper and oregano. Cook, covered, on low until meat is tender, 8-10 hours. Remove oregano sprigs; discard. Remove meat; shred with 2 forks. Return to slow cooker; heat through. Serve with rice and, if desired, additional oregano, lime wedges and green olives.
1 serving: 278 cal., 11g fat (5g sat. fat), 72mg chol., 611mg sod., 10g carb. (5g sugars, 2g fiber), 32g pro. **Diabetic exchanges:** 4 lean meat, 1 vegetable.

SLOW-COOKER SECRETS
For a spicier version, add sliced serrano or jalapeno peppers. For a tangier version, add 2 tablespoons lemon juice or apple cider vinegar. For a sweeter version, add more carrots.

INDIAN CURRIED BEEF WITH RICE

My family loves Indian food. Instead of always going to an Indian restaurant, I created this recipe.
—Nancy Heishman, Las Vegas, NV

Prep: 30 min. • **Cook:** 4½ hours
Makes: 6 servings

- 1½ tsp. salt, divided
- 1 tsp. ground cardamom
- ½ tsp. ground allspice
- 1 boneless beef chuck roast (2 lbs.), cut into 1 in. cubes
- 1 Tbsp. olive oil
- 2 medium onions, chopped
- 1 Tbsp. minced fresh gingerroot
- 2 garlic cloves, minced
- 2 tsp. curry powder
- 1 tsp. ground cumin
- 1 pkg. (10 oz.) frozen chopped spinach, thawed and squeezed dry
- ¾ cup plain Greek yogurt
  Hot cooked rice
  Optional: Additional plain Greek yogurt and chopped red onion

INDIAN CURRIED BEEF WITH RICE

1. In a large bowl, combine ½ tsp. salt, cardamom and allspice. Add beef; turn to coat. In a large skillet, heat oil over medium heat; brown meat in batches. Transfer meat to a 3- or 4-qt. slow cooker. In the same skillet, cook onions until tender, 4-5 minutes. Add ginger, garlic, curry powder, cumin and remaining 1 tsp. salt; cook 1 minute longer. Transfer to slow cooker.
2. Cook, covered, on low until meat is tender, 4-5 hours. Stir in spinach; cook until heated through, about 30 minutes. Just before serving, stir in the yogurt. Serve with the rice and, if desired, additional yogurt and red onion.

1 serving: 343 cal., 20g fat (8g sat. fat), 106mg chol., 707mg sod., 8g carb. (3g sugars, 3g fiber), 33g pro.

To prepare in an electric pressure cooker, in a large bowl, combine ½ tsp. salt, cardamom and allspice. Add beef; turn to coat. Select saute or browning setting on a 6-qt. electric pressure cooker. Adjust for medium heat; add oil. When oil is hot, brown beef in batches. Add onions; cook and stir until tender, 4-5 minutes. Add ginger, garlic, curry powder, cumin and remaining 1 tsp. salt; cook 1 minute longer. Add ¾ cup water to pressure cooker. Cook 1 minute, stirring to loosen browned bits from pan. Press cancel. Return beef to pressure cooker.

Lock lid; close pressure-release valve. Adjust to pressure-cook on high for 20 minutes. Allow pressure to release naturally for 10 minutes, then quick-release any remaining pressure. Select saute setting and adjust for low heat. Add spinach; simmer, uncovered, until heated through and sauce is slightly thickened, 8-10 minutes, stirring occasionally. Press cancel. Just before serving, stir in yogurt. Serve with rice.

SPICY SAUSAGE MEATBALL SAUCE

I threw together spicy sausage and three of our favorite veggies for this incredible sauce that makes our mouths water the whole time it's cooking. Besides serving this with pasta (refrigerated tortellini is best), we've had it with brown basmati rice, on toasted Italian rolls to make sloppy subs and as a stew with garlic bread.
—Ann Sheehy, Lawrence, MA

- -

Prep: 40 min. • **Cook:** 5 hours
Makes: 12 servings (3¾ qt.)

2 cans (28 oz. each) crushed tomatoes
2 cans (14½ oz. each) diced tomatoes, undrained
¾ lb. sliced fresh mushrooms
5 garlic cloves, minced
4 tsp. Italian seasoning
1 tsp. pepper
¼ tsp. salt
¼ tsp. crushed red pepper flakes
1 large sweet onion
1 large green pepper
1 medium sweet red pepper
1 medium sweet orange pepper
1 medium sweet yellow pepper
10 hot Italian sausage links (4 oz. each), casings removed
¼ cup all-purpose flour
2 Tbsp. canola oil
Hot cooked pasta

1. Place the first 8 ingredients in a 6-qt. slow cooker. Chop onion and peppers; stir into tomato mixture.
2. Shape sausage into 1¾-in. balls; roll in flour to coat lightly. In a large skillet, heat oil over medium-high heat; cook meatballs in batches until lightly browned, 5-8 minutes, turning occasionally. Drain on paper towels. Add to the slow cooker, stirring gently into sauce.
3. Cook, covered, on low 5-6 hours or until meatballs are cooked through and vegetables are tender. Serve with pasta.
Freeze option: Freeze cooled meatball mixture in freezer containers. To use, partially thaw in refrigerator overnight. Place meatball mixture in a large skillet. Heat through, stirring occasionally; add a little water if necessary.
1¼ cups meatball sauce: 343 cal., 23g fat (7g sat. fat), 51mg chol., 984mg sod., 22g carb. (11g sugars, 5g fiber), 15g pro.

> **SLOW-COOKER SECRETS**
> This is a hearty take on meatballs with sauce. If you aren't a fan of heat, use sweet sausage links.

SPICY SAUSAGE
MEATBALL SAUCE

SLOW-COOKER
CHICKEN STROGANOFF

SLOW-COOKER CHICKEN STROGANOFF

This recipe is creamy, warm, satisfying and fairly inexpensive—and it needs just a few ingredients! Who could ask for more on a chilly evening? I will admit, though, that I have been known to make it during summer, too.
—Jason Kretzer, Grants Pass, OR

Prep: 15 min. • **Cook:** 4½ hours
Makes: 8 servings

- 3 lbs. boneless skinless chicken thighs, cut into 1-in. pieces
- 2 cans (10½ oz. each) condensed cream of chicken with herbs soup, undiluted
- ½ cup dry white wine or chicken broth
- ½ lb. sliced baby portobello mushrooms
- 2 cups sour cream
- ¾ tsp. salt
   Hot cooked egg noodles
   Pepper
   Chopped fresh parsley, optional

1. Place chicken, soup and wine in a 5- or 6-qt. slow cooker. Cook, covered, on high until a thermometer inserted into chicken reads at least 165°, about 3 hours. Cut chicken into bite-sized pieces; return to slow cooker.
2. Add mushrooms. Cook, covered, on high until mushrooms are tender, 1½-2 hours longer. Stir in sour cream and salt. Serve with egg noodles; sprinkle with pepper and, if desired, chopped parsley.

1⅓ cups: 447 cal., 29g fat (12g sat. fat), 133mg chol., 877mg sod., 9g carb. (3g sugars, 2g fiber), 36g pro.

EASY CHICKEN TAMALE PIE

EASY CHICKEN TAMALE PIE

This savory dinner is so worth the wait! I love the fact I can toss it all together and go fishing while it cooks.
—Peter Halferty, Corpus Christi, TX

Prep: 20 min. • **Cook:** 7 hours
Makes: 8 servings

- 1 lb. ground chicken
- 1 tsp. ground cumin
- 1 tsp. chili powder
- ½ tsp. salt
- ¼ tsp. pepper
- 1 can (15 oz.) black beans, rinsed and drained
- 1 can (14½ oz.) diced tomatoes, undrained
- 1 can (11 oz.) whole kernel corn, drained
- 1 can (10 oz.) enchilada sauce
- 2 green onions, chopped
- ¼ cup minced fresh cilantro
- 1 pkg. (8½ oz.) cornbread/ muffin mix
- 2 large eggs, lightly beaten
- 1 cup shredded Mexican cheese blend
   Optional toppings: Sour cream, salsa and minced fresh cilantro

1. In a large skillet, cook the chicken over medium heat until no longer pink, 6-8 minutes, breaking it into crumbles. Stir in seasonings.
2. Transfer to a 4-qt. slow cooker. Stir in beans, tomatoes, corn, enchilada sauce, green onions and cilantro. Cook, covered, on low until heated through, 6-8 hours.
3. In a small bowl, combine muffin mix and eggs; spoon over chicken mixture. Cook, covered, on low until a toothpick inserted in cornbread layer comes out clean, 1-1½ hours longer.
4. Sprinkle with the cheese; let stand, covered, 5 minutes. If desired, serve with toppings.

1 serving: 359 cal., 14g fat (5g sat. fat), 110mg chol., 1021mg sod., 40g carb. (11g sugars, 5g fiber), 20g pro.

GREEN CHILE ADOBADO POUTINE

This Canadian classic is even better when served southwestern-style as either an entree or a party appetizer. Although these ribs are done without fuss in a slow cooker, you can also bake them at 325°, covered with foil, for about 45 minutes. Then uncover and bake for another 20 minutes.
—Johnna Johnson, Scottsdale, AZ

- -

Prep: 50 min. • **Cook:** 3 hours
Makes: 8 servings

- 3 **garlic cloves, unpeeled**
- 4 **dried guajillo or ancho chiles, stemmed and seeded**
- 1 **can (10 oz.) enchilada sauce, divided**
- 3 **cans (4 oz. each) chopped green chiles, divided**
- 1 **Tbsp. cider vinegar**
- 2 **tsp. dried oregano**
- ½ **tsp. ground cumin**
- ½ **tsp. salt**
- ½ **tsp. pepper**
- ⅛ **tsp. ground cinnamon**
- 2 **lbs. boneless country-style pork ribs, cut into 2-in. pieces**
- 1 **pkg. (32 oz.) frozen french-fried potatoes**
- 1 **cup queso fresco**
  Pico de gallo, optional

1. Lightly smash garlic cloves with the bottom of a heavy skillet to flatten. Cook in a large skillet over medium-low heat until softened and browned, about 10 minutes. Cool and peel.

2. In the same skillet at the same time, cook dried chiles, pressing them against the bottom with a spatula or tongs until lightly toasted and fragrant, 1-2 minutes. Transfer to a bowl. Pour boiling water over chiles to cover; let stand about 15 minutes. Drain.

3. Place chiles and garlic in a food processor. Add ½ cup enchilada sauce, 2 cans green chiles, vinegar, oregano, cumin, salt, pepper and cinnamon; process until blended. Stir in remaining enchilada sauce and green chiles. Transfer to a 5- or 6-qt. slow cooker. Add ribs; turn to coat. Cover and cook on high until meat is tender, 3-4 hours. During the final 30 minutes, cook fries according to package directions.

4. Remove pork; shred with 2 forks. Top fries with meat, queso fresco, enchilada gravy and, if desired, pico de gallo.

1 serving: 434 cal., 19g fat (7g sat. fat), 75mg chol., 1065mg sod., 31g carb. (2g sugars, 5g fiber), 28g pro.

SLOW-COOKER SECRETS
Cutting back on your carbs? Substitute some steamed or roasted cauliflower for the french fries.

GREEN CHILE
ADOBADO POUTINE

CHERRY PORK CHOPS

I mixed and matched several recipes to come up with this one. I'm always happy to adapt recipes for my slow cooker. It's so easy to prepare a meal that way.
—Mildred Sherrer, Fort Worth, TX

Prep: 10 min. • **Cook:** 3 hours
Makes: 6 servings

- 6 **bone-in pork loin chops (8 oz. each)**
- ⅛ **tsp. salt**
  Dash pepper
- 1 **cup canned cherry pie filling**
- 2 **tsp. lemon juice**
- ½ **tsp. chicken bouillon granules**
- ⅛ **tsp. ground mace**
  Additional cherry pie filling, warmed, optional

1. In a large skillet coated with cooking spray, brown the pork chops on both sides over medium heat. Season with salt and pepper.

2. In a 3-qt. slow cooker, combine pie filling, lemon juice, bouillon and mace. Add pork chops. Cover and cook on low until meat is no longer pink, 3-4 hours. Serve with additional cherry pie filling if desired.

1 serving: 371 cal., 18g fat (7g sat. fat), 111mg chol., 203mg sod., 13g carb. (0 sugars, 0 fiber), 36g pro.

UPSIDE-DOWN FRITO PIE

Using ground turkey is a smart way to lighten this hearty family pleaser!
—Mary Berg, Lake Elmo, MN

- -

Prep: 15 min. • **Cook:** 2 hours 5 min.
Makes: 6 servings

- 2 **lbs. ground turkey or beef**
- 1 **medium onion, chopped**
- 2 **envelopes chili seasoning mix**
- 1 **can (10 oz.) diced tomatoes and green chiles, undrained**
- 1 **can (8 oz.) tomato sauce**
- 1 **can (15 oz.) pinto beans, rinsed and drained**
- 1 **cup shredded cheddar cheese**
- 3 **cups corn chips**
  Optional: Sour cream, minced fresh cilantro and additional chopped onion

1. In a large skillet, cook turkey and onion over medium heat until no longer pink, 8-10 minutes, breaking meat into crumbles; stir in chili seasoning. Transfer to a 3- or 4-qt. slow cooker. Pour the tomatoes and tomato sauce over turkey.

2. Cook, covered, on low 2-3 hours or until heated through. Stir the turkey mixture to combine. Top with beans. Sprinkle with cheese. Cook, covered, 5-10 minutes or until cheese is melted. Top with chips. If desired, serve with sour cream, minced cilantro and additional onion.

1⅓ cups: 524 cal., 26g fat (8g sat. fat), 118mg chol., 1662mg sod., 33g carb. (5g sugars, 6g fiber), 41g pro.

GERMAN SCHNITZEL & POTATOES WITH GORGONZOLA CREAM

I lived in Germany for five years and ate a lot of schnitzel. I developed this recipe so it wasn't so time-consuming to put together. I get asked for the recipe every time I make it.
—Beth Taylor, Pleasant Grove, UT

- -

Prep: 20 min. • **Cook:** 4 hours
Makes: 4 servings

- 1 **pork tenderloin (1 lb.)**
- 1 **cup dry bread crumbs**
- 2 **lbs. medium Yukon Gold potatoes, peeled and cut into ¼-in. slices**
- 2 **cups heavy whipping cream**
- ⅔ **cup crumbled Gorgonzola cheese**
- 1 **tsp. salt**
- ¼ **cup minced fresh Italian parsley Lemon wedges**

1. Cut tenderloin into 12 slices. Pound with a meat mallet to ¼-in. thickness. Place 4 slices in a 3- or 4-qt. slow cooker. Layer with ¼ cup bread crumbs and a third of the potatoes. Repeat layers twice; top with the remaining bread crumbs.

2. In a small bowl, combine cream, Gorgonzola and salt. Pour over the pork mixture; cook on low, covered, 4-6 hours or until meat and potatoes are tender. Sprinkle with parsley; serve with lemon wedges.

3 slices pork with 1 cup potato mixture: 926 cal., 54g fat (33g sat. fat), 216mg chol., 1132mg sod., 73g carb. (9g sugars, 5g fiber), 38g pro.

GERMAN SCHNITZEL & POTATOES WITH GORGONZOLA CREAM

SLOW-COOKER
TURKEY PESTO LASAGNA

turkey into crumbles; drain. Stir in Italian seasoning and salt.

3. In a small bowl, mix 1 cup mozzarella cheese, ricotta cheese and pesto. In prepared slow cooker, layer a third each of the following: marinara sauce, noodles (breaking noodles if necessary to fit), turkey mixture and cheese mixture. Repeat layers twice. Sprinkle with remaining mozzarella cheese.

4. Cook, covered, on low until noodles are tender, 3-4 hours. Turn off slow cooker; remove insert. Let stand, uncovered, 30 minutes before serving. Using foil strips, remove lasagna to a platter. Serve with Parmesan cheese.

1 slice: 397 cal., 19g fat (8g sat. fat), 79mg chol., 883mg sod., 28g carb. (9g sugars, 3g fiber), 28g pro.

READER RAVE...
"Simply delicious! I love how easy this was to put together. My 3-year-old son especially loved the dish. He ate every bite off his plate."
—ANGEL182009, TASTEOFHOME.COM

SLOW-COOKER
TURKEY PESTO LASAGNA

My cheesy, noodley lasagna makes any slow-cooker skeptic a believer. It's easy to prep while my kids nap, and dinner's ready when their dad walks in the door at night. We bring more pesto and marinara to the table for our resident sauce lovers.
—Blair Lonergan, Rochelle, VA

Prep: 25 min. • **Cook:** 3 hours + standing
Makes: 8 servings

- 1 lb. ground turkey
- 1 small onion, chopped
- 2 tsp. Italian seasoning
- ½ tsp. salt
- 2 cups shredded part-skim mozzarella cheese, divided
- 1 container (15 oz.) whole-milk ricotta cheese
- ¼ cup prepared pesto
- 1 jar (24 oz.) marinara sauce
- 9 no-cook lasagna noodles
   Grated Parmesan cheese

1. Cut three 25x3-in. strips of heavy-duty foil; crisscross so they resemble spokes of a wheel. Place strips on bottom and up sides of a greased 5-qt. slow cooker. Coat strips with cooking spray.

2. In a large skillet, cook turkey and onion over medium heat 6-8 minutes or until turkey is no longer pink, breaking

TOMATO-BASIL STEAK

SLOW-COOKER CURRY PORK

I'm a stay-at-home mom, and the slow cooker helps me create dishes like this pork with a curry and cumin rub. I also add a splash of coconut milk.
—Beverly Peychal, Waukesha, WI

Prep: 15 min. • **Cook:** 3½ hours + standing
Makes: 10 servings

- 1½ tsp. salt
- 1½ tsp. hot or regular curry powder
- 1 tsp. ground cumin
- 1 tsp. dried oregano
- ¾ tsp. onion powder
- ¾ tsp. garlic powder
- ½ tsp. pepper
- ¼ tsp. cayenne pepper
- ¼ tsp. paprika
- ¼ tsp. ground chipotle pepper
- 1½ lbs. potatoes, cut into ½-in. pieces
- 4 medium carrots, thinly sliced
- 3 cups cubed peeled butternut squash (about 1 lb.)
- 1 can (14½ oz.) reduced-sodium chicken broth
- 1 boneless pork loin roast (3 to 4 lbs.)

1. In a small bowl, mix seasonings. In a 6-qt. slow cooker, combine the vegetables, broth and 2 tsp. seasoning mixture. Rub the remaining seasoning mixture over roast; place on vegetables. Cook, covered, on low 3½-4½ hours or until meat and vegetables are tender (a thermometer inserted in roast should read at least 145°).
2. Remove roast from slow cooker; tent with foil. Let stand 15 minutes before slicing. Serve with vegetables.
4 oz. slow-cooked pork with ½ cup vegetables: 261 cal., 7g fat (2g sat. fat), 68mg chol., 523mg sod., 21g carb. (3g sugars, 4g fiber), 29g pro. **Diabetic exchanges:** 4 lean meat, 1½ starch.

TOMATO-BASIL STEAK

I use basil and bell peppers from my herb and vegetable garden to make this dish. It's so easy to prepare and so rich and delicious.
—Sherry Little, Cabot, AR

Prep: 15 min. • **Cook:** 6 hours
Makes: 4 servings

- 1¼ lbs. boneless beef shoulder top blade or flat iron steaks
- ½ lb. whole fresh mushrooms, quartered
- 1 medium sweet yellow pepper, julienned
- 1 can (14½ oz.) stewed tomatoes, undrained
- 1 can (8 oz.) tomato sauce
- 1 envelope onion soup mix
- 2 Tbsp. minced fresh basil Hot cooked rice

1. Place steaks in a 4-qt. slow cooker. Add mushrooms and pepper. In a small bowl, mix tomatoes, tomato sauce, soup mix and basil; pour over top.
2. Cook, covered, on low 6-8 hours or until beef and vegetables are tender. Serve with rice.
1 serving: 324 cal., 14g fat (5g sat. fat), 92mg chol., 1116mg sod., 19g carb. (8g sugars, 3g fiber), 32g pro.

SLOW-COOKER CURRY PORK

GERMAN BRATWURST WITH SAUERKRAUT & APPLES

I created this old-world favorite based on a dish I tasted during my travels. The entree is perfect for weeknights or special occasions. I like to serve it with pasta.
—Gerald Hetrick, Erie, PA

- -

Prep: 15 min. • **Cook:** 6 hours
Makes: 15 servings

- 4 lbs. uncooked bratwurst links
- 3 bottles (12 oz. each) German-style beer or 4½ cups reduced-sodium chicken broth
- 1 jar (32 oz.) sauerkraut, rinsed and well drained
- 4 medium Granny Smith apples (about 1¼ lbs.), cut into wedges
- 1 medium onion, halved and thinly sliced
- 1½ tsp. caraway seeds
- ¼ tsp. pepper

1. In a large nonstick skillet, brown bratwursts over medium-high heat in batches. Transfer to a 7-qt. slow cooker. Add remaining ingredients.
2. Cook, covered, on low 6-8 hours or until a thermometer inserted in sausage reads at least 160°.
1 serving: 445 cal., 35g fat (12g sat. fat), 90mg chol., 1424mg sod., 13g carb. (6g sugars, 3g fiber), 17g pro.

SLOW-COOKER SECRETS
This recipe pairs well with spaetzle. You could also serve the brats on pretzel buns.

MOROCCAN POT ROAST

MOROCCAN POT ROAST

My husband loves meat and I love veggies, so we're both happy with this spicy twist on beefy pot roast. With garbanzo beans, eggplant, honey and mint, it's like something you'd eat at a Marrakech bazaar.
—Catherine Dempsey, Clifton Park, NY

Prep: 25 min. • **Cook:** 7 hours
Makes: 8 servings

- 2 **Tbsp. olive oil**
- 3 **small onions, chopped**
- 3 **Tbsp. paprika**
- 1 **Tbsp. plus ½ tsp. garam masala, divided**
- 1¼ **tsp. salt, divided**
- ¼ **tsp. cayenne pepper**
- 2 **Tbsp. tomato paste**
- 1 **can (15 oz.) garbanzo beans or chickpeas, rinsed and drained**
- 1 **can (14½ oz.) beef broth**
- ¼ **tsp. pepper**
- 1 **boneless beef chuck roast (3 lbs.)**
- 4 **medium carrots, cut diagonally into ¾-in. pieces**
- 1 **small eggplant, cubed**
- 2 **Tbsp. honey**
- 2 **Tbsp. minced fresh mint**
  Optional: Hot cooked couscous or flatbreads

1. In a large skillet, heat oil over medium heat; saute onions with paprika, 1 Tbsp. garam masala, ½ tsp. salt and cayenne until tender, 4-5 minutes. Stir in tomato paste; cook and stir 1 minute. Stir in garbanzo beans and broth; transfer to a 5- or 6-qt. slow cooker.

2. Mix pepper and the remaining ½ tsp. garam masala and ¾ tsp. salt; rub over roast. Place in slow cooker. Add carrots and eggplant. Cook, covered, until meat and vegetables are tender, 7-9 hours.

3. Remove roast from slow cooker; break into pieces. Remove vegetables with a slotted spoon; skim fat from cooking juices. Stir in honey. Return beef and vegetables to slow cooker and heat through. Sprinkle with mint. If desired, serve with couscous.

Freeze option: Freeze cooled beef and vegetable mixture in freezer containers. To use, partially thaw in refrigerator overnight. Microwave, covered, on high in a microwave-safe dish until heated through, stirring gently.

1 serving: 435 cal., 21g fat (7g sat. fat), 111mg chol., 766mg sod., 23g carb. (10g sugars, 6g fiber), 38g pro.

MAMA'S CARNITAS

My husband loves to cook Mexican dishes, while I'm more of an Italian-style cook. The joke in our house is that I should leave all the Mexican cooking to him. However, this dish of mine turned out so amazing that my husband fell in love! It's all in the meat. If you can get an all-natural pork shoulder, it really makes a difference.
—Chelsea Wickman, Painesville, OH

- -

Prep: 25 min. • **Cook:** 9 hours
Makes: 16 servings

MAMA'S CARNITAS

3	garlic cloves, minced
1	Tbsp. minced fresh cilantro
½	tsp. salt
½	tsp. dried oregano
½	tsp. chili powder
½	tsp. ground cumin
½	tsp. paprika
½	tsp. pepper
¼	tsp. cayenne pepper
1	bone-in pork shoulder roast (5 to 7 lbs.)
½	cup unsweetened pineapple juice
½	cup reduced-sodium soy sauce
½	cup beef stock
¼	cup lime juice
2	Anaheim peppers, seeded and diced
16	flour tortillas (8 in.)
1	cup creme fraiche or sour cream
2	cups shredded Monterey Jack cheese

1. In a small bowl, combine the first 9 ingredients. Cut roast in half; rub all sides with spice mixture. Place in a 5-qt. slow cooker coated with cooking spray. Combine the pineapple juice, soy sauce, stock, lime juice and peppers; pour around meat.

2. Cover and cook on low for 9-11 hours or until meat is tender.

3. Remove meat from slow cooker; skim fat from cooking juices. When cool enough to handle, remove meat from bones; discard bones. Shred meat and return to slow cooker; heat through.

4. With a slotted spoon, spoon ½ cup filling off center on each tortilla. Top each with 1 Tbsp. creme fraiche and 2 Tbsp. cheese. Fold sides and ends over filling and roll up.

Freeze option: Place cooked shredded pork in freezer containers; top with cooking juices. Cool and freeze. To use, partially thaw in refrigerator overnight.

Heat through in a covered saucepan, stirring occasionally; add a little broth if necessary.

Note: Wear disposable gloves when cutting hot peppers; the oils can burn skin. Avoid touching your face.

1 filled tortilla: 494 cal., 26g fat (12g sat. fat), 97mg chol., 758mg sod., 31g carb. (1g sugars, 2g fiber), 32g pro.

CHICKPEA & POTATO CURRY

I make chana masala, the classic Indian dish, in my slow cooker. First browning the onion, ginger and garlic really makes the sauce amazing.
—Anjana Devasahayam, San Antonio, TX

Prep: 25 min. • **Cook:** 6 hours
Makes: 6 servings

1 Tbsp. canola oil
1 medium onion, chopped
2 garlic cloves, minced
2 tsp. minced fresh gingerroot
2 tsp. ground coriander
1 tsp. garam masala
1 tsp. chili powder
½ tsp. salt
½ tsp. ground cumin
¼ tsp. ground turmeric
1 can (15 oz.) crushed tomatoes
2 cans (15 oz. each) chickpeas or garbanzo beans, rinsed and drained
1 large baking potato, peeled and cut into ¾-in. cubes
2½ cups vegetable stock
1 Tbsp. lime juice
 Chopped fresh cilantro
 Hot cooked rice
 Optional: Sliced red onion and lime wedges

CHICKPEA & POTATO CURRY

1. In a large skillet, heat the oil over medium-high heat; saute onion until tender, 2-4 minutes. Add garlic, ginger and dry seasonings; cook and stir 1 minute. Stir in tomatoes; transfer to a 3- or 4-qt. slow cooker.
2. Stir in the chickpeas, potato and stock. Cook, covered, on low until the potato is tender and flavors are blended, 6-8 hours.
3. Stir in the lime juice; sprinkle with cilantro. Serve with rice and, if desired, red onion and lime wedges.

1¼ cups chickpea mixture: 240 cal., 6g fat (0 sat. fat), 0 chol., 767mg sod., 42g carb. (8g sugars, 9g fiber), 8g pro.

SLOW-COOKER
STUFFED SHELLS

SLOW-COOKER STUFFED SHELLS

There's no need to precook the shells in this simple pasta dish. It's almost like magic to lift the lid and find such deliciousness ready to serve. Add garlic bread and you're golden!
—Sherry Day, Pinckney, MI

Prep: 30 min. • **Cook:** 4 hours
Makes: 10 servings

- 1 carton (15 oz.) part-skim ricotta cheese
- 1 pkg. (10 oz.) frozen chopped spinach, thawed and squeezed dry
- 2½ cups shredded Italian cheese blend
- ½ cup diced red onion
- ½ tsp. garlic powder
- 2 tsp. dried basil
- ½ tsp. dried oregano
- ½ tsp. dried thyme
- 2 jars (24 oz. each) roasted garlic Parmesan pasta sauce
- 2 cups water
- 1 pkg. (12 oz.) jumbo pasta shells
  Optional: Additional shredded Italian cheese blend and sliced fresh basil

1. Mix the first 8 ingredients (mixture will be stiff). In a greased 6-qt. slow cooker, mix 1 jar pasta sauce with water. Fill shells with ricotta mixture; layer in slow cooker. Top with the remaining jar pasta sauce.
2. Cook, covered, on low until pasta is tender, 4-5 hours. If desired, serve with additional cheese and fresh basil.
4 stuffed shells: 303 cal., 10g fat (6g sat. fat), 34mg chol., 377mg sod., 34g carb. (4g sugars, 3g fiber), 17g pro. **Diabetic exchanges:** 2 starch, 2 medium-fat meat.

SWEET & SOUR PORK WRAPS

SWEET & SOUR PORK WRAPS

We always make these wraps at our family's annual party, and they're a true favorite. The cabbage and cilantro give them tempting texture and flavor.
—Andrew DeVito, Hartford, CT

Prep: 15 min. • **Cook:** 6 hours
Makes: 8 servings (16 wraps)

- 1 boneless pork shoulder butt roast (3 to 4 lbs.)
- 1 medium onion, chopped
- 1 cup water
- 1 cup sweet-and-sour sauce
- ¼ cup sherry or chicken broth
- ¼ cup reduced-sodium soy sauce
- 1 envelope onion soup mix
- 1 Tbsp. minced fresh gingerroot
- 3 garlic cloves, minced
- 16 flour tortillas (6 in.), warmed
- 4 cups shredded cabbage
- ¼ cup minced fresh cilantro

1. Place roast and onion in a 6-qt. slow cooker. In a small bowl, whisk water, sweet-and-sour sauce, sherry, soy sauce, soup mix, ginger and garlic until blended; pour over pork. Cook, covered, on low until meat is tender, 6-8 hours.
2. When cool enough to handle, shred pork with 2 forks. To serve, spoon about ⅓ cup pork mixture onto the center of each tortilla. Top with ¼ cup cabbage; sprinkle with cilantro. Fold bottom of the tortilla over the filling; fold both sides to close.
2 wraps: 523 cal., 23g fat (6g sat. fat), 101mg chol., 1357mg sod., 42g carb. (8g sugars, 1g fiber), 36g pro.

SIDES

CORN & ONION STUFFING

CORN & ONION STUFFING

I like something different for a side dish and this is it! This stuffing is perfect with poultry, pork or even beef. You can leave it in the slow cooker until it's time to eat—or make it early, refrigerate it until almost serving time and then simply reheat it.
—Patricia Swart, Galloway, NJ

- -

Prep: 10 min. • **Cook:** 3 hours
Makes: 8 servings

- 1   can (14¾ oz.) cream-style corn
- 1   pkg. (6 oz.) stuffing mix
- 1   small onion, chopped
- 1   celery rib, chopped
- ¼   cup water
- 2   large eggs
- 1   tsp. poultry seasoning
- ⅛   tsp. pepper
- ¼   cup butter, melted

Combine first 8 ingredients. Transfer to a greased 3-qt. slow cooker. Drizzle with butter. Cook, covered, on low until set, 3-4 hours.

½ cup: 192 cal., 8g fat (4g sat. fat), 63mg chol., 530mg sod., 26g carb. (4g sugars, 1g fiber), 5g pro.

CRAN-APPLE CHUTNEY

CRAN-APPLE CHUTNEY

My crew isn't crazy for cranberries, but they can't get enough of this delicious chutney. I highly recommend it for Thanksgiving since it tastes amazing paired with turkey, but it's also good on its own.
—Raquel Haggard, Edmond, OK

- -

Prep: 10 min. • **Cook:** 3 hours + chilling
Makes: 3 cups

- 1   pkg. (12 oz.) fresh or frozen cranberries, thawed
- 1   medium Gala apple, peeled and finely chopped
- ⅔   cup sugar or sugar substitute equivalent to ⅔ cup sugar
- ⅓   cup honey
- 2   Tbsp. brown sugar
- 2   Tbsp. frozen orange juice concentrate, thawed
- 1   tsp. ground cinnamon
- 1   tsp. cider vinegar
     Dash ground ginger

1. In a 1½-qt. slow cooker, combine all ingredients. Cook, covered, on low 3-4 hours or until cranberries pop and mixture is slightly thickened.
2. Transfer to a small bowl; cool slightly. Refrigerate until cold.

¼ cup: 103 cal., 0 fat (0 sat. fat), 0 chol., 2mg sod., 27g carb. (24g sugars, 1g fiber), 0 pro.

AUTUMN'S BEST SCALLOPED POTATOES

I jazzed up sliced potatoes with mushrooms, onions, canned soup and cheese to create this versatile side. With its comforting flavor, it's an ideal accompaniment to a holiday meal.
—Linda Bernard, Golden Meadow, LA

Prep: 25 min. • **Cook:** 6 hours
Makes: 10 servings

- 7   medium potatoes, peeled and thinly sliced
- 1   medium onion, sliced
- 4   garlic cloves, minced
- 2   green onions, chopped
- 1   can (8 oz.) mushroom stems and pieces, drained
- ¼   cup all-purpose flour
- 2   tsp. salt
- ½   tsp. pepper
- ¼   cup butter, cubed
- 1   can (10¾ oz.) condensed cream of mushroom soup, undiluted
- 1   cup shredded Colby-Monterey Jack cheese

In a 3-qt. slow cooker, layer half each of the potatoes, onion, garlic, green onions, mushrooms, flour, salt, pepper and butter. Repeat layers. Pour soup over the top. Cover and cook on low until potatoes are tender, 6-8 hours; sprinkle with cheese during the last 30 minutes of cooking time.

¾ cup: 249 cal., 9g fat (6g sat. fat), 23mg chol., 893mg sod., 35g carb. (4g sugars, 4g fiber), 7g pro.

SLOW-COOKER SECRETS
Use thinly sliced fresh mushrooms for a strong mushroom flavor.

AUTUMN'S BEST
SCALLOPED POTATOES

SLOW-COOKER ITALIAN MUSHROOMS

For big family gatherings, I love to make these mushrooms—everyone always wants to know what the secret ingredient is! They're a star as a side dish, and leftovers go well with steaks or a roast.

—Becky Schmitz, Fond du Lac, WI

Prep: 10 min. • **Cook:** 5 hours
Makes: 8 servings

- 3 **lbs. medium fresh mushrooms**
- ¾ **cup butter, melted**
- ¼ **cup Italian salad dressing**
- 3 **Tbsp. chicken bouillon granules**
- 1 **envelope zesty Italian salad dressing mix**
- ½ **tsp. onion powder**
- ½ **tsp. dried oregano**
- ½ **tsp. Worcestershire sauce**

Place the mushrooms in a 6-qt. slow cooker. Mix remaining ingredients; pour over mushrooms. Cook, covered, on low until mushrooms are tender, 5-6 hours. Serve with a slotted spoon.

½ cup: 221 cal., 19g fat (11g sat. fat), 46mg chol., 1394mg sod., 9g carb. (2g sugars, 0 fiber), 4g pro.

MUSHROOM STUFFING

My grandmother created this recipe after my grandfather left the well-drilling business and invested all their money in a mushroom farm. The farm was a success and saw the family through the Great Depression.
—Eric Cooper, Durham, NC

- -

Prep: 30 min. • **Cook:** 3 hours
Makes: 16 servings

- ¼ cup butter, cubed
- 1 lb. baby portobello mushrooms, coarsely chopped
- 4 celery ribs, chopped
- 1 large onion, chopped
- 12 cups unseasoned stuffing cubes
- ¼ cup chopped fresh parsley
- 1½ tsp. rubbed sage
- 1 tsp. salt
- 1 tsp. dried thyme
- 1 tsp. poultry seasoning
- ½ tsp. dried marjoram
- ½ tsp. pepper
- 2 large eggs, lightly beaten
- 3 cups vegetable broth

1. In a 6-qt. stockpot, heat butter over medium-high heat. Add mushrooms, celery and onion; cook and stir until crisp-tender, 5-7 minutes. Transfer to a bowl. Add stuffing cubes, parsley and seasonings; toss. Whisk together eggs and broth. Pour over stuffing mixture; stir to combine.
2. Transfer to a greased 6-qt. slow cooker. Cook, covered, on low until heated through, 3-4 hours.
¾ cup: 190 cal., 5g fat (2g sat. fat), 31mg chol., 625mg sod., 32g carb. (3g sugars, 3g fiber), 7g pro. **Diabetic exchanges:** 2 starch, 1 fat.

CREAMY POLENTA WITH
BALSAMIC GLAZE

CREAMY POLENTA WITH BALSAMIC GLAZE

This scrumptious, easy side dish goes incredibly well with braised meat. It makes any fall meal feel just a little more elevated.
—Sarah Vasques, Milford, NH

- -

Prep: 15 min. • **Cook:** 2 hours
Makes: 4 servings

- 4 Tbsp. butter, divided
- 1½ cups half-and-half cream, divided
- 1 cup 2% milk
- ¼ tsp. salt
- ⅓ cup cornmeal
- 1 cup balsamic vinegar
- 1 Tbsp. sugar
- ½ cup grated Parmesan cheese

1. In a medium saucepan, melt 2 Tbsp. butter over medium heat. Add 1 cup cream, the milk and salt. Bring to a low simmer. Gradually whisk in cornmeal. Cook and stir for 3 minutes.
2. Pour the polenta into a 3-qt. slow cooker coated with cooking spray. Cook, covered, on low for 2 hours, stirring every 30 minutes. Meanwhile, in a small saucepan, bring vinegar and sugar to a boil. Reduce heat; simmer, uncovered, until reduced to ⅓ cup. Just before serving, stir cheese and the remaining cream and butter into polenta. To serve, drizzle with balsamic glaze.
½ cup polenta with 1 Tbsp. glaze: 415 cal., 25g fat (16g sat. fat), 89mg chol., 494mg sod., 37g carb. (25g sugars, 1g fiber), 9g pro.

BUFFALO WING POTATOES

I was getting tired of mashed and baked potatoes, so I created something new. This potluck-ready recipe is a simple and tasty twist on the usual potato side dish.
—Summer Feaker, Ankeny, IA

Prep: 15 min. • **Cook:** 6¼ hours
Makes: 12 servings

4 lbs. large Yukon Gold potatoes, cut into 1-in. cubes
1 medium sweet yellow pepper, chopped
1 small red onion, chopped
½ cup Buffalo wing sauce
1 cup shredded cheddar cheese
Optional toppings: Crumbled cooked bacon, sliced green onions and sour cream

1. Place potatoes, yellow pepper and red onion in a 6-qt. slow cooker. Add Buffalo wing sauce; stir to coat. Cook, covered, on low 6 hours or until potatoes are tender, stirring halfway through. Stir potato mixture; sprinkle with cheese. Cover and cook until cheese is melted, about 15 minutes.
2. Transfer to a serving bowl. If desired, top with bacon, green onions and sour cream.

¾ cup: 182 cal., 4g fat (2g sat. fat), 9mg chol., 382mg sod., 32g carb. (3g sugars, 3g fiber), 6g pro. **Diabetic exchanges:** 2 starch, ½ fat.

SLOW-COOKER SECRETS
Serve these potatoes alongside chicken strips and celery sticks (or iceberg wedges) with blue cheese dressing for an easy crowd-pleasing buffet perfect for game time.

BUFFALO WING POTATOES

OREGANO GREEN BEANS
WITH TOASTED PINE NUTS

SAVORY RICE-STUFFED APPLES

My family loves apples. Since we have several trees, I am challenged to create new recipes every fall. This side dish is fabulous with pork roast and so effortless due to the use of the slow cooker. This is a win for me!
—Roxanne Chan, Albany, CA

- -

Prep: 15 min. • **Cook:** 1½ hours
Makes: 6 servings

- 6   medium apples
- ½   cup cooked brown rice
- 1   Tbsp. thinly sliced green onions
- 1   Tbsp. chopped sweet red pepper
- 1   Tbsp. minced fresh parsley
- 1   Tbsp. finely chopped celery
- 1   Tbsp. chopped carrot
- 1   Tbsp. chopped walnuts
- ½   tsp. ground cinnamon
- 2   Tbsp. shredded cheddar cheese
- 1   cup unsweetened apple juice
- 1   Tbsp. chili sauce

Core apples, leaving bottoms intact. In a medium bowl, combine brown rice and the next 8 ingredients; mix well. Fill each apple with about 2 Tbsp. filling, packing it well. Place the stuffed apples in a greased 4-qt. slow cooker. Pour in the apple juice and chili sauce. Cover and cook on high until the apples are soft, 1½-2 hours. Spoon liquid over each apple serving.

1 stuffed apple: 139 cal., 2g fat (1g sat. fat), 2mg chol., 60mg sod., 31g carb. (20g sugars, 4g fiber), 2g pro. **Diabetic exchanges:** 1 starch, 1 fruit.

OREGANO GREEN BEANS WITH TOASTED PINE NUTS

This super easy side dish is a wonderful potluck recipe. It's a surprising mix that leaves guests and family raving. You can substitute any kind of nut for the pine nuts or even replace them with fresh berries.
—Wolfgang Hanau,
West Palm Beach, FL

- -

Prep: 15 min. • **Cook:** 5 hours
Makes: 8 servings

- 2   lbs. fresh thin french-style green beans, cut into 2-in. pieces
- ½   cup water
- 2   Tbsp. minced fresh oregano
- ½   tsp. onion powder
- ½   tsp. salt
- ¼   tsp. celery salt
- ¼   tsp. pepper
- ½   cup pine nuts or sliced almonds, toasted

In a 6-qt. slow cooker, combine all ingredients except pine nuts. Cook, covered, on low until beans are tender, 5-6 hours. Remove with a slotted spoon. Top with pine nuts.

1 cup: 94 cal., 6g fat (0 sat. fat), 0 chol., 191mg sod., 10g carb. (3g sugars, 4g fiber), 3g pro. **Diabetic exchanges:** 1 vegetable, 1 fat.

SAVORY RICE-STUFFED
APPLES

SPICED CARROTS & BUTTERNUT SQUASH

When I've got a lot going on, my slow cooker is my go-to tool for cooking veggies. The sweetness of the squash and carrots really complements the spicy seasonings.
—Courtney Stultz, Weir, KS

- -

Prep: 15 min. • **Cook:** 4 hours
Makes: 6 servings

- 5 **large carrots, cut into ½-in. pieces (about 3 cups)**
- 2 **cups cubed peeled butternut squash (1-in. pieces)**
- 1 **Tbsp. balsamic vinegar**
- 1 **Tbsp. olive oil**
- 1 **Tbsp. honey**
- 1 **tsp. ground cinnamon**
- ½ **tsp. salt**
- ½ **tsp. ground cumin**
- ¼ **tsp. chili powder**

Place carrots and squash in a 3-qt. slow cooker. In a small bowl, mix remaining ingredients; drizzle over vegetables and toss to coat. Cook, covered, on low 4-5 hours or until vegetables are tender. Gently stir before serving.

⅔ cup: 85 cal., 3g fat (0 sat. fat), 0 chol., 245mg sod., 16g carb. (8g sugars, 3g fiber), 1g pro. **Diabetic exchanges:** 1 vegetable, ½ starch, ½ fat.

BACON & SAUSAGE STUFFING

BACON & SAUSAGE STUFFING

This was inspired by my mother's stuffing recipe. It smells like heaven while you're making it, and people can never seem to get enough.
—Stephan-Scott Rugh, Portland, OR

Prep: 25 min. • **Cook:** 4 hours + standing
Makes: 20 servings

- 1   **lb. bulk pork sausage**
- 1   **lb. thick-sliced bacon strips, chopped**
- ½   **cup butter, cubed**
- 1   **large onion, chopped**
- 3   **celery ribs, sliced**
- 10½ **cups unseasoned stuffing cubes**
- 1   **cup sliced fresh mushrooms**
- 1   **cup chopped fresh parsley**
- 4   **tsp. dried sage leaves**
- 4   **tsp. dried thyme**
- 6   **large eggs**
- 2   **cans (10¾ oz. each) condensed cream of chicken soup, undiluted**
- 1¼ **cups chicken stock**

1. In a large skillet, cook sausage over medium heat 6-8 minutes or until no longer pink, breaking it into crumbles. Remove with a slotted spoon; drain on paper towels. Discard drippings.
2. Add bacon to pan; cook over medium heat until crisp. Remove to paper towels to drain. Discard drippings. Wipe out pan. In the same pan, heat butter over medium-high heat. Add onion and celery; cook and stir 6-8 minutes or until tender. Remove from heat.
3. In a large bowl, combine stuffing cubes, sausage, bacon, onion mixture, mushrooms, parsley, sage and thyme. In a small bowl, whisk eggs, soup and stock; pour over the stuffing mixture and toss to coat.
4. Transfer to a greased 6-qt. slow cooker. Cook, covered, on low for 4-5 hours or until a thermometer reads 160°. Remove lid; let stand 15 minutes before serving.

¾ cup: 290 cal., 17g fat (6g sat. fat), 89mg chol., 823mg sod., 25g carb. (2g sugars, 2g fiber), 11g pro.

CHEESY CAULIFLOWER

When my main course took up the entire oven, I needed a vegetable that I could make in the slow cooker. After searching for a recipe, I ended up writing my own. My dish turned out better than I could have hoped!
—Heather Corson, Casper, WY

- -

Prep: 10 min. • **Cook:** 5 hours
Makes: 16 servings

- 2 **medium heads cauliflower, cut into florets (about 18 cups)**
- 1 **can (10¾ oz.) condensed cream of chicken soup, undiluted**
- 2 **cups shredded cheddar cheese**
- 1 **cup sour cream**
- ½ **tsp. salt**
- ½ **tsp. pepper**
- ¼ **cup butter, cubed**
- 1 **cup dry bread crumbs**

1. In a 6-qt. slow cooker, combine cauliflower, soup and cheese. Cook, covered, on low for 5-6 hours or until cauliflower is tender. Stir in sour cream, salt and pepper.
2. In a small skillet, melt butter over medium heat. Add bread crumbs; cook and stir until golden brown, 2-3 minutes. Sprinkle over cauliflower.
¾ cup: 178 cal., 12g fat (7g sat. fat), 27mg chol., 411mg sod., 11g carb. (3g sugars, 2g fiber), 6g pro.

GOLDEN MASHED POTATOES

Making a special holiday meal can be a little daunting, even for the most experienced cook. The convenience of the slow cooker for these classic spuds makes your task one step easier and allows you to spend more time with family.
—Samantha Six, Fredricksburg, IN

- -

Prep: 20 min. • **Cook:** 4 hours
Makes: 14 servings

- 5 **lbs. Yukon Gold potatoes (about 10 medium), chopped**
- 1 **cup butter, cubed**
- 1 **cup water**
- 3 **tsp. salt**
- ¾ **tsp. pepper**
- ½ **cup mayonnaise**
- ¼ **cup grated Parmesan cheese**
- 1 **to 1½ cups 2% milk**

1. In a 6-qt. slow cooker, combine the first 5 ingredients. Cook, covered, on high 4-5 hours or until potatoes are tender (do not drain liquid).
2. Mash potatoes, gradually adding mayonnaise, cheese and enough milk to achieve desired consistency.
¾ cup: 327 cal., 20g fat (10g sat. fat), 38mg chol., 703mg sod., 33g carb. (3g sugars, 3g fiber), 5g pro.

GOLDEN MASHED POTATOES

prepared slow cooker. If desired, sprinkle cinnamon sugar over the top of batter. Cover slow cooker with a double layer of white paper towels; place lid securely over towels.

2. Cook, covered, on high until bread is lightly browned, 2½-3 hours. To avoid scorching, rotate slow cooker insert a half turn midway through cooking, lifting carefully with oven mitts. Remove bread from slow cooker using parchment to lift; cool slightly before slicing.

Note: As a substitute for each cup of self-rising flour, place 1½ tsp. baking powder and ½ tsp. salt in a measuring cup. Add all-purpose flour to measure 1 cup.

1 slice: 210 cal., 3g fat (2g sat. fat), 11mg chol., 276mg sod., 41g carb. (23g sugars, 2g fiber), 5g pro.

SLOW-COOKER SECRETS
Try stirring a little vanilla or coconut extract into the batter of this banana bread.

SLOW-COOKER
BANANA BREAD

SLOW-COOKER BANANA BREAD

I love to use my slow cooker. I started to experiment with making bread in it so I wouldn't have to heat up my kitchen by turning on my oven. It's so easy and simple. I now make bread this way all the time.
—Nicole Gackowski, Antioch, CA

- -

Prep: 10 min. • **Cook:** 2½ hours
Makes: 16 servings

5 medium ripe bananas
2½ cups self-rising flour
1 can (14 oz.) sweetened
   condensed milk
1 tsp. ground cinnamon
   Cinnamon sugar, optional

1. Place a piece of parchment into a 5-qt. slow cooker, letting ends extend up sides. Grease paper with cooking spray. Combine the first 4 ingredients in a large bowl. Pour the batter into

WILD RICE WITH
DRIED BLUEBERRIES

WILD RICE WITH DRIED BLUEBERRIES

I love the combination of rice and fruit, so this is a go-to Thanksgiving side dish at my house. I toss in mushrooms and toasted almonds; you can also include dried cherries or cranberries if you'd like.
—Janie Colle, Hutchinson, KS

Prep: 15 min. • **Cook:** 3¼ hours
Makes: 16 servings

- 2 **Tbsp. butter**
- 8 **oz. sliced fresh mushrooms**
- 3 **cups uncooked wild rice**
- 8 **green onions, sliced**
- 1 **tsp. salt**
- ½ **tsp. pepper**
- 4 **cans (14½ oz. each)**
  vegetable broth
- 1 **cup chopped pecans, toasted**
- 1 **cup dried blueberries**

In a large skillet, heat butter over medium heat. Add mushrooms; cook and stir 4-5 minutes or until tender. In a 5-qt. slow cooker, combine the rice, mushrooms, onions, salt and pepper. Pour broth over rice mixture. Cook, covered, on low 3-4 hours or until rice is tender. Stir in pecans and blueberries. Cook, covered, 15 minutes longer or until heated through. If desired, top with additional sliced green onions.
¾ cup: 199 cal., 7g fat (1g sat. fat), 4mg chol., 163mg sod., 31g carb. (5g sugars, 4g fiber), 6g pro. **Diabetic exchanges:** 2 starch, 1½ fat.

APPLE-BROWN SUGAR GLAZED CARROTS

APPLE-BROWN SUGAR GLAZED CARROTS

Carrots seem so simple, but this recipe is truly something special. Sweet and buttery, it was a favorite my mother always served around the holidays.
—Darlis Wilfer, West Bend, WI

Prep: 10 min. • **Cook:** 3¼ hours
Makes: 4 servings

- 2 **lbs. medium carrots,**
  cut into 1-in. pieces
- ½ **cup unsweetened apple juice**
- ½ **cup packed brown sugar**
- ¼ **cup butter, cubed**
- ¼ **tsp. salt**
- ¼ **cup chopped pecans or**
  walnuts, toasted, optional

1. In a 3-qt. slow cooker, combine the carrots and apple juice. Cook, covered, on high until the carrots are tender, 3-4 hours.
2. Remove carrots from slow cooker; discard juices. Return carrots to slow cooker. Stir in brown sugar, butter and salt. Cook, covered, on high until the carrots are glazed, 15-20 minutes longer. If desired, sprinkle with pecans.
¾ cup: 314 cal., 12g fat (7g sat. fat), 31mg chol., 404mg sod., 52g carb. (41g sugars, 6g fiber), 2g pro.

PUMPKIN YEAST BREAD

Savor the rich flavors of fall with this homey loaf you can bake up in the slow cooker. Butterscotch chips add a sweet surprise.
—Erica Polly, Sun Prairie, WI

Prep: 20 min. • **Cook:** 2½ hours + cooling
Makes: 1 loaf (12 slices)

- ⅓ **cup packed brown sugar**
- 1 **pkg. (¼ oz.) quick-rise yeast**
- 2 **tsp. pumpkin pie spice**
- ¾ **tsp. salt**
- 3½ **to 4 cups all-purpose flour**
- ¾ **cup 2% milk**
- 2 **Tbsp. butter, cubed**
- ¾ **cup canned pumpkin**
- 1 **large egg, lightly beaten**
- ⅓ **cup raisins**
- ⅓ **cup chopped pecans, toasted**
- ⅓ **cup butterscotch chips, optional**

1. In a large bowl, mix brown sugar, yeast, pie spice, salt and 1½ cups flour. In a small saucepan, heat milk and butter to 120°-130°; stir into the dry ingredients. Stir in the pumpkin, egg and enough remaining flour to form a soft dough (dough will be sticky).

2. Turn dough onto a floured surface; knead dough until smooth and elastic, 6-8 minutes. During the last few minutes of kneading, add raisins, pecans and, if desired, chips. Shape into a 6-in. round loaf; transfer to a greased double thickness of heavy-duty foil (about 12 in. square). Lifting with foil, place in a 6-qt. slow cooker. Press foil against bottom and sides of slow cooker.

3. Cook, covered, on high 2½-3 hours or until a thermometer reads 190°-200°. Remove to a wire rack; cool completely before slicing.

1 slice: 228 cal., 5g fat (2g sat. fat), 22mg chol., 180mg sod., 40g carb. (10g sugars, 2g fiber), 6g pro.

PUMPKIN YEAST BREAD

BACON MAC & CHEESE

I'm all about easy slow-cooker meals. Using more cheese than ever, I developed an addictive spin on this casserole favorite.
—Kristen Heigl, Staten Island, NY

Prep: 20 min. • **Cook:** 3 hours + standing
Makes: 18 servings

- 2 large eggs, lightly beaten
- 4 cups whole milk
- 1 can (12 oz.) evaporated milk
- ¼ cup butter, melted
- 1 Tbsp. all-purpose flour
- 1 tsp. salt
- 1 pkg. (16 oz.) small pasta shells
- 1 cup shredded provolone cheese
- 1 cup shredded Manchego or Monterey Jack cheese
- 1 cup shredded white cheddar cheese
- 8 bacon strips, cooked and crumbled

1. In a large bowl, whisk the first 6 ingredients until blended. Stir in pasta and cheeses; transfer to a 4- or 5-qt. slow cooker.
2. Cook, covered, on low until pasta is tender, 3-3½ hours. Turn off slow cooker; remove insert. Let stand, uncovered, 15 minutes before serving. Top with bacon.
½ cup: 272 cal., 14g fat (8g sat. fat), 59mg chol., 400mg sod., 24g carb. (5g sugars, 1g fiber), 13g pro.

DESSERTS

PUMPKIN APPLE COBBLER

PUMPKIN APPLE COBBLER

This spiced cobbler with apples and cranberries is sure to please all of your holiday guests. It's perfect for fall but can be made year-round since it uses fresh or frozen cranberries.
—Joan Hallford,
North Richland Hills, TX

Prep: 20 min. • **Cook:** 4 hours
Makes: 8 servings

- 5 cups sliced peeled tart apples (about 4 medium)
- 1 cup fresh or frozen cranberries
- 1 cup packed dark brown sugar, divided
- 2 tsp. ground cinnamon, divided
- 1 tsp. vanilla extract
- ½ cup butter, softened
- 3 large eggs, room temperature
- 1 can (15 oz.) pumpkin
- 2 cups all-purpose flour
- 2 tsp. baking powder
- ½ tsp. baking soda
- ¼ tsp. salt
  Chopped pecans, optional
  Vanilla ice cream or whipped cream

1. In a 4- or 5-qt. greased slow cooker, combine apples, cranberries, ½ cup brown sugar, 1 tsp. cinnamon and the vanilla.
2. In a large bowl, cream butter and remaining ½ cup brown sugar until light and fluffy, 5-7 minutes. Add eggs, 1 at a time, beating well after each addition. Beat in pumpkin. In another bowl, whisk flour, baking powder, baking soda, salt and remaining 1 tsp. cinnamon; beat into pumpkin mixture.
3. Spread over apple mixture. If desired, sprinkle with pecans. Cook, covered, on high until apple mixture is bubbling

WARM AUTUMN APPLES

around edges and cake is set, about 4 hours. Serve with ice cream or whipped cream.
1 serving: 407 cal., 14g fat (8g sat. fat), 100mg chol., 402mg sod., 66g carb. (36g sugars, 4g fiber), 7g pro.

WARM AUTUMN APPLES

I have given people this recipe more than any other. It has a delicious nutty flavor. Use it to top waffles or pancakes. Or mix it with vanilla or plain yogurt for a light and quick dessert.
—Rosemary Franta, New Ulm, MN

Prep: 5 min. • **Cook:** 3 hours
Makes: 5 cups

- 8 baking apples (about 3½ lbs.), peeled and sliced
- ½ to 1 cup chopped pecans
- ¾ cup raisins
- ½ cup butter, melted
- ⅓ cup sugar
- ¼ cup old-fashioned oats
- 2 Tbsp. lemon juice
- ¼ tsp. ground cinnamon

Combine all ingredients in a 1½-qt. slow cooker. Cook on high heat for 3 hours, stirring occasionally.
¼ cup: 133 cal., 7g fat (3g sat. fat), 12mg chol., 47mg sod., 19g carb. (15g sugars, 2g fiber), 1g pro.

CARAMEL PECAN PUMPKIN CAKE

Use your slow cooker as a cake maker for a seriously yummy dessert that is easy enough for any weekday and tasty enough for a holiday meal. It frees up oven space, too.
—Julie Peterson, Crofton, MD

- -

Prep: 15 min. • **Cook:** 2 hours
Makes: 10 servings

- 1   **cup butter, softened**
- 1¼ **cups sugar**
- 4   **large eggs, room temperature**
- 2   **cups all-purpose flour**
- 2   **tsp. baking powder**
- 1   **tsp. baking soda**
- 1   **tsp. pumpkin pie spice**
     or ground cinnamon
- ½   **tsp. salt**
- 1   **can (15 oz.) pumpkin**
- ½   **cup caramel sundae syrup**
- ½   **cup chopped pecans**

1. In large bowl, cream butter and sugar until light and fluffy, 5-7 minutes. Add eggs, 1 at a time, beating well after each addition. In another bowl, whisk the next 5 ingredients; add to creamed mixture alternately with pumpkin, beating well after each addition.

2. Line a 5-qt. round slow cooker with heavy-duty foil extending over sides; spray with cooking spray. Spread batter evenly into slow cooker. Cook, covered, on high until a toothpick inserted in center comes out clean, about 2 hours. To avoid scorching, rotate cooker insert a half turn midway through cooking, lifting carefully with oven mitts. Turn off slow cooker; let stand, uncovered, 10 minutes. Using foil, carefully lift cake out and invert onto a serving plate.

3. Drizzle caramel syrup over cake; top with pecans. Serve warm.

1 slice: 473 cal., 25g fat (13g sat. fat), 123mg chol., 561mg sod., 59g carb. (35g sugars, 2g fiber), 7g pro.

SLOW-COOKER SECRETS
For variety, try this cake using canned pureed sweet potato instead of canned pumpkin.

CARAMEL PECAN
PUMPKIN CAKE

MOM'S HAZELNUT & CHOCOLATE BREAD PUDDING

Mom combined her love of hazelnut spread and bread pudding into one delicious recipe. It's a fabulous make-ahead dessert for cozy nights and game-day parties.
—Jo Hahn, Newport News, VA

Prep: 15 min. • **Cook:** 4 hours
Makes: 12 servings

- ¼ **cup unsalted butter**
- 2 **Tbsp. semisweet chocolate chips**
- 8 **cups cubed challah or brioche**
- ½ **cup chopped hazelnuts**
- 4 **large eggs**
- 1½ **cups fat-free milk**
- ½ **cup fat-free half-and-half**
- ½ **cup Nutella**
- ¼ **cup sugar**
- ½ **tsp. vanilla extract**
- ¼ **tsp. salt**
  Sweetened whipped cream, optional

1. Microwave butter and chocolate chips until melted, 30-45 seconds; stir until smooth. Cool. In a 3- or 4-qt. slow cooker coated with cooking spray, combine bread cubes and hazelnuts. In a large bowl, combine the next 7 ingredients, mixing well. Add the chocolate mixture to bowl; whisk until smooth.

2. Pour egg mixture over bread and hazelnuts, gently pressing bread cubes to help them absorb liquid. Cook, covered, on low 4-5 hours or until a knife inserted in center comes out clean. Serve warm, dolloped with whipped cream if desired.

½ cup: 259 cal., 14g fat (4g sat. fat), 85mg chol., 190mg sod., 28g carb. (15g sugars, 1g fiber), 7g pro.

BUTTER PECAN SYRUP

My family loves butter pecan anything, and this recipe is amazing over vanilla ice cream, cake or waffles. It's a special treat we all enjoy.
—Angela Lively, Conroe, TX

Prep: 10 min. • **Cook:** 3 hours
Makes: 2 cups

- 1 cup packed brown sugar
- 5 tsp. cornstarch
  Dash salt
- 1 cup water
- ⅓ cup butter, cubed
- ¾ cup chopped pecans, toasted
- 1 tsp. vanilla extract
  Vanilla ice cream

In a 1½-qt. slow cooker, mix brown sugar, cornstarch and salt. Whisk in water. Cover and cook on high until thickened and bubbly, 3-3½ hours, stirring every 30 minutes. Whisk in butter until melted. Stir in pecans and vanilla. Serve with ice cream.
¼ cup: 251 cal., 15g fat (5g sat. fat), 20mg chol., 87mg sod., 30g carb. (27g sugars, 1g fiber), 1g pro.

CRANBERRY
STUFFED APPLES

CRANBERRY STUFFED APPLES

Cinnamon, nutmeg and walnuts add a homey autumn flavor to these stuffed apples, while the slow cooker does most of the work.
—Grace Sandvigen, Rochester, NY

Prep: 10 min. • **Cook:** 3 hours
Makes: 5 servings

- 5 medium apples
- ⅓ cup fresh or frozen cranberries, thawed and chopped
- ¼ cup packed brown sugar
- 2 Tbsp. chopped walnuts
- ¼ tsp. ground cinnamon
- ⅛ tsp. ground nutmeg
  Optional: Whipped cream or vanilla ice cream

1. Core apples, leaving bottoms intact. Peel top third of each apple; place in a 5-qt. slow cooker. Combine the cranberries, brown sugar, walnuts, cinnamon and nutmeg; carefully spoon into apples.
2. Cover and cook on low for 3-4 hours or until apples are tender. Serve with whipped cream or ice cream if desired.
1 stuffed apple: 136 cal., 2g fat (0 sat. fat), 0 chol., 6mg sod., 31g carb. (25g sugars, 4g fiber), 1g pro. **Diabetic exchanges:** 1 starch, 1 fruit.

INDIAN RICE & CARROT PUDDING

This recipe is rich in flavor and very easy to prepare.
—Daljeet Singh, Coral Springs, FL

- -

Prep: 15 min. • **Cook:** 2¾ hours
Makes: 9 servings

    3½ cups 1% milk
    1 cup shredded carrots
    ½ cup uncooked basmati rice, washed and drained
    ¾ tsp. ground cardamom
    ½ tsp. ground cinnamon
    ¼ tsp. ground ginger
    ¼ cup unsalted pistachios, chopped, divided
    ½ cup agave nectar
    ⅓ cup raisins
    ¼ tsp. rose water, optional

Combine milk, carrots, rice, cardamom, cinnamon and ginger in a 4-qt. slow cooker. Stir in half chopped pistachios. Cook, covered, on high heat 2½ hours, stirring occasionally. Add the agave and raisins; reduce heat to low. Cover and cook until rice is tender, 15 minutes longer. If desired, stir in rose water. Serve warm, or refrigerate and serve chilled. Garnish each serving with remaining pistachios.

½ cup: 176 cal., 3g fat (1g sat. fat), 5mg chol., 66mg sod., 35g carb. (23g sugars, 1g fiber), 5g pro.

CINNAMON SPICED APPLES

If you're feeling festive, scoop some vanilla ice cream over a bowl of these heartwarming cinnamon spiced apples. They're comforting, aromatic and just plain heavenly.
—Amie Powell, Knoxville, TN

- -

Prep: 15 min. • **Cook:** 3 hours
Makes: 6 cups

    ⅓ cup sugar
    ¼ cup packed brown sugar
    1 Tbsp. cornstarch
    3 tsp. ground cinnamon
    ⅛ tsp. ground nutmeg
    6 large Granny Smith apples, peeled and cut into eighths
    ¼ cup butter, cubed

In a small bowl, mix first 5 ingredients. Place apples in a greased 5-qt. slow cooker; add sugar mixture and toss to coat. Top with butter. Cook, covered, on low 3-4 hours or until apples are tender, stirring halfway through cooking.

¾ cup: 181 cal., 6g fat (4g sat. fat), 15mg chol., 48mg sod., 34g carb. (29g sugars, 2g fiber), 0 pro.

INDIAN RICE & CARROT PUDDING

QUINOA CHILI, PAGE 248

WINTER

SNACKS & APPETIZERS

CHEDDAR BACON
BEER DIP

CHEDDAR BACON BEER DIP

My tangy, smoky dip won the top prize in our office party recipe contest. Other beers can work for this, but be sure to steer clear of dark varieties.
—Ashley Lecker, Green Bay, WI

- -

Prep: 15 min. • **Cook:** 3 hours
Makes: 4½ cups

- 18 oz. cream cheese, softened
- ¼ cup sour cream
- 1½ Tbsp. Dijon mustard
- 1 tsp. garlic powder
- 1 cup amber beer or nonalcoholic beer
- 2 cups shredded cheddar cheese
- 1 lb. bacon strips, cooked and crumbled, divided
- ¼ cup heavy whipping cream
- 1 green onion, thinly sliced
  Soft pretzel bites

1. In a greased 3-qt. slow cooker, combine cream cheese, sour cream, mustard and garlic powder until smooth. Stir in beer, cheese and all but 2 Tbsp. bacon. Cook, covered, on low, stirring occasionally, until heated through, 3-4 hours.
2. In the last 30 minutes, stir in heavy cream. Top with onion and remaining bacon. Serve with soft pretzel bites.
¼ cup: 213 cal., 19g fat (10g sat. fat), 60mg chol., 378mg sod., 2g carb. (1g sugars, 0 fiber), 8g pro.

APPLE SPRITZER

APPLE SPRITZER

This is an easy beverage to offer guests for the holidays. Serve it hot or cold.
—Courtney Stultz, Weir, KS

- -

Prep: 10 min. • **Cook:** 3 hours
Makes: 12 servings

- 1 bottle (2 liters) lemon-lime soda
- 6 medium apples, peeled and chopped
- 1 medium navel orange, sliced
- 1 cup fresh or frozen cranberries
- 5 cinnamon sticks (3 in.)
- 2 to 4 Tbsp. honey, optional
  Apple slices

In a 4- or 5-qt. slow cooker, combine the first 5 ingredients and, if desired, honey. Cover and cook on high 3-4 hours or until heated through. If desired, strain before serving. Garnish with apple slices and additional cinnamon sticks.
¾ cup: 137 cal., 0 fat (0 sat. fat), 0 chol., 17mg sod., 35g carb. (31g sugars, 2g fiber), 0 pro.

SLOW-COOKER MEXICAN DIP

My husband and I love to entertain, and we make this hearty seven-ingredient dip often. Using our slow cooker leaves us free to share quality time with our guests. After all, isn't that the purpose of a party?
—Heather Courtney, Ames, IA

- -

Prep: 15 min. • **Cook:** 1½ hours
Makes: 8 cups

    1½ lbs. ground beef
    1   lb. bulk hot Italian sausage
    1   cup chopped onion
    1   pkg. (8.8 oz.) ready-to-serve
        Spanish rice
    1   can (16 oz.) refried beans
    1   can (10 oz.) enchilada sauce
    1   lb. Velveeta, cubed
        Tortilla chip scoops

1. In a Dutch oven, cook the beef, sausage and onion over medium heat until meat is no longer pink, breaking it into crumbles; drain. Heat rice according to package directions.
2. In a 3-qt. slow cooker, combine the meat mixture, rice, beans, enchilada sauce and cheese. Cover and cook on low for 1½-2 hours or until cheese is melted. Serve with tortilla scoops.
2 Tbsp.: 75 cal., 5g fat (2g sat. fat), 17mg chol., 215mg sod., 3g carb. (1g sugars, 0 fiber), 4g pro.

HOT CHILI CHEESE DIP

To simplify party preparation, I use my slow cooker to create a thick, cheesy dip. Your guests won't believe how delicious this is!
—Jeanie Carrigan, Madera, CA

- -

Prep: 20 min. • **Cook:** 4 hours
Makes: 6 cups

    1   medium onion, finely chopped
    2   tsp. canola oil
    2   garlic cloves, minced
    2   cans (15 oz. each) chili
        without beans
    2   cups salsa
    2   pkg. (3 oz. each) cream cheese,
        cubed
    2   cans (2¼ oz. each) sliced
        ripe olives, drained
        Tortilla chips

1. In a small skillet, saute the onion in oil until tender. Add garlic; cook 1 minute longer.
2. Transfer to a 3-qt. slow cooker. Stir in the chili, salsa, cream cheese and olives. Cover and cook on low for 4 hours or until heated through, stirring occasionally. Stir before serving with tortilla chips.
2 Tbsp.: 38 cal., 2g fat (1g sat. fat), 7mg chol., 144mg sod., 3g carb. (1g sugars, 0 fiber), 1g pro.

HOT CHILI CHEESE DIP

CHRISTMAS PUNCH

This holiday, why not indulge in a warm ruby red punch made in the slow cooker? We use cinnamon and Red Hots to give it that cozy spiced flavor and welcome-home aroma.
—Angie Goins, Tazewell, TN

Prep: 5 min. • **Cook:** 3 hours
Makes: 10 servings

- 4 **cups unsweetened pineapple juice**
- 4 **cups cranberry juice**
- ⅓ **cup Red Hots**
- 2 **cinnamon sticks (3 in.)**
  Fresh cranberries and additional cinnamon sticks

In a 3- or 4-qt. slow cooker, combine the first 4 ingredients. Cook, covered, on low until heated through and the candies are melted, 3-4 hours. Garnish with fresh cranberries and additional cinnamon sticks.

¾ cup: 129 cal., 0 fat (0 sat. fat), 0 chol., 4mg sod., 33g carb. (28g sugars, 0 fiber), 1g pro.

GARLIC SWISS FONDUE

I've been making this recipe for years—everyone flips over the wonderful flavors. When cooled, this cheesy appetizer is also fantastic as a cracker spread.
—Cleo Gonske, Redding, CA

- -

Prep: 10 min. • **Cook:** 2 hours
Makes: 3 cups

- **4** cups shredded Swiss cheese
- **1** can (10¾ oz.) condensed cheddar cheese soup, undiluted
- **2** Tbsp. sherry or chicken broth
- **1** Tbsp. Dijon mustard
- **2** garlic cloves, minced
- **2** tsp. hot pepper sauce
  Cubed French bread baguette, sliced apples and seedless red grapes

In a 1½-qt. slow cooker, mix the first 6 ingredients. Cook, covered, on low 2-2½ hours or until cheese is melted, stirring every 30 minutes. Serve warm with bread cubes and fruit.
¼ cup: 159 cal., 11g fat (7g sat. fat), 35mg chol., 326mg sod., 4g carb. (2g sugars, 0 fiber), 11g pro.

PEPPERED MEATBALLS

PEPPERED MEATBALLS

Plenty of ground pepper gives these saucy meatballs their irresistible zip. I sometimes serve them over noodles as an entree.
—Darla Schroeder, Stanley, ND

- -

Prep: 35 min. • **Cook:** 2 hours
Makes: 1½ dozen

- **½** cup sour cream
- **2** tsp. grated Parmesan or Romano cheese
- **2** to 3 tsp. pepper
- **1** tsp. salt
- **1** tsp. dry bread crumbs
- **½** tsp. garlic powder
- **1½** lbs. ground beef
SAUCE
- **1** can (10¾ oz.) condensed cream of mushroom soup, undiluted
- **1** cup sour cream

- **2** tsp. dill weed
- **½** tsp. sugar
- **½** tsp. pepper
- **¼** tsp. garlic powder

1. In a large bowl, combine sour cream and cheese. Add pepper, salt, bread crumbs and garlic powder. Crumble meat over mixture and mix well. Shape into 1-in. balls.
2. Place meatballs on a greased rack in a shallow baking pan. Bake at 350° for 20-25 minutes or until meatballs are no longer pink; drain.
3. Transfer to a 1½-qt. slow cooker. Combine sauce ingredients; pour over meatballs. Cover and cook on high for 2-3 hours or until heated through.
2 meatballs: 259 cal., 18g fat (9g sat. fat), 77mg chol., 565mg sod., 5g carb. (2g sugars, 0 fiber), 17g pro.

SLAW-TOPPED BEEF SLIDERS

When I was working full time, I relied on these delicious, fast-to-fix appetizer sliders for simple meals. To speed prep time a bit and avoid extra cleanup, I used bagged coleslaw mix and bottled slaw dressing.
—Jane Whittaker, Pensacola, FL

Prep: 20 min. • **Cook:** 6 hours
Makes: 1 dozen

3 cups coleslaw mix
½ medium red onion, chopped (about ⅔ cup)
⅛ tsp. celery seed
¼ tsp. pepper
⅓ cup coleslaw salad dressing

SANDWICHES

1 boneless beef chuck roast (2 lbs.)
1 tsp. salt
½ tsp. pepper
1 can (6 oz.) tomato paste

¼ cup water
1 tsp. Worcestershire sauce
1 small onion, diced
1 cup barbecue sauce
12 slider buns or dinner rolls, split

1. Combine coleslaw, onion, celery seed and pepper. Add salad dressing; toss to coat. Refrigerate until serving.
2. Sprinkle roast with salt and pepper; transfer roast to a 5-qt. slow cooker. Mix tomato paste, water and Worcestershire sauce; pour over roast. Top with onion. Cook, covered, on low 6-8 hours or until meat is tender.
3. Shred meat with 2 forks; return to slow cooker. Stir in barbecue sauce; heat through. Serve beef on buns; top with coleslaw. Replace bun tops.
1 slider: 322 cal., 12g fat (4g sat. fat), 67mg chol., 726mg sod., 34g carb. (13g sugars, 3g fiber), 20g pro.

SLAW-TOPPED
BEEF SLIDERS

READER RAVE...

"Very delicious and easy to make. I always take a long time whenever I cook anything, but the preparation for this recipe took almost no time."
—GREENBEE, TASTEOFHOME.COM

PIZZA DIP

PIZZA DIP

I created this dip for my daughter's pizza-themed birthday party. It was an instant hit and I've continued to take it along to other gatherings. Everyone just loves it!
—Stephanie Gates, Waterloo, IA

Prep: 15 min. • **Cook:** 2 hours
Makes: 20 servings

- ½ lb. ground beef
- ½ lb. bulk pork sausage
- 1 can (28 oz.) crushed tomatoes
- ½ cup diced green pepper
- ¼ cup grated Parmesan cheese
- 2 Tbsp. tomato paste
- 2 tsp. Italian seasoning
- 1 garlic clove, minced
- ¾ tsp. crushed red pepper flakes
- ¼ tsp. salt
- ¼ tsp. pepper
  Hot garlic bread

1. In a large skillet, cook and crumble beef and sausage over medium heat until no longer pink, 5-7 minutes. Using a slotted spoon, transfer the meat to a 3-qt. slow cooker. Stir in all remaining ingredients except garlic bread.
2. Cook, covered, on low 2-3 hours or until heated through. Serve with hot garlic bread.
Freeze option: Freeze cooled dip in freezer containers. To use, partially thaw in the refrigerator overnight. Heat through in a saucepan, stirring occasionally.
¼ cup dip: 68 cal., 4g fat (1g sat. fat), 14mg chol., 198mg sod., 4g carb. (2g sugars, 1g fiber), 4g pro.

SWEET-AND-SOUR
CHICKEN WINGS

SWEET-AND-SOUR CHICKEN WINGS

These wings are a fun appetizer for gatherings. I also like to serve them over rice as a main dish. Any way you do it, they'll be a hit!
—June Eberhardt, Marysville, CA

Prep: 15 min. • **Cook:** 3 hours
Makes: 32 appetizers

- 1 cup sugar
- 1 cup cider vinegar
- ½ cup ketchup
- 2 Tbsp. reduced-sodium soy sauce
- 1 tsp. chicken bouillon granules
- 16 chicken wings
- 3 Tbsp. cornstarch
- ½ cup cold water

1. In a small saucepan, combine the first 5 ingredients. Bring to a boil; cook and stir until sugar is dissolved.

2. Meanwhile, using a sharp knife, cut through the 2 wing joints; discard wing tips. Transfer wings to a 5-qt. slow cooker; add sugar mixture. Cover and cook on low until chicken juices run clear, 3-3½ hours.
3. Transfer wings to a serving dish; keep warm. Skim fat from cooking juices; transfer to a small saucepan. Bring liquid to a boil. Combine the cornstarch and water until smooth. Gradually stir into pan. Bring to a boil; cook and stir until thickened, about 2 minutes. Spoon over the chicken. Serve with a slotted spoon.
Note: Uncooked chicken wing sections (wingettes) may be substituted for whole chicken wings.
1 piece: 87 cal., 3g fat (1g sat. fat), 15mg chol., 126mg sod., 9g carb. (7g sugars, 0 fiber), 5g pro.

HOT SPICED BERRY PUNCH

I like to make punch in the slow cooker for winter parties. Add a splash of bourbon or whiskey for an adult crowd. It's also superb for poaching pears.
—Judy Batson, Tampa, FL

Prep: 10 min. • **Cook:** 2 hours
Makes: 10 servings

- 4 cups frozen unsweetened mixed berries
- ¼ cup sugar
- 2 cinnamon sticks (3 in.)
- 6 whole star anise
- 8 cups cranberry-raspberry juice
  Mixed fresh berries, optional

In a 5- or 6-qt. slow cooker, combine the first 5 ingredients. Cook, covered, on low 2-3 hours or until heated through. Strain punch, discarding fruit and spices. If desired, serve punch with fresh berries.

¾ cup: 148 cal., 0 fat (0 sat. fat), 0 chol., 8mg sod., 36g carb. (32g sugars, 1g fiber), 0 pro.

SLOW-COOKER CAPONATA

SLOW-COOKER CAPONATA

This Italian eggplant dip preps quickly and actually gets better as it stands. Serve it warm or at room temperature. Try adding a little leftover caponata to scrambled eggs for a savory breakfast.
—Nancy Beckman, Helena, MT

Prep: 20 min. • **Cook:** 5 hours
Makes: 6 cups

- 2 medium eggplants, cut into ½-in. pieces
- 1 medium onion, chopped
- 1 can (14½ oz.) diced tomatoes, undrained
- 12 garlic cloves, sliced
- ½ cup dry red wine
- 3 Tbsp. olive oil
- 2 Tbsp. red wine vinegar
- 4 tsp. capers, undrained
- 5 bay leaves
- 1½ tsp. salt
- ¼ tsp. coarsely ground pepper
  French bread baguette slices, toasted
  Optional: Fresh basil leaves, toasted pine nuts and additional olive oil

Place first 11 ingredients in a 6-qt. slow cooker (do not stir). Cook, covered, on high for 3 hours. Stir gently; replace cover. Cook on high 2 hours longer or until vegetables are tender. Cool slightly; discard bay leaves. Serve with toasted baguette slices, adding toppings as desired.
¼ cup: 34 cal., 2g fat (0 sat. fat), 0 chol., 189mg sod., 4g carb. (2g sugars, 2g fiber), 1g pro.

POTLUCK ENCHILADA MEATBALLS

This is a twist on the ordinary potluck meatballs. These are easy, inexpensive and a hit for any occasion.
—Terina Lewis, Decatur, IL

Prep: 1 hour + cooling • **Cook:** 3 hours
Makes: 6 dozen

- 2 pkg. (8½ oz. each) cornbread/muffin mix
- 2 envelopes reduced-sodium taco seasoning, divided
- 2 large eggs, lightly beaten
- 3 cans (10 oz. each) enchilada sauce, divided
- 2 lbs. lean ground beef (90% lean)
- 1 jar (16 oz.) salsa
- 1 can (4 oz.) chopped green chiles
- 1 cup shredded Mexican cheese blend, divided

1. Preheat oven to 400°. Prepare and bake muffin mix according to the package directions. Cool completely and crumble; transfer to a large bowl. Add 1 envelope taco seasoning, eggs, 1½ cups enchilada sauce and meat; mix lightly but thoroughly. Shape the meat mixture into 1½-in. balls; bake on greased racks in 15x10x1-in. baking pans lined with foil until lightly browned, 10-12 minutes.
2. Place meatballs in a 5- or 6-qt. slow cooker. Combine remaining enchilada sauce, salsa, chiles, ½ cup cheese and remaining envelope taco seasoning; pour over meatballs. Sprinkle with remaining cheese. Cook, covered, on low until meatballs are cooked through, about 3 hours.
1 meatball: 68 cal., 3g fat (1g sat. fat), 20mg chol., 227mg sod., 7g carb. (2g sugars, 0 fiber), 4g pro.

SOUPS & SANDWICHES

BACON CHEESEBURGER SOUP

BACON CHEESEBURGER SOUP

This creamy recipe brings two of my absolute favorite foods together in one meal! The tomato, fresh lettuce and crisp bacon toppers make this soup taste as if it's burger time.
—Geoff Bales, Hemet, CA

Prep: 20 min. • **Cook:** 4 hours
Makes: 6 servings (1½ qt.)

- 1½ lbs. lean ground beef (90% lean)
- 1 large onion, chopped
- ⅓ cup all-purpose flour
- ½ tsp. pepper
- 2½ cups chicken broth
- 1 can (12 oz.) evaporated milk
- 1½ cups shredded cheddar cheese
- 8 slices American cheese, chopped
- 1½ cups shredded lettuce
- 2 medium tomatoes, chopped
- 6 bacon strips, cooked and crumbled

1. In a large skillet, cook the beef with onion over medium-high heat until no longer pink, 6-8 minutes, breaking beef into crumbles; drain. Stir in flour and pepper; transfer to a 5-qt. slow cooker.
2. Stir in the broth and milk. Cook, covered, on low for 4-5 hours or until flavors are blended. Stir in cheeses until melted. Top individual servings with remaining ingredients.
1 cup: 557 cal., 32g fat (17g sat. fat), 135mg chol., 1160mg sod., 18g carb. (10g sugars, 1g fiber), 42g pro.

ITALIAN SAUSAGE HOAGIES

ITALIAN SAUSAGE HOAGIES

In southeastern Wisconsin, our cuisine is influenced by both Germans and Italians who immigrated to this area. When preparing this recipe, we often substitute German bratwurst for the Italian sausage, so we blend the two influences with delicious results.
—Craig Wachs, Racine, WI

Prep: 15 min. • **Cook:** 4 hours
Makes: 10 servings

- 10 Italian sausage links
- 2 Tbsp. olive oil
- 1 jar (24 oz.) meatless spaghetti sauce
- ½ medium green pepper, julienned
- ½ medium sweet red pepper, julienned
- ½ cup water
- ¼ cup grated Romano cheese
- 2 Tbsp. dried oregano
- 2 Tbsp. dried basil
- 2 loaves French bread (20 in.)

1. In a large skillet over medium-high heat, brown the sausage in oil; drain. Transfer to a 5-qt. slow cooker. Add spaghetti sauce, peppers, water, cheese, oregano and basil. Cover and cook on low for 4 hours or until sausage is no longer pink.
2. Slice each French bread loaf lengthwise but not all the way through; cut each loaf widthwise into 5 pieces. Fill each with sausage, peppers and sauce.
1 sandwich: 509 cal., 21g fat (7g sat. fat), 48mg chol., 1451mg sod., 56g carb. (7g sugars, 5g fiber), 22g pro.

QUINOA CHILI

This recipe turned my husband into a quinoa lover. I made it the day he got good news on a new job, and we'll always remember how excited we were as we ate this beautiful meal.
—Claire Gallam, Alexandria, VA

- -

Prep: 25 min. • **Cook:** 4 hours
Makes: 10 servings (3¾ qt.)

- 1   **lb. lean ground beef (90% lean)**
- 1   **medium onion, chopped**
- 2   **garlic cloves, minced**
- 1   **can (28 oz.) diced tomatoes with mild green chiles, undrained**
- 1   **can (14 oz.) fire-roasted diced tomatoes, undrained**
- 1   **can (15 oz.) garbanzo beans or chickpeas, rinsed and drained**
- 1   **can (15 oz.) black beans, rinsed and drained**
- 2   **cups reduced-sodium beef broth**
- 1   **cup quinoa, rinsed**
- 2   **tsp. onion soup mix**
- 1   **to 2 tsp. crushed red pepper flakes**
- 1   **tsp. garlic powder**
- ¼   **to ½ tsp. cayenne pepper**
- ¼   **tsp. salt**
      Optional: Shredded cheddar cheese, chopped avocado, chopped red onion, sliced jalapeno, sour cream and cilantro

1. In a large skillet, cook beef, onion and garlic over medium-high heat 6-8 minutes or until meat is no longer pink, breaking it into crumbles; drain.
2. Transfer mixture to a 5- or 6-qt. slow cooker. Add next 11 ingredients; stir to combine. Cook, covered, on low 4-5 hours, until quinoa is tender.
3. Serve with optional toppings as desired.

1½ cups: 318 cal., 7g fat (2g sat. fat), 37mg chol., 805mg sod., 41g carb. (7g sugars, 8g fiber), 21g pro. **Diabetic exchanges:** 2½ starch, 2 lean meat.

SLOW-COOKER SECRETS
To make this chili vegetarian, simply omit the ground beef.

QUINOA CHILI

WHISKEY BARBECUE PORK

The ingredient list may seem long for this saucy pork, but most of these items are things you'll already have in your kitchen. Plus, once the sauce is mixed, the slow cooker does the rest.
—Rebecca Horvath, Johnson City, TN

- -

Prep: 15 min. • **Cook:** 6 hours
Makes: 8 servings

- ½ to ¾ cup packed brown sugar
- 1 can (6 oz.) tomato paste
- ⅓ cup barbecue sauce
- ¼ cup whiskey
- 2 Tbsp. liquid smoke
- 2 Tbsp. Worcestershire sauce
- 3 garlic cloves, minced
- ½ tsp. chili powder
- ½ tsp. salt
- ½ tsp. pepper
- ½ tsp. hot pepper sauce
- ¼ tsp. ground cumin
- 1 boneless pork shoulder butt roast (3 to 4 lbs.)
- 1 medium onion, quartered
- 8 hamburger buns, split

1. In a small bowl, mix the first 12 ingredients. Place pork roast and onion in a 5-qt. slow cooker. Add the sauce mixture. Cook, covered, on low 6-8 hours or until pork is tender.
2. Remove roast and onion. Cool pork slightly; discard the onion. Meanwhile, skim fat from sauce. If desired, transfer sauce to a small saucepan; bring to a boil and cook to thicken slightly.
3. Shred pork with 2 forks. Return pork and sauce to slow cooker; heat through. Serve on buns.
1 sandwich: 505 cal., 19g fat (7g sat. fat), 101mg chol., 618mg sod., 43g carb. (21g sugars, 2g fiber), 35g pro.

SLOW-COOKER ITALIAN SLOPPY JOES

These tasty sloppy joes with plenty of mass appeal are perfect for a cold-weather gathering. If you're taking them to an event, simplify things by cooking the beef mixture and stirring in other ingredients the night before. Cool the meat sauce in shallow bowls in the fridge, then cover and refrigerate them overnight. The next day, transfer the meat mixture to the slow cooker to keep it warm for the party.
—Hope Wasylenki, Gahanna, OH

Prep: 30 min. • **Cook:** 4 hours
Makes: 36 servings

- 2 **lbs. lean ground beef (90% lean)**
- 2 **lbs. bulk Italian sausage**
- 2 **medium green peppers, chopped**
- 1 **large onion, chopped**
- 4 **cups spaghetti sauce**
- 1 **can (28 oz.) diced tomatoes, undrained**
- ½ **lb. sliced fresh mushrooms**
- 1 **can (6 oz.) tomato paste**
- 2 **garlic cloves, minced**
- 2 **bay leaves**
- 36 **hamburger buns, split**

Cook the beef, sausage, peppers and onion in a Dutch oven over medium heat until meat is no longer pink, breaking meat into crumbles; drain. Transfer to a 6-qt. slow cooker. Stir in the spaghetti sauce, tomatoes, mushrooms, tomato paste, garlic and bay leaves. Cover and cook on high until flavors are blended, 4-5 hours. Discard bay leaves. Serve on buns, ½ cup on each.
Freeze option: Freeze cooled meat mixture in freezer containers. To use, partially thaw in refrigerator overnight.

PHILLY CHEESE SANDWICHES

Heat through in a saucepan, stirring occasionally; add broth or water if necessary.
1 sandwich: 246 cal., 9g fat (3g sat. fat), 29mg chol., 522mg sod., 27g carb. (6g sugars, 2g fiber), 13g pro. **Diabetic exchanges:** 2 starch, 2 lean meat.

PHILLY CHEESE SANDWICHES

I'm a big fan of Phillies, so this throw-together recipe is right up my alley. Plus, my slow cooker does all the work. It's a win-win!
—Christina Addison, Blanchester, OH

Prep: 20 min. • **Cook:** 8 hours
Makes: 8 servings

- 1 **boneless beef chuck roast (2½ to 3 lbs.), trimmed and cut into 1-in. cubes**
- 2 **medium onions, halved and sliced**
- ¼ **cup Worcestershire sauce**
- 2 **garlic cloves, minced**
- 1 **tsp. dried oregano**
- ½ **tsp. dried basil**
- 1 **medium sweet red pepper, sliced**
- 1 **medium green pepper, sliced**
- 8 **slices American cheese or pepper jack cheese**
- 8 **hoagie buns, split and toasted**

1. In a 3- or 4-qt. slow cooker, combine the first 6 ingredients. Cook, covered, on low 7 hours. Stir in peppers; cook, covered, until the meat and peppers are tender, 1-3 hours.
2. Stir to break up meat. Serve beef mixture and cheese on buns.
1 sandwich: 546 cal., 23g fat (9g sat. fat), 97mg chol., 754mg sod., 42g carb. (9g sugars, 2g fiber), 40g pro.

STUFFED PEPPER SOUP

I tweaked a recipe I got from one of my best friends, and I couldn't believe how much it really does taste like stuffed green peppers! With beef and brown rice, it makes a hearty meal on a cold winter day.

—Gina Baxter, Plainfield, IL

Prep: 15 min. • **Cook:** 5 hours
Makes: 12 servings (4½ qt.)

- 1 lb. extra-lean ground beef (95% lean)
- 1 medium onion, chopped
- 2 medium green peppers, chopped
- 1 pkg. (8.8 oz.) ready-to-serve brown rice
- 3 Tbsp. packed brown sugar
- ½ tsp. salt
- ½ tsp. dried basil
- ½ tsp. dried oregano
- 2 cans (15 oz. each) tomato sauce
- 2 cans (14½ oz. each) diced tomatoes, undrained
- 1 carton (32 oz.) beef broth

1. In a large skillet, cook and crumble beef with onion over medium heat until meat is no longer pink, 5-7 minutes; transfer to a 6-qt. slow cooker. Stir in remaining ingredients.

2. Cook, covered, on low until flavors are blended, 5-6 hours.

Freeze option: Freeze cooled soup in freezer containers. To use, partially thaw in refrigerator overnight. Heat through in a saucepan, stirring occasionally; add a little broth or water if necessary.

1½ cups: 141 cal., 3g fat (1g sat. fat), 22mg chol., 852mg sod., 18g carb. (8g sugars, 3g fiber), 11g pro.

READER RAVE...

"Made this exactly as written. It was so rich and flavorful! Perfect on a cold winter night with crusty French rolls. Thank you for this easy recipe!"

—BJPALMER, TASTEOFHOME.COM

STUFFED PEPPER SOUP

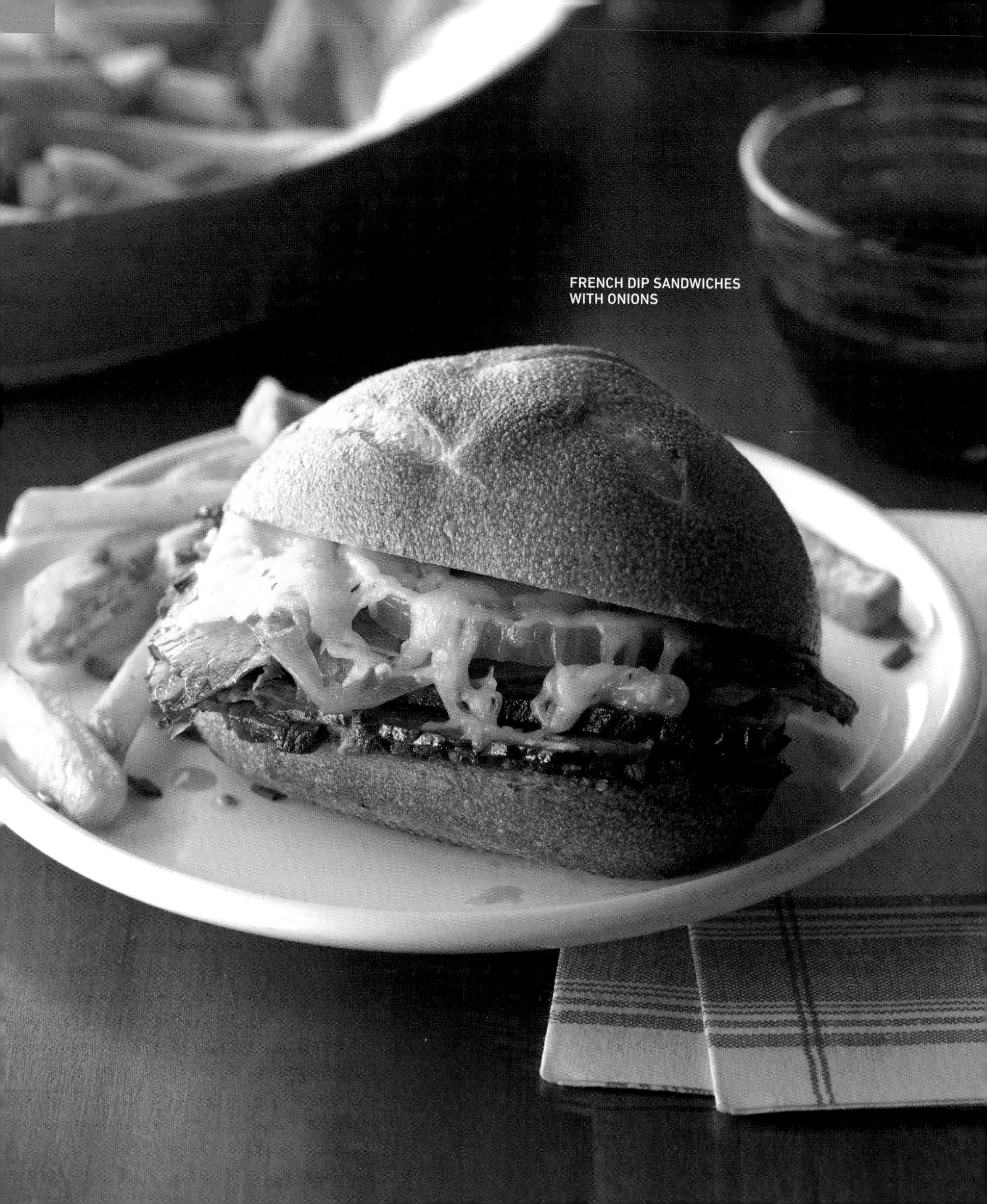

FRENCH DIP SANDWICHES
WITH ONIONS

FRENCH DIP SANDWICHES WITH ONIONS

When I want to impress company, these satisfying sandwiches are my first pick for the menu. I serve them au jus, with the cooking juices in individual bowls for dipping.
—Florence Robinson, Lenox, IA

Prep: 30 min. • **Cook:** 7 hours + standing
Makes: 14 servings

- 2 large onions, cut into ¼-in. slices
- ¼ cup butter, cubed
- 1 beef rump roast or bottom round roast (3 to 4 lbs.)
- 5 cups water
- ½ cup soy sauce
- 1 envelope onion soup mix
- 1½ tsp. browning sauce, optional
- 1 garlic clove, minced
- 14 French rolls, split
- 2 cups shredded Swiss cheese

1. In a large skillet, saute onions in butter until tender. Transfer to a 5-qt. slow cooker. Cut roast in half; place over onions.
2. In a large bowl, combine the water, soy sauce, soup mix, browning sauce if desired and garlic; pour over roast. Cover and cook on low until meat is tender, 7-9 hours.
3. Remove roast with a slotted spoon and let stand for 15 minutes. Thinly slice the meat across the grain. Place on roll bottoms; sprinkle with Swiss cheese. Place on an ungreased baking sheet.
4. Broil 3-4 in. from the heat until cheese is melted, about 1 minute. Replace tops. Skim fat from cooking juices; strain and serve as a dipping sauce if desired.
1 sandwich: 399 cal., 15g fat (7g sat. fat), 81mg chol., 1099mg sod., 34g carb. (2g sugars, 2g fiber), 30g pro.

BEAN & BEEF
SLOW-COOKED CHILI

BEAN & BEEF SLOW-COOKED CHILI

This chili may be already chock-full, but we love to build it up even more with toppings like pico de gallo, red onion, cilantro and cheese.
—Mallory Lynch, Madison, WI

Prep: 20 min. • **Cook:** 6 hours
Makes: 6 servings (2¼ qt.)

- 1 lb. lean ground beef (90% lean)
- 1 large sweet onion, chopped
- 3 garlic cloves, minced
- 2 cans (14½ oz. each) diced tomatoes with mild green chiles
- 2 cans (15 oz. each) pinto beans, rinsed and drained
- 2 cans (15 oz. each) black beans, rinsed and drained
- 2 to 3 Tbsp. chili powder
- 2 tsp. ground cumin
- ½ tsp. salt
  Optional toppings: Sour cream, chopped red onion and minced fresh cilantro

1. In a large skillet, cook beef, onion and garlic over medium heat 6-8 minutes or until beef is no longer pink, breaking beef into crumbles; drain.
2. Transfer the beef mixture to a 5-qt. slow cooker. Drain 1 can of tomatoes, discarding liquid; add to slow cooker. Stir in beans, chili powder, cumin, salt and remaining tomatoes. Cook, covered, on low 6-8 hours to allow the flavors to blend.
3. Mash beans to desired consistency. Serve with toppings as desired.
Freeze option: Freeze cooled chili in freezer containers. To use, partially thaw in the refrigerator overnight. Heat through in a saucepan, stirring occasionally; add a little water if necessary.
1½ cups: 427 cal., 7g fat (3g sat. fat), 47mg chol., 1103mg sod., 58g carb. (11g sugars, 15g fiber), 30g pro.

HEARTY BAKED POTATO SOUP

I got this recipe from my aunt, a terrific cook. Loaded up with bacon, cheese and chives, the soup tastes just like a loaded baked potato. My husband and I love to hunker down with it on chilly winter nights.

—Molly Seidel, Edgewood, NM

- -

Prep: 25 min. • **Cook:** 6 hours
Makes: 10 servings (3½ qt.)

- 5 lbs. baking potatoes, cut into ½-in. cubes (about 13 cups)
- 1 large onion, chopped
- ¼ cup butter
- 4 garlic cloves, minced
- 1 tsp. salt
- ½ tsp. pepper
- 3 cans (14½ oz. each) chicken broth
- 1 cup shredded sharp cheddar cheese
- 1 cup half-and-half cream
- 3 Tbsp. minced fresh chives
  Optional toppings: Shredded cheddar cheese, sour cream, crumbled cooked bacon and minced chives

1. Place the first 7 ingredients in a 6-qt. slow cooker. Cook, covered, on low until potatoes are very tender, 6-8 hours.
2. Mash potatoes slightly to break up and thicken soup. Add 1 cup cheese and the cream and chives; heat through, stirring until blended. Serve with the toppings as desired.

Freeze option: Freeze cooled soup in freezer containers. To use, partially thaw in refrigerator overnight. Heat through in a saucepan, stirring occasionally.

1⅓ cups: 310 cal., 11g fat (7g sat. fat), 38mg chol., 906mg sod., 43g carb. (4g sugars, 5g fiber), 9g pro.

CUBANO PORK SANDWICHES

CUBANO PORK SANDWICHES

When a hungry crowd is coming over, we plan to make our juicy pork a day ahead. I call the sauce "Mojo" because it's loaded with zingy flavors.
—Theresa Yardas, Sheridan, IN

Prep: 1¾ hours + marinating
Cook: 8 hours • **Makes:** 24 servings

- ⅓ cup ground cumin
- ¼ cup sugar
- 2 Tbsp. onion powder
- 1 Tbsp. kosher salt
- ½ tsp. pepper
- 1 boneless pork shoulder roast (6 to 7 lbs.)
- 2 tsp. olive oil
- 1 large onion, quartered
- 1 cup dry red wine or beef broth
- ⅔ cup lime juice
- ⅓ cup lemon juice
- ⅓ cup orange juice
- 1 bay leaf
- 1 tsp. dried cilantro flakes
- 1 tsp. dried oregano
- 1 tsp. dried thyme
- 1 tsp. ground allspice
- 4 tsp. olive oil

SANDWICHES

- 2 loaves unsliced French bread (1 lb. each)
- ¼ cup sweet pickle relish
- ¼ cup Dijon mustard
- 8 slices Swiss cheese

1. In a small bowl, mix the first 5 ingredients. Cut roast into thirds; rub with oil. Rub spice mixture over meat. Cover and refrigerate 24 hours.

2. In a large saucepan, combine onion, wine, juices, bay leaf and seasonings. Bring to a boil. Reduce heat; simmer, covered, 45 minutes. Strain sauce, discarding onion and seasonings.

3. In a large skillet, heat oil over medium heat. Brown roast on all sides; drain. Transfer to a 6-qt. slow cooker. Pour sauce over meat. Cook, covered, on low 8-10 hours or until meat is tender. Remove roast; cool slightly. Skim fat from cooking juices. Shred pork with 2 forks. Return pork to slow cooker; heat through.

4. Preheat oven to 325°. Split bread horizontally. Hollow out bottoms of loaves, leaving ¾-in. shells. Spread relish and mustard inside shells. Layer with the meat and cheese. Replace tops.

5. Wrap sandwiches tightly in heavy-duty foil. Place on baking sheets. Bake 20-25 minutes or until heated through. Cut each crosswise into 12 slices.

1 slice: 368 cal., 16g fat (6g sat. fat), 76mg chol., 648mg sod., 28g carb. (5g sugars, 2g fiber), 26g pro.

BRISKET SLIDERS WITH CARAMELIZED ONIONS

For a dear friend's going-away party, I made a juicy brisket and turned it into sliders. If you cook the brisket ahead, slider assembly is a breeze.
—Marlies Coventry,
North Vancouver, BC

Prep: 25 min. + marinating
Cook: 7 hours • **Makes:** 2 dozen

2   **Tbsp. plus ⅛ tsp. salt, divided**
2   **Tbsp. sugar**
2   **Tbsp. whole peppercorns, crushed**
5   **garlic cloves, minced**
1   **fresh beef brisket (about 4 lbs.)**
1   **cup mayonnaise**
½   **cup crumbled blue cheese**
2   **tsp. horseradish**
⅛   **tsp. cayenne pepper**
3   **medium carrots, cut into 1-in. pieces**
2   **medium onions, chopped**
2   **celery ribs, chopped**
1   **cup dry red wine or beef broth**
¼   **cup stone-ground mustard**
3   **bay leaves**
1   **Tbsp. olive oil**
3   **medium onions, sliced**
24 **mini buns**
    Optional: Arugula and tomato slices

1. In a small bowl, combine 2 Tbsp. salt, sugar, peppercorns and garlic; rub onto all sides of brisket. Cover brisket and refrigerate 8 hours or overnight. In a small bowl, combine mayonnaise, blue cheese, horseradish and cayenne. Refrigerate until assembling.
2. Place carrots, chopped onions and celery in a 6- or 7-qt. slow cooker. Place brisket on top of vegetables. In a small bowl, combine red wine, mustard and bay leaves; pour over brisket. Cook, covered, on low 7-9 hours or until meat is fork-tender.
3. Meanwhile, in a large skillet, heat oil over medium heat. Add sliced onions and remaining salt; cook and stir until softened. Reduce heat to medium-low; cook 30-35 minutes or until deep golden brown, stirring occasionally.
4. Remove brisket; cool slightly. Reserve 1 cup cooking juices; discard remaining juices. Skim fat from reserved juices. Thinly slice brisket across the grain; return to slow cooker. Pour juices over the brisket.
5. Serve the brisket on buns with mayonnaise mixture and caramelized onions and, if desired, arugula and tomato slices.

1 slider: 272 cal., 13g fat (3g sat. fat), 36mg chol., 876mg sod., 17g carb. (3g sugars, 1g fiber), 19g pro.

BRISKET SLIDERS WITH CARAMELIZED ONIONS

SWEET POTATO CHILI WITH TURKEY

crumbles; drain. Transfer to a 3- or 4-qt. slow cooker.

2. Stir in broth, sweet potato puree, chiles and seasonings. Cook, covered, on low 4-5 hours. Stir in beans; cook until heated through, about 1 hour. If desired, top with sour cream, cilantro and red onions.

Freeze option: Freeze cooled chili in freezer containers. To use, partially thaw in the refrigerator overnight. Heat through in a saucepan, stirring occasionally; add broth if necessary.

1½ cups: 243 cal., 6g fat (1g sat. fat), 52mg chol., 606mg sod., 27g carb. (5g sugars, 7g fiber), 20g pro. **Diabetic exchanges:** 2 starch, 2 lean meat.

SLOW-COOKER SECRETS
Chili is the perfect food to make in a slow cooker on a cold winter day. The longer you let chili simmer on low, the better the flavors blend.

SWEET POTATO CHILI WITH TURKEY

This chili is packed with flavor. Ground turkey lightens it, and sweet potato puree sneaks in a healthy dose of vitamin A.
—Rachel Lewis, Danville, VA

Prep: 20 min. • **Cook:** 5 hours
Makes: 6 servings (2¼ qt.)

- 1 lb. ground turkey
- 1 small onion, chopped
- 2 cups chicken broth
- 1 can (15 oz.) sweet potato puree or canned pumpkin
- 1 can (4 oz.) chopped green chiles
- 1 Tbsp. chili powder
- 1 tsp. garlic powder
- 1 tsp. ground cumin
- 1 tsp. curry powder
- ½ tsp. dried oregano
- ½ tsp. salt
- 1 can (15½ oz.) great northern beans, rinsed and drained
  Optional: Sour cream, fresh cilantro and sliced red onions

1. In a large skillet, cook turkey and onion over medium heat until turkey is no longer pink and onion is tender, 5-7 minutes, breaking turkey into

SHREDDED STEAK SANDWICHES

ITALIAN SAUSAGE & KALE SOUP

The first time I made this colorful soup, our home smelled wonderful. We knew it was a keeper to see us through cold winter days.
—Sarah Stombaugh, Chicago, IL

- -

Prep: 20 min. • **Cook:** 8 hours
Makes: 8 servings (3½ qt.)

- 1 **lb. bulk hot Italian sausage**
- 6 **cups chopped fresh kale**
- 2 **cans (15½ oz. each) great northern beans, rinsed and drained**
- 1 **can (28 oz.) crushed tomatoes**
- 4 **large carrots, finely chopped (about 3 cups)**
- 1 **medium onion, chopped**
- 3 **garlic cloves, minced**
- 1 **tsp. dried oregano**
- ¼ **tsp. salt**
- ⅛ **tsp. pepper**
- 5 **cups chicken stock**
  Grated Parmesan cheese

1. In a large skillet, cook sausage over medium heat 6-8 minutes or until no longer pink, breaking it into crumbles; drain. Transfer to a 5-qt. slow cooker.
2. Add kale, beans, tomatoes, carrots, onion, garlic, seasonings and stock to slow cooker. Cook, covered, on low 8-10 hours or until the vegetables are tender. Top each serving with cheese.
1¾ cups: 297 cal., 13g fat (4g sat. fat), 31mg chol., 1105mg sod., 31g carb. (7g sugars, 9g fiber), 16g pro.

SHREDDED STEAK SANDWICHES

I received this recipe when I was a newlywed, and it's been a favorite since then. The saucy steak barbecue makes a quick meal served on sliced buns or over rice, potatoes or buttered noodles.
—Lee Steinmetz, Lansing, MI

- -

Prep: 15 min. • **Cook:** 6 hours
Makes: 14 servings

- 3 **lbs. beef top round steak, cut into large pieces**
- 2 **large onions, chopped**
- ¾ **cup thinly sliced celery**
- 1½ **cups ketchup**
- ½ **to ¾ cup water**
- ⅓ **cup lemon juice**
- ⅓ **cup Worcestershire sauce**
- 3 **Tbsp. brown sugar**
- 3 **Tbsp. cider vinegar**
- 2 **to 3 tsp. salt**
- 2 **tsp. prepared mustard**
- 1½ **tsp. paprika**
- 1 **tsp. chili powder**
- ½ **tsp. pepper**
- ⅛ **to ¼ tsp. hot pepper sauce**
- 14 **sandwich rolls, split**

1. Place meat in a 5-qt. slow cooker. Add the onions and celery. In a bowl, combine the ketchup, water, lemon juice, Worcestershire sauce, brown sugar, vinegar, salt, mustard, paprika, chili powder, pepper and hot pepper sauce. Pour over the meat.
2. Cover and cook on high for 6-8 hours. Remove meat; cool slightly. Shred meat with 2 forks. Return to the slow cooker and heat through. Serve on rolls.
1 sandwich: 347 cal., 7g fat (2g sat. fat), 39mg chol., 1100mg sod., 44g carb. (13g sugars, 2g fiber), 27g pro.

ITALIAN SAUSAGE & KALE SOUP

SMOKY PEANUT BUTTER CHILI

I eliminated beans from my standard chili recipe and added peanut butter and peanuts just for fun. Wow, was it amazing! I tried it on my family and everyone loved it.

—Nancy Heishman, Las Vegas, NV

- -

Prep: 25 min. • **Cook:** 4 hours
Makes: 12 servings (3 qt.)

- 1 Tbsp. peanut oil or canola oil
- 2½ lbs. lean ground beef (90% lean)
- 1 large green pepper, chopped
- 1 large red onion, chopped
- 1 large carrot, peeled and chopped
- 2 garlic cloves, minced
- 2 cans (15 oz. each) tomato sauce
- 2 cans (14½ oz. each) diced tomatoes with basil, oregano and garlic, undrained
- 2 cans (4 oz. each) chopped green chiles
- ½ cup creamy peanut butter
- 1 to 2 Tbsp. ground ancho chile pepper
- 1 tsp. kosher salt
- 1 tsp. smoked paprika
  Optional: Shredded smoked cheddar cheese and chopped peanuts

1. In a large skillet, heat the oil over medium-high heat; add beef and cook in batches until no longer pink, 7-10 minutes, breaking it into crumbles. Remove with a slotted spoon; drain. Add green pepper, onion and carrot; cook and stir until slightly browned, about 2 minutes. Add the garlic; cook 1 minute longer. Transfer meat, vegetables and drippings to a 5- or 6-qt. slow cooker.
2. Stir in the next 7 ingredients until combined. Cook, covered, on low 4 hours or until the vegetables are tender. If desired, sprinkle servings with shredded cheese and peanuts.
1 cup: 279 cal., 15g fat (4g sat. fat), 59mg chol., 878mg sod., 13g carb. (6g sugars, 4g fiber), 23g pro.

SLOW-COOKER SECRETS
Paprika derives from peppers that have been dried and ground. Smoked paprika reverses the process and smokes the peppers before the grinding process.

SMOKY
PEANUT BUTTER CHILI

SAUSAGE PEPPER SANDWICHES

Peppers and onions add fresh flavor to this sausage filling for sammies. It's simple to assemble, and it's always gobbled up quickly.
—Suzette Gessel, Albuquerque, NM

Prep: 15 min. • **Cook:** 3 hours
Makes: 6 servings

- 6 **Italian sausage links (4 oz. each)**
- 1 **medium green pepper, cut into 1-in. pieces**
- 1 **large onion, cut into 1-in. pieces**
- 1 **can (8 oz.) tomato sauce**
- ⅛ **tsp. pepper**
- 6 **hoagie or submarine sandwich buns, split**

1. In a large skillet, brown the sausage links over medium heat. Cut into ½-in. slices; place in a 3-qt. slow cooker. Stir in the green pepper, onion, tomato sauce and pepper.

2. Cover and cook on low for 3-4 hours or until sausage is no longer pink and vegetables are tender. Use a slotted spoon to serve on buns.

1 sandwich: 389 cal., 17g fat (7g sat. fat), 38mg chol., 965mg sod., 42g carb. (9g sugars, 3g fiber), 18g pro.

PULLED BRISKET SANDWICHES

Don't let the number of ingredients in this recipe scare you; I'll bet you have most of them in your pantry already. The sauce is what makes this dish so special. It's hard not to like ketchup, brown sugar and a little butter drizzled over tender beef brisket.

—Jane Guilbeau, New Orleans, LA

- -

Prep: 25 min. • **Cook:** 8 hours
Makes: 12 servings

- 1   **fresh beef brisket (4 to 5 lbs.)**
- 1½ **cups water**
- ½   **cup Worcestershire sauce**
- 2   **Tbsp. cider vinegar**
- 2   **garlic cloves, minced**
- 1½ **tsp. beef bouillon granules**
- 1½ **tsp. chili powder**
- 1   **tsp. ground mustard**
- ½   **tsp. cayenne pepper**
- ¼   **tsp. garlic salt**
- ½   **cup ketchup**
- 2   **Tbsp. brown sugar**
- 2   **Tbsp. butter**
- ½   **tsp. hot pepper sauce**
- 12 **kaiser rolls, split**

PULLED BRISKET SANDWICHES

1. Cut brisket in half; place in a 5-qt. slow cooker. In a small bowl, combine water, Worcestershire sauce, vinegar, garlic, bouillon, chili powder, mustard, cayenne and garlic salt. Cover and refrigerate ½ cup mixture for sauce; pour remaining mixture over beef. Cover and cook on low 8-10 hours or until meat is tender.

2. Remove beef; cool slightly. Skim fat from cooking juices. Shred meat with 2 forks and return to the slow cooker; heat through.

3. In a small saucepan, combine the ketchup, brown sugar, butter, pepper sauce and reserved water mixture. Bring to a boil; reduce heat. Simmer, uncovered, for 2-3 minutes to allow flavors to blend. Using a slotted spoon, place beef on rolls; drizzle with sauce.
Note: This was tested with a fresh beef brisket, not corned beef.
1 sandwich: 405 cal., 11g fat (4g sat. fat), 69mg chol., 753mg sod., 38g carb. (7g sugars, 1g fiber), 37g pro.

READER RAVE...
"It was delicious, my family loved it, and I had every ingredient in my pantry but the brisket! The recipe made plenty, and the leftovers froze well for a really easy future meal. This recipe is a keeper."
—CHSMOAK, TASTEOFHOME.COM

TOMATO BASIL TORTELLINI SOUP

When my family tried this soup, they all had to have seconds, and my husband is happy any time I put it on the table. Sometimes I include cooked, crumbled bacon and serve it with some shredded mozzarella cheese.

—Christina Addison, Blanchester, OH

Prep: 25 min. • **Cook:** 6¼ hours
Makes: 18 servings (4½ qt.)

- 2 Tbsp. olive oil
- 1 medium onion, chopped
- 3 medium carrots, chopped
- 5 garlic cloves, minced
- 3 cans (28 oz. each) crushed tomatoes, undrained
- 1 carton (32 oz.) vegetable broth
- 1 Tbsp. sugar
- 1 tsp. dried basil
- 1 bay leaf
- 3 pkg. (9 oz. each) refrigerated cheese tortellini
- ¾ cup half-and-half cream
  Shredded Parmesan cheese and minced fresh basil

1. In a large skillet, heat the oil over medium-high heat. Add the onion and carrots; cook and stir until crisp-tender, 5-6 minutes. Add the garlic; cook 1 minute longer.

2. Transfer to a 6- or 7-qt. slow cooker. Add the tomatoes, broth, sugar, basil and bay leaf. Cook, covered, on low until vegetables are tender, 6-7 hours.

3. Stir in tortellini. Cook, covered, on high 15 minutes. Reduce heat to low; stir in cream until heated through. Discard bay leaf. Serve with Parmesan cheese and basil.

Freeze option: Before stirring in the half-and-half, cool soup and freeze in freezer containers. To use, partially thaw in refrigerator overnight. Heat through in a saucepan, stirring occasionally; add half-and-half as directed.

1 cup: 214 cal., 7g fat (3g sat. fat), 23mg chol., 569mg sod., 32g carb. (9g sugars, 4g fiber), 9g pro. **Diabetic exchanges:** 2 starch, 1 fat.

SLOW-COOKER SECRETS

If you're cooking for a smaller group, make just a third of the recipe in a small slow cooker and decrease the cooking time slightly.

TOMATO BASIL
TORTELLINI SOUP

SPICED PULLED PORK
SANDWICHES

SPICED PULLED PORK SANDWICHES

This pulled pork is tender and has a savory spice rub on it. It is my sweetie's favorite meal, and I love that it is so easy. What a fantastic way to warm up chilly afternoons. Add more or less salt to taste if you'd like.
—Katie Citrowske, Bozeman, MT

- -

Prep: 30 min. • **Cook:** 6 hours
Makes: 10 servings

1½ tsp. salt
1½ tsp. garlic powder
1½ tsp. ground cumin
1½ tsp. ground cinnamon
1½ tsp. chili powder
1½ tsp. coarsely ground pepper
1 boneless pork shoulder butt roast (3 to 4 lbs.), halved
2 Tbsp. olive oil
2 medium onions, halved and sliced
8 garlic cloves, coarsely chopped
1½ cups water
1 Tbsp. liquid smoke, optional
10 hamburger buns, split and toasted
   Barbecue sauce
   Sliced jalapeno pepper, optional

ITALIAN SIRLOIN BEEF SANDWICHES

1. Mix seasonings; rub over pork. In a large skillet, heat oil over medium heat. Brown pork on all sides. Transfer to a 5- or 6-qt. slow cooker.
2. In the same pan, cook and stir onions over medium heat until lightly browned, 4-5 minutes. Add garlic; cook and stir about 1 minute. Add water; bring to a boil, stirring to loosen browned bits from pan. If desired, stir in liquid smoke. Add to pork.
3. Cook, covered, on low until meat is tender, 6-8 hours. Remove the roast; discard onion mixture. Shred pork with 2 forks; return to slow cooker and heat through. Serve on buns with barbecue sauce and, if desired, jalapeno slices.
1 sandwich: 386 cal., 18g fat (6g sat. fat), 81mg chol., 669mg sod., 26g carb. (4g sugars, 2g fiber), 28g pro.

ITALIAN SIRLOIN BEEF SANDWICHES

After a hectic winter day, our family loves coming home to the inviting smell of this Italian beef wafting from our slow cooker.
—Keith Sadler, Oran, MO

- -

Prep: 20 min. • **Cook:** 6 hours
Makes: 8 servings

1 beef sirloin tip roast (2 lbs.), cut into ¼-in. strips
2 jars (11½ oz. each) pepperoncini, undrained
1 small onion, sliced and separated into rings
3 tsp. dried oregano
¾ tsp. garlic powder
1 can (12 oz.) beer or nonalcoholic beer
   Mayonnaise, optional
8 hoagie buns, split
8 slices provolone cheese

1. In a 5-qt. slow cooker, layer the beef, pepperoncinis and onion; sprinkle with oregano and garlic powder. Pour beer over the top. Cover and cook on low for 6 hours or until meat is tender.
2. Spread mayonnaise on cut sides of rolls if desired. Place cheese on roll bottoms. With a slotted spoon, place meat mixture over cheese.
1 sandwich: 502 cal., 17g fat (8g sat. fat), 92mg chol., 1729mg sod., 41g carb. (7g sugars, 1g fiber), 38g pro.

ROSEMARY LAMB SHANKS
WITH ROOT VEGETABLES

ROSEMARY LAMB SHANKS WITH ROOT VEGETABLES

When I was young, my family lived in New Zealand for two years after World War II. Some things were in short supply, but one item that was always available was lamb shanks. Mother cooked them all the time with root vegetables, and to this day I love lamb!
—Nancy Heishman, Las Vegas, NV

- -

Prep: 25 min. • **Cook:** 6 hours
Makes: 8 servings

- 1 tsp. salt
- ¾ tsp. pepper
- 4 lamb shanks (about 20 oz. each)
- 1 Tbsp. butter
- ½ cup white wine
- 3 medium parsnips, peeled and cut into 1-in. chunks
- 2 large carrots, peeled and cut into 1-in. chunks
- 2 medium turnips, peeled and cut into 1-in. chunks
- 2 large tomatoes, chopped
- 1 large onion, chopped
- 4 garlic cloves, minced
- 2 cups beef broth
- 1 pkg. (10 oz.) frozen peas, thawed
- ⅓ cup chopped fresh parsley
- 2 Tbsp. minced fresh rosemary

1. Rub salt and pepper over lamb. In a large skillet, heat butter over medium-high heat; brown meat. Transfer meat to a 6- or 7-qt. slow cooker. Add wine to skillet; cook and stir 1 minute to loosen brown bits. Pour over lamb. Add the parsnips, carrots, turnips, tomatoes, onion, garlic and broth. Cook, covered, on low 6-8 hours or until meat is tender.
2. Remove lamb; keep warm. Stir in peas, parsley and rosemary; heat through. Serve lamb with vegetables.

SOY-GARLIC CHICKEN

½ lamb shank with 1 cup vegetables: 350 cal., 15g fat (6g sat. fat), 103mg chol., 668mg sod., 22g carb. (8g sugars, 6g fiber), 31g pro. **Diabetic exchanges:** 4 lean meat, 1 starch, 1 vegetable, ½ fat.

SOY-GARLIC CHICKEN

Because I'm a full-time mom and I help my husband on our ranch, I'm always looking for simple yet hearty meals for the slow cooker. My family really likes this one.
—Colleen Faber, Buffalo, MT

- -

Prep: 10 min. • **Cook:** 4 hours
Makes: 6 servings

- 6 chicken leg quarters, skin removed
- 1 can (8 oz.) tomato sauce
- ½ cup reduced-sodium soy sauce
- ¼ cup packed brown sugar
- 2 tsp. minced garlic

1. With a sharp knife, cut leg quarters at the joints if desired. Place in a 4-qt. slow cooker. In a small bowl, combine the tomato sauce, soy sauce, brown sugar and garlic; pour over chicken.
2. Cover and cook on low for 4-5 hours or until chicken is tender.
Freeze option: Cool chicken in sauce. Freeze in freezer containers. To use, partially thaw in refrigerator overnight. Heat through slowly in a covered skillet until a thermometer inserted in chicken reads 165°, stirring occasionally and adding a little chicken broth or water if necessary.
1 chicken leg quarter: 246 cal., 8g fat (2g sat. fat), 90mg chol., 1022mg sod., 13g carb. (10g sugars, 1g fiber), 29g pro.

CREAMY CURRY VEGETABLE STEW

Our family loves to eat Indian food, and this recipe is quick and easy to prepare using jarred korma sauce and fresh vegetables. If you want it hotter, add cayenne pepper to taste. Sometimes I add cooked chicken. I serve this stew with naan bread, chutney and flaked coconut for condiments.
—Nancy Heishman, Las Vegas, NV

Prep: 25 min. • **Cook:** 7 hours
Makes: 6 servings

- 2   jars (15 oz. each) korma curry sauce
- 2   Tbsp. curry powder
- 2   tsp. garam masala
- 1½ tsp. ground mustard
- 2   lbs. red potatoes (about 6 medium), cubed
- 2   cups small fresh mushrooms
- 2   cups fresh baby carrots
- 1½ cups frozen corn, thawed
- 5   green onions, chopped
- 2   cups cut fresh asparagus (2-in. pieces)
- 2   Tbsp. water
- 1½ cups frozen peas, thawed
- ¼   cup chopped fresh parsley
     Naan flatbreads or cooked basmati rice, optional

1. In a greased 5-qt. slow cooker, combine curry sauce, curry powder, garam masala and mustard. Stir in potatoes, mushrooms, carrots, corn and green onions. Cook, covered, on low 7-9 hours or until vegetables are tender.
2. In a microwave-safe bowl, combine asparagus and water; microwave, covered, on high for 2-3 minutes or until crisp-tender. Drain. Stir asparagus and peas into slow cooker; heat through. Sprinkle with parsley. If desired, serve with naan.

Note: Look for garam masala in the spice aisle.

1¾ cups: 455 cal., 20g fat (10g sat. fat), 5mg chol., 495mg sod., 61g carb. (18g sugars, 11g fiber), 11g pro.

CREAMY CURRY VEGETABLE STEW

CHIPOTLE PORK CHOPS

Here's a great way to enjoy summer flavors during winter. I love the tender texture of pork chops made in the slow cooker! The flavor of this sauce is similar to barbecue but with a little extra kick. The crispy onions on top add an extra, delectable crunch.
—Elisabeth Larsen, Pleasant Grove, UT

- -

Prep: 15 min. • **Cook:** 4 hours
Makes: 8 servings

- 8 **bone-in pork loin chops (7 oz. each)**
- 1 **small onion, finely chopped**
- ⅓ **cup chopped chipotle peppers in adobo sauce**
- ¼ **cup packed brown sugar**
- 2 **Tbsp. red wine vinegar**
- 2 **garlic cloves, minced**
- ½ **tsp. salt**
- ¼ **tsp. pepper**
- 1 **can (15 oz.) tomato sauce**
- 1 **can (14½ oz.) fire-roasted diced tomatoes, undrained**

TOPPINGS
- 1 **can (6 oz.) french-fried onions**
- ¼ **cup minced fresh cilantro**

Place all ingredients except toppings in a 5-qt. slow cooker. Cook, covered, on low until a thermometer inserted in pork reads at least 145°, 4-5 hours. Top with french-fried onions and cilantro just before serving.

1 pork chop: 408 cal., 20g fat (6g sat. fat), 86mg chol., 844mg sod., 24g carb. (10g sugars, 2g fiber), 32g pro.

TOP-RATED ITALIAN POT ROAST

I'm always collecting recipes from newspapers and magazines, and this one just sounded too good not to try! You'll love the the blend of hearty ingredients and aromatic spices.
—Karen Burdell, Lafayette, CO

Prep: 30 min. • **Cook:** 6 hours
Makes: 8 servings

- 1 **cinnamon stick (3 in.)**
- 6 **whole peppercorns**
- 4 **whole cloves**
- 3 **whole allspice berries**
- 2 **tsp. olive oil**
- 1 **boneless beef chuck roast (2 lbs.)**
- 2 **celery ribs, sliced**
- 2 **medium carrots, sliced**
- 1 **large onion, chopped**
- 4 **garlic cloves, minced**
- 1 **cup dry sherry or reduced-sodium beef broth**
- 1 **can (28 oz.) crushed tomatoes**
- ¼ **tsp. salt**
  Hot cooked egg noodles and minced parsley, optional

1. Place cinnamon stick, peppercorns, cloves and allspice on a double thickness of cheesecloth. Gather corners of cloth to enclose spices; tie securely with string.
2. In a large skillet, heat the oil over medium-high heat. Brown roast on all sides; transfer to a 4-qt. slow cooker. Add celery, carrots and spice bag.
3. Add onion to same skillet; cook and stir until tender. Add garlic; cook 1 minute longer. Add sherry, stirring to loosen browned bits from pan. Bring to a boil; cook and stir until liquid is reduced to ⅔ cup. Stir in tomatoes and salt; pour over roast and vegetables.

4. Cook, covered, on low 6-7 hours or until meat and vegetables are tender. Remove roast from slow cooker; keep warm. Discard spice bag; skim fat from sauce. Serve roast and sauce with noodles and parsley if desired.
Freeze option: Place sliced pot roast in freezer containers; top with sauce. Cool and freeze. To use, partially thaw in refrigerator overnight. Heat through in a covered saucepan, stirring gently and adding a little broth if necessary.

3 oz. cooked beef with ⅔ cup sauce: 251 cal., 12g fat (4g sat. fat), 74mg chol., 271mg sod., 11g carb. (2g sugars, 3g fiber), 24g pro. **Diabetic exchanges:** 3 lean meat, 2 vegetable, ½ fat.

TOP-RATED ITALIAN POT ROAST

½ cup shredded Monterey
  Jack cheese
  Optional toppings: Sour cream
  and fresh jalapeno pepper slices

1. In a 3-qt. slow cooker, combine broth and cornmeal. Let stand for 5 minutes. In a large skillet, cook beef over medium heat until no longer pink; drain. Stir in chili powder and cumin. Transfer to slow cooker. Stir in the salsa, corn, beans and olives. Cover and cook on low for 6-8 hours or until heated through.
2. Sprinkle with cheese. Cover and cook 5-10 minutes longer or until cheese is melted. If desired, top with sour cream and jalapeno slices.
1⅓ cups: 455 cal., 16g fat (6g sat. fat), 66mg chol., 1112mg sod., 45g carb. (7g

SLOW-COOKER SECRETS

Serve comforting tamale pie with lemonade, margarita, white sangria, wine or beer. You can also pair it with chili con queso, tortilla soup or Spanish rice. End the meal with fresh pineapple or mango sorbet.

CALIFORNIA
TAMALE PIE

CALIFORNIA TAMALE PIE

When I serve this dish, I know I'll see smiles on the faces of everyone at the table. With this recipe, you'll enjoy the taste and texture of classic tamales but without the time and hassle.
—Patricia Nieh, Portola Valley, CA

- -

Prep: 15 min. • **Cook:** 6 hours
Makes: 5 servings

1 **cup beef broth**
¾ **cup cornmeal**
1 **lb. ground beef**
1 **tsp. chili powder**
½ **tsp. ground cumin**
1 **jar (16 oz.) chunky salsa**
1 **can (15¼ oz.) whole
   kernel corn, drained**
1 **can (15 oz.) black beans,
   rinsed and drained**
¼ **cup sliced ripe olives**

COUNTRY FRENCH PORK WITH PRUNES & APPLES

The flavors of herbes de Provence, apples and dried plums make this easy dish taste like a meal at a French cafe.
—Suzanne Banfield, Basking Ridge, NJ

Prep: 20 min. • **Cook:** 4 hours + standing
Makes: 10 servings

2	Tbsp. all-purpose flour
1	Tbsp. herbes de Provence
1½	tsp. salt
¾	tsp. pepper
1	boneless pork loin roast (3 to 4 lbs.)
2	Tbsp. olive oil
2	medium onions, halved and thinly sliced
1	cup apple cider or unsweetened apple juice
1	cup beef stock
2	bay leaves
2	large tart apples, peeled, cored and chopped
1	cup pitted dried plums (prunes)

1. Mix flour, herbes de Provence, salt and pepper; rub over pork. In a large skillet, heat oil over medium-high heat. Brown roast on all sides. Place roast in a 5- or 6-qt. slow cooker. Add onions, apple cider, beef stock and bay leaves.
2. Cook, covered, on low 3 hours. Add apples and dried plums. Cook, covered, on low 1 to 1½ hours longer or until apples and pork are tender. Remove roast, onions, apples and plums to a serving platter, discarding bay leaves; tent with foil. Let stand 15 minutes before slicing.

4 oz. cooked pork with ¾ cup fruit mixture: 286 cal., 9g fat (3g sat. fat), 68mg chol., 449mg sod., 22g carb. (13g sugars, 2g fiber), 28g pro.

SLOW-COOKED VEGETABLE CURRY

SLOW-COOKED VEGETABLE CURRY

I love the fuss-free nature of the slow cooker, but I don't want to sacrifice flavor for convenience. This cozy, spiced-up dish has both.
—Susan Smith, Mead, WA

Prep: 35 min. • **Cook:** 5 hours
Makes: 6 servings

- 1 Tbsp. canola oil
- 1 medium onion, finely chopped
- 4 garlic cloves, minced
- 3 tsp. ground coriander
- 1½ tsp. ground cinnamon
- 1 tsp. ground ginger
- 1 tsp. ground turmeric
- ½ tsp. cayenne pepper
- 2 Tbsp. tomato paste
- 2 cans (15 oz. each) garbanzo beans or chickpeas, rinsed and drained
- 3 cups cubed peeled sweet potatoes (about 1 lb.)
- 3 cups fresh cauliflower florets (about 8 oz.)
- 4 medium carrots, cut into ¾-in. pieces (about 2 cups)
- 2 medium tomatoes, seeded and chopped
- 2 cups chicken broth
- 1 cup light coconut milk
- ½ tsp. pepper
- ¼ tsp. salt
  Minced fresh cilantro
  Hot cooked brown rice
  Lime wedges
  Plain yogurt, optional

1. In a large skillet, heat oil over medium heat; saute onion until soft and lightly browned, 5-7 minutes. Add garlic and spices; cook and stir 1 minute. Stir in tomato paste; cook 1 minute. Transfer to a 5- or 6-qt. slow cooker.
2. Mash 1 can of beans until smooth; add to slow cooker. Stir in remaining beans, vegetables, broth, coconut milk, pepper and salt.
3. Cook, covered, on low until vegetables are tender, 5-6 hours. Sprinkle with cilantro. Serve with rice, lime wedges and, if desired, yogurt.

1⅔ cups curry: 304 cal., 8g fat (2g sat. fat), 2mg chol., 696mg sod., 49g carb. (12g sugars, 12g fiber), 9g pro.

SLOW-COOKER SECRETS
Garbanzo beans are a smart way to add a dose of protein to any meatless main. A good source of fiber, folate and vitamin B6, garbanzo beans hold up well when simmered in a slow cooker.

TURKEY BREAST
WITH GRAVY

TURKEY BREAST WITH GRAVY

This quick-prep recipe lets you feast on turkey no matter what your schedule might be. We save the rich broth for gravy, noodles and soup making.
—Joyce Hough, Annapolis, MD

Prep: 25 min. • **Cook:** 5 hours + standing
Makes: 12 servings

- 2 tsp. dried parsley flakes
- 1 tsp. salt
- 1 tsp. poultry seasoning
- ½ tsp. paprika
- ½ tsp. pepper
- 2 medium onions, chopped
- 3 medium carrots, cut into ½-in. slices
- 3 celery ribs, coarsely chopped
- 1 bone-in turkey breast (6 to 7 lbs.), skin removed
- ¼ cup all-purpose flour
- ½ cup water

1. Mix the first 5 ingredients in a small bowl. Place vegetables in a 6- or 7-qt. slow cooker; top with turkey. Rub turkey with seasoning mixture.
2. Cook, covered, on low 5-6 hours or until a thermometer inserted in turkey reads at least 170°. Remove from slow cooker; let stand, covered, 15 minutes before slicing.
3. Meanwhile, strain cooking juices into a small saucepan. Mix flour and water until smooth; stir into cooking juices. Bring to a boil; cook and stir until thickened, 1-2 minutes. Serve with the turkey.

6 oz. cooked turkey with 3 Tbsp. gravy : 200 cal., 1g fat (0 sat. fat), 117mg chol., 270mg sod., 2g carb. (0 sugars, 0 fiber), 43g pro.

CURRIED CHICKEN CACCIATORE

CURRIED CHICKEN CACCIATORE

With a family, a full-time load at college and a part-time job, I've found that the slow cooker is my best friend when it comes to getting hot, homemade meals like this one on the table.
—Laura Gier, Rensselaer, NY

Prep: 30 min. • **Cook:** 6¼ hours
Makes: 4 servings

- 1 broiler/fryer chicken (3 to 4 lbs.), cut up and skin removed
- 2 small zucchini, halved and sliced
- ½ lb. sliced fresh mushrooms
- 1 small green pepper, chopped
- 1 small onion, chopped
- 1 jar (24 oz.) spaghetti sauce
- 1 can (14½ oz.) diced tomatoes, undrained
- ⅔ cup dry red wine
- ⅓ cup chicken broth
- 1 Tbsp. minced fresh parsley
- 2 garlic cloves, minced
- 1½ tsp. dried thyme
- 1½ tsp. curry powder
- ½ tsp. pepper
- 2 Tbsp. cornstarch
- 2 Tbsp. cold water
  Hot cooked rice

1. Place chicken and vegetables in a 5-qt. slow cooker. In a large bowl, mix spaghetti sauce, tomatoes, wine, broth, parsley, garlic and seasonings; pour over chicken. Cook, covered, on low 6-8 hours or until chicken is tender.
2. In a bowl, mix cornstarch and water until smooth; gradually stir into stew. Cook, covered, on high 15 minutes or until sauce is thickened. Serve with rice.

1 serving: 452 cal., 16g fat (4g sat. fat), 115mg chol., 1167mg sod., 33g carb. (17g sugars, 7g fiber), 44g pro.

ROOT VEGETABLE POT ROAST

During the hectic holiday season, I make this roast a lot. We've scarfed it down before and after shopping and while wrapping presents. Root vegetables and roast beef make everyone feel cozy and calm.
—Pat Dazis, Charlotte, NC

Prep: 30 min. • **Cook:** 7 hours
Makes: 8 servings

ROOT VEGETABLE POT ROAST

- 1   can (14½ oz.) reduced-sodium beef broth
- 2   chai black tea bags
- 2   medium potatoes (about 1 lb.), cut into 1½-in. cubes
- 2   medium turnips (about 9 oz.), cut into 1½-in. pieces
- 4   medium carrots, cut into ½-in. pieces
- 2   medium parsnips, peeled and cut into ½-in. pieces
- 1   large onion, cut into 1-in. wedges
- 2   celery ribs, cut into ½-in. pieces
- 1   Tbsp. olive oil
- 1   boneless beef chuck roast (about 3 lbs.)
- 1   tsp. salt
- ½   tsp. pepper
- 1   medium lemon, thinly sliced
- 3   Tbsp. cornstarch
- 3   Tbsp. cold water

1. In a small saucepan, bring the broth to a boil; remove from heat. Add tea bags; steep, covered, 3-5 minutes according to taste. Discard tea bags. Meanwhile, combine vegetables in a 6-qt. slow cooker.

2. In a large skillet, heat oil over medium-high heat; brown roast on all sides. Place over vegetables; pour tea-steeped broth over the top.

Sprinkle roast with salt and pepper; top with lemon slices. Cook, covered, on low until beef and vegetables are tender, 7-9 hours.

3. Discard lemon slices. Remove the roast and vegetables from slow cooker; keep warm.

4. Transfer cooking juices to a saucepan; skim off fat. Bring juices to a boil. In a small bowl, mix cornstarch and water until smooth; stir into juices. Return to a boil, stirring constantly; cook and stir until thickened, 1-2 minutes. Serve with roast and vegetables.

1 serving: 421 cal., 18g fat (7g sat. fat), 112mg chol., 523mg sod., 27g carb. (7g sugars, 5g fiber), 36g pro.

SLOW-COOKER SECRETS
The flavor of chai tea varies quite a bit by brand. We tested this recipe with Twinings, and it added a subtle spiced flavor. If you want stronger chai flavor, use more tea bags rather than steeping longer. Too much steeping can turn the flavor bitter.

TURKEY WITH HERBED STUFFING

I'm all for turkey dinner, especially around the holidays. A whole turkey won't fit in my slow cooker, so thank goodness for turkey breast. I cook it with my grandma's easy stuffing recipe for a happy meal that doesn't require any hard work.
—Camille Beckstrand, Layton, UT

- -

Prep: 20 min. • **Cook:** 3 hours + standing
Makes: 8 servings

1   boneless skinless turkey breast half (2 lbs.) or 2 lbs. turkey breast tenderloins
1   jar (12 oz.) turkey gravy, divided
1   can (10½ oz.) reduced-fat reduced-sodium condensed cream of mushroom soup, undiluted
½   tsp. salt
½   tsp. poultry seasoning
¼   tsp. pepper
1   medium Granny Smith apple, finely chopped
2   celery ribs, thinly sliced
1   small onion, finely chopped
1   cup sliced fresh mushrooms, optional
6   cups seasoned stuffing cubes

1. Place turkey in a 5- or 6-qt. slow cooker. Whisk ¼ cup gravy, condensed soup and seasonings. Cover and refrigerate remaining gravy. Stir the apple, celery, onion and, if desired, mushrooms into gravy mixture. Stir in the stuffing cubes; spoon over turkey. Cook, covered, on low until a thermometer reads 170° and the turkey meat is tender, 3-4 hours.
2. Remove turkey from slow cooker; tent with foil. Let stand 10 minutes before slicing. Warm remaining gravy. Serve with turkey and stuffing.

4 oz. cooked turkey with ¾ cup stuffing and 2 Tbsp. gravy: 324 cal., 4g fat (1g sat. fat), 70mg chol., 1172mg sod., 38g carb. (5g sugars, 3g fiber), 32g pro.

TURKEY WITH
HERBED STUFFING

SPICY KALE & HERB PORCHETTA

Serve this classic Italian specialty as an entree or with crusty artisan bread as a sandwich. Combine the liquid from the slow cooker with your favorite seasonings to make a sauce or gravy.
—Sandi Sheppard, Norman, OK

- -

Prep: 30 min. + chilling • **Cook:** 5 hours
Makes: 12 servings

1½ cups packed torn fresh
    kale leaves (no stems)
¼ cup chopped fresh sage
¼ cup chopped fresh rosemary
¼ cup chopped fresh parsley
2 Tbsp. kosher salt
1 Tbsp. crushed fennel seed
1 tsp. crushed red pepper flakes
4 garlic cloves, halved
1 boneless pork shoulder roast
    (about 6 lbs.), butterflied
2 tsp. grated lemon zest
1 large sweet onion, thickly sliced
¼ cup white wine or chicken broth
1 Tbsp. olive oil
3 Tbsp. cornstarch
3 Tbsp. water

1. In a blender or food processor, pulse the first 8 ingredients until finely chopped. In a 15x10x1-in. baking pan, open the roast flat. Spread the herb mixture evenly over meat to within ½ in. of edges; sprinkle lemon zest over herb mixture.

2. Starting at a long side, roll up pork jelly-roll style. Using a sharp knife, score fat on outside of roast. Tie at 2-in. intervals with kitchen string. Secure ends with toothpicks. Refrigerate, covered, at least 4 hours or overnight.

3. In a 6-qt. slow cooker, combine onion and wine. Place porchetta seam side down on top of onion. Cook, covered, on low 5-6 hours or until tender. Remove toothpicks. Reserve cooking juices.

4. In a large skillet, heat oil over medium heat. Brown porchetta on all sides; remove from heat. Tent with foil. Let stand 15 minutes.

5. Meanwhile, strain and skim fat from cooking juices. Transfer to a large saucepan; bring to a boil. In a small bowl, mix cornstarch and water until smooth; stir into juices. Return to a boil, stirring constantly; cook and stir until thickened, 1-2 minutes. Cut string on roast and slice. Serve with gravy.

1 serving: 402 cal., 24g fat (8g sat. fat), 135mg chol., 1104mg sod., 5g carb. (1g sugars, 1g fiber), 39g pro.

SLOW-COOKER SECRETS
To butterfly the pork shoulder, make a cut starting 1 in. from the bottom of the roast and stopping 1 in. from the other side (it's easier to do this with the roast on its side). Lay open the roast like a book. It's easy, but if you don't feel up to the challenge, you can simply ask the butcher to butterfly it for you.

SPICY KALE & HERB PORCHETTA

BEEF IN MUSHROOM GRAVY

This is one of the best and easiest meals I've ever made. It has only four ingredients, and they all go into the pot at once. The meat is nicely seasoned and makes its own gravy. It tastes wonderful over mashed potatoes.
—Margery Bryan, Moses Lake, WA

Prep: 10 min. • **Cook:** 7 hours
Makes: 6 servings

2½ lbs. beef top round steak
1 to 2 envelopes onion soup mix
1 can (10¾ oz.) condensed cream of mushroom soup, undiluted
½ cup water
Mashed potatoes, optional

1. Cut steak into 6 serving pieces; place in a 3-qt. slow cooker. Combine the soup mix, soup and water; pour over beef. Cover and cook on low for 7-8 hours or until meat is tender. If desired, serve with mashed potatoes.

Freeze option: Place beef in freezer containers; top with gravy. Cool and freeze. To use, partially thaw in refrigerator overnight. Heat through in a covered saucepan, stirring occasionally; add a little water if necessary.

1 serving: 241 cal., 7g fat (2g sat. fat), 87mg chol., 810mg sod., 7g carb. (1g sugars, 1g fiber), 35g pro.

TURKEY TACO MACARONI

CREAMY ONION PORK CHOPS

This easy dish just might initiate your gang into the clean-plate club!
—Kristina Wyatt, Catawba, VA

Prep: 10 min. • **Cook:** 8 hours
Makes: 6 servings

- 6   bone-in pork loin chops (8 oz. each)
- ¼   tsp. pepper
- ⅛   tsp. salt
- 1¼ cups 2% milk
- 1   can (10¾ oz.) condensed cream of onion soup, undiluted
- 1   can (10¾ oz.) reduced-fat reduced-sodium condensed cream of mushroom soup, undiluted
- ⅔   cup white wine or chicken broth
- 1   envelope ranch salad dressing mix
- 3   Tbsp. cornstarch
- 2   Tbsp. water
      Minced fresh parsley, optional

1. Sprinkle chops with pepper and salt; transfer to a 4-qt slow cooker. In a large bowl, combine the milk, soups, wine and dressing mix; pour over pork. Cover and cook on low for 8-10 hours or until the pork is tender.
2. Remove pork to a serving platter and keep warm. Skim fat from cooking juices; transfer to a large saucepan. Bring liquid to a boil. Combine the cornstarch and water until smooth; gradually stir into the pan. Bring to a boil; cook and stir for 2 minutes or until thickened. Serve with pork. Sprinkle with parsley if desired.

1 pork chop with ⅔ cup gravy: 446 cal., 22g fat (8g sat. fat), 123mg chol., 1105mg sod., 18g carb. (5g sugars, 1g fiber), 39g pro.

TURKEY TACO MACARONI

Turkey and taco seasoning make for a nice twist on a classic dish. If you love cheese, feel free to add more. You can even add some green peppers.
—Barb Kondolf, Hamlin, NY

Prep: 15 min. • **Cook:** 3 hours + standing
Makes: 10 servings

- 2   Tbsp. canola oil, divided
- 4   cups uncooked elbow macaroni
- 2   lbs. ground turkey
- 1   medium onion, chopped
- 4   cans (8 oz. each) tomato sauce
- 1   cup water
- 1   cup salsa
- 1   envelope taco seasoning
- 2   cups shredded cheddar cheese

1. In a large skillet, heat 1 Tbsp. oil over medium heat. Add pasta; cook and stir 2-3 minutes or until pasta is toasted. Transfer to a 5-qt. slow cooker. In same skillet, heat remaining 1 Tbsp. oil over medium-high heat. Add turkey and onion; cook 6-8 minutes or until meat is no longer pink, breaking into crumbles.
2. Transfer to slow cooker. Stir in tomato sauce, water, salsa and taco seasoning. Cook, covered, 3-4 hours or until pasta is tender.
3. Remove insert; top with cheese. Let stand, covered, 15 minutes.

1 cup: 402 cal., 19g fat (6g sat. fat), 83mg chol., 1063mg sod., 32g carb. (4g sugars, 3g fiber), 29g pro.

CREAMY ONION PORK CHOPS

SLOW-COOKER SHORT RIBS

These ribs are an easy alternative to traditionally braised short ribs—you don't need to pay any attention to them once you get them started.
—Rebekah Beyer, Sabetha, KS

Prep: 30 min. • **Cook:** 6¼ hours
Makes: 6 servings

3 lbs. bone-in beef short ribs
½ tsp. salt
½ tsp. pepper
1 Tbsp. canola oil
4 medium carrots, cut into 1-in. pieces
1 cup beef broth
4 fresh thyme sprigs
1 bay leaf
2 large onions, cut into ½-in. wedges
6 garlic cloves, minced
1 Tbsp. tomato paste
2 cups dry red wine or beef broth
4 tsp. cornstarch
3 Tbsp. cold water
  Salt and pepper to taste

1. Sprinkle the ribs with salt and pepper. In a large skillet, heat oil over medium heat. In batches, brown ribs on all sides; transfer to a 4- or 5-qt. slow cooker. Add the carrots, broth, thyme and bay leaf to the ribs.
2. Add onions to the same skillet; cook and stir over medium heat 8-9 minutes or until tender. Add garlic and tomato paste; cook and stir 1 minute longer. Stir in the wine. Bring to a boil; cook 8-10 minutes or until liquid is reduced by half. Add to slow cooker. Cook, covered, on low 6-8 hours or until meat is tender.
3. Remove ribs and vegetables; keep warm. Transfer cooking juices to a small saucepan; skim off fat. Discard thyme and bay leaf. Bring juices to a boil. In a small bowl, mix the cornstarch and water until smooth; stir into cooking juices. Return to a boil; cook and stir 1-2 minutes or until thickened. If desired, sprinkle with additional salt and pepper. Serve with ribs and vegetables.

1 serving: 250 cal., 13g fat (5g sat. fat), 55mg chol., 412mg sod., 12g carb. (4g sugars, 2g fiber), 20g pro.

SLOW-COOKER SECRETS

When you are preparing veggies, such as carrots, in the slow cooker, remember to cut them into uniform sizes to ensure even cooking.

SLOW-COOKER SHORT RIBS

1. In a large bowl, mix bread crumbs, cheese, pepper and salt; stir in eggs. Add beef; mix lightly but thoroughly. Shape into 1½-in. balls. In a large skillet, brown meatballs in batches over medium heat; drain.

2. Place the first 5 sauce ingredients in a 6-qt. slow cooker; stir in garlic and seasonings. Add meatballs, stirring gently to coat. Cook, covered, on low 5-6 hours, until the meatballs are cooked through.

3. Carefully remove the bay leaves. Serve with spaghetti.

About 3 meatballs with ¾ cup sauce: 250 cal., 11g fat (4g sat. fat), 79mg chol., 1116mg sod., 20g carb. (7g sugars, 4g fiber), 20g pro.

SLOW-COOKED SPAGHETTI & MEATBALLS

SLOW-COOKED SPAGHETTI & MEATBALLS

I've been cooking for 50 years, and this dish is still one that guests request frequently. It is my No. 1 standby recipe and also makes amazing meatball sandwiches. The sauce works for any type of pasta.
—Jane Whittaker, Pensacola, FL

- -

Prep: 50 min. • **Cook:** 5 hours
Makes: 12 servings

- 1 cup seasoned bread crumbs
- 2 Tbsp. grated Parmesan and Romano cheese blend
- 1 tsp. pepper
- ½ tsp. salt
- 2 large eggs, lightly beaten
- 2 lbs. ground beef

SAUCE
- 1 large onion, finely chopped
- 1 medium green pepper, finely chopped
- 3 cans (15 oz. each) tomato sauce
- 2 cans (14½ oz. each) diced tomatoes, undrained
- 1 can (6 oz.) tomato paste
- 6 garlic cloves, minced
- 2 bay leaves
- 1 tsp. each dried basil, oregano and parsley flakes
- 1 tsp. salt
- ½ tsp. pepper
- ¼ tsp. crushed red pepper flakes
     Hot cooked spaghetti

PULLED PORK TATERS

This recipe is as hearty as it gets. It's part barbecued pork, part potatoes, completely delicious. My family can't get enough of this comforting warm-you-up baked potato rendition.
—Shannon Harris, Tyler, TX

- -

Prep: 15 min. • **Cook:** 6 hours
Makes: 6 servings

- 1 boneless pork loin roast (2 to 3 lbs.)
- 1 medium onion, chopped
- 1 cup ketchup
- 1 cup root beer
- ¼ cup cider vinegar
- 2 Tbsp. Worcestershire sauce
- 1 Tbsp. Louisiana-style hot sauce
- 2 tsp. salt
- 2 tsp. pepper
- 1 tsp. ground mustard
- 6 large potatoes
- 1 Tbsp. cornstarch
- 1 Tbsp. cold water
- 6 Tbsp. butter
- 6 Tbsp. sour cream
- 1½ cups shredded cheddar cheese
  Thinly sliced green onions, optional

1. Place roast in a 5-qt. slow cooker. Top with onion. Combine the ketchup, root beer, vinegar, Worcestershire, hot sauce, salt, pepper and mustard; pour over top. Cover and cook on low until meat is tender, 6-8 hours.

2. Meanwhile, scrub and pierce potatoes. Bake at 400° until tender, 50-55 minutes.

3. Remove pork; shred meat with 2 forks. Skim fat from cooking juices; transfer to a large saucepan. Bring liquid to a boil. Combine cornstarch and water until smooth; gradually stir into the pan. Bring to a boil; cook and stir until thickened, 2 minutes. Return meat to cooking juices; heat through.

4. With a sharp knife, cut an "X" in each potato; fluff with a fork. Top each with butter and pork mixture; top with sour cream. Sprinkle with cheese and, if desired, green onions.

1 serving: 795 cal., 29g fat (18g sat. fat), 145mg chol., 1677mg sod., 89g carb. (24g sugars, 7g fiber), 44g pro.

SLOW-COOKER SECRETS
Sharp cheddar cheese has been aged longer than regular cheddar. As cheese ages, its flavor becomes more pronounced. That's why using aged cheese in a slow-cooker recipe can add complexity and rich flavor, even to humble favorites like mac & cheese.

PULLED PORK TATERS

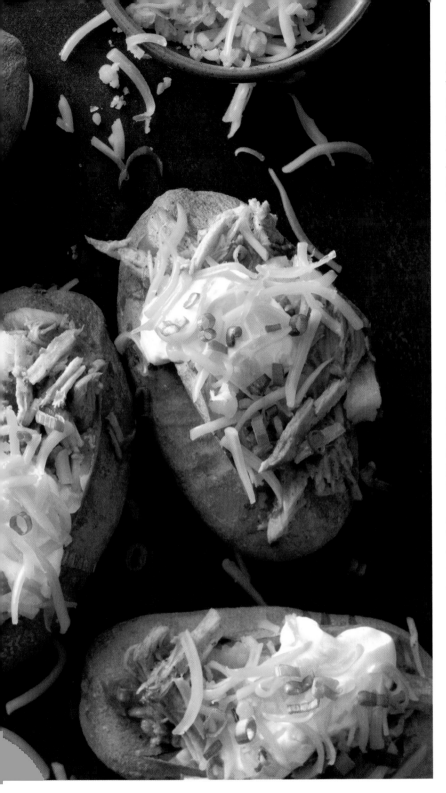

SWEET & TANGY BEEF ROAST

This is a tasty change to the classic beef roast. I love to serve this for cozy family dinners because I know it will be well-appreciated.
—Rachel Van Orden, Annville, PA

Prep: 10 min. • **Cook:** 7 hours + standing
Makes: 8 servings

1	Tbsp. canola oil
1	boneless beef chuck roast (4 lbs.)
2	medium onions, sliced into ½-in. rings
1	cup plus 2 Tbsp. water, divided
¾	cup honey barbecue sauce
½	cup red pepper jelly
3	Tbsp. hoisin sauce
2	Tbsp. cornstarch

1. In a large skillet, heat oil over medium heat. Brown roast on all sides. Transfer to a 5-qt. slow cooker; add onions and 1 cup water.

2. In a small bowl, mix barbecue sauce, jelly and hoisin sauce; pour over meat. Cook, covered, on low 7-9 hours or until meat is tender. Carefully remove roast and onions from slow cooker; tent roast with foil. Let stand 10 minutes before slicing meat.

3. Meanwhile, skim fat from cooking juices; transfer juices to a small saucepan. Bring to a boil. Mix the cornstarch and remaining water until smooth. Stir into pan. Return to a boil; cook and stir 1-2 minutes or until thickened. Serve with roast and onions.

5 oz. cooked beef with ⅓ cup sauce and ¼ cup onion: 516 cal., 25g fat (8g sat. fat), 135mg chol., 499mg sod., 31g carb. (22g sugars, 1g fiber), 39g pro.

CHICKEN & ARTICHOKE LASAGNA

My family loves lasagna, and I love the slow cooker. I wanted to try something a little different from the lasagna we usually make. This recipe not only tastes incredible, but it's hearty and convenient, too.
—Kelly Silvers, Edmond, OK

- -

Prep: 30 min. • **Cook:** 3 hours + standing
Makes: 8 servings

- 2 **cans (14 oz. each) water-packed artichoke hearts, drained and finely chopped**
- 1 **cup shredded Parmesan cheese, divided**
- ¼ **cup loosely packed basil leaves, finely chopped**
- 3 **garlic cloves, minced, divided**
- 1 **lb. ground chicken**
- 1 **Tbsp. canola oil**
- 1 **cup finely chopped onion**
- ¾ **tsp. salt**
- ½ **tsp. pepper**
- ½ **cup white wine**
- 1 **cup half-and-half cream**
- 1 **pkg. (8 oz.) cream cheese, softened**
- 1 **cup shredded Monterey Jack cheese**
- 1 **large egg**
- 1½ **cups 2% cottage cheese**
- 9 **no-cook lasagna noodles**
- 2 **cups shredded part-skim mozzarella cheese**
  Prepared pesto, optional
  Additional basil, optional

1. Fold two 18-in. square pieces of foil into thirds. Crisscross the strips and place strips on bottom and up sides of a 6-qt. slow cooker. Coat the strips with cooking spray. Combine the artichoke hearts, ½ cup Parmesan cheese, basil and 2 garlic cloves.

2. In a large skillet, crumble chicken over medium heat 6-8 minutes or until no longer pink; drain. Set chicken aside. Add oil and onion; cook and stir just until tender, 6-8 minutes. Add salt, pepper and remaining garlic; cook 1 minute longer. Stir in the wine. Bring to a boil; cook until the liquid is reduced by half, 4-5 minutes. Stir in cream, cream cheese and Monterey Jack cheese. Return chicken to pan. In a bowl, combine egg, cottage cheese and remaining ½ cup Parmesan.

3. Spread ¾ cup chicken mixture into slow cooker. Layer with 3 noodles (breaking noodles as necessary to fit), ¾ cup chicken mixture, ½ cup cottage cheese mixture, 1 cup artichoke mixture and ½ cup mozzarella cheese. Repeat layers twice; top with remaining ½ cup mozzarella cheese. Cook, covered, on low until noodles are tender, 3-4 hours. Remove slow cooker insert and let stand 30 minutes. If desired, serve with pesto and sprinkle with additional basil.
1 serving: 588 cal., 34g fat (18g sat. fat), 144mg chol., 1187mg sod., 31g carb. (6g sugars, 1g fiber), 36g pro.

CHICKEN & ARTICHOKE LASAGNA

⅓ cup sliced onion
1½ cups hot cooked egg noodles

1. Rub pork with salt and pepper; cut in half. In a 1½-qt. slow cooker, combine the cornstarch, ½ cup crushed tomatoes, sun-dried tomatoes and savory. Top with mushrooms, onion and pork. Pour remaining tomatoes over pork. Cover and cook on low 3-4 hours, until meat is tender.
2. Remove meat and cut into slices. Stir cooking juices until smooth; serve with pork and noodles.

1 serving: 360 cal., 7g fat (2g sat. fat), 122mg chol., 309mg sod., 32g carb. (3g sugars, 3g fiber), 40g pro. **Diabetic exchanges:** 5 lean meat, 2 vegetable, 1 starch.

Baked Mushroom Pork Ragout: Assemble as directed, using a greased 1½-qt. baking dish. Cover and bake at 425° for 30-35 minutes or until a meat thermometer reads 160°. Serve as directed.

MUSHROOM PORK RAGOUT

MUSHROOM PORK RAGOUT

Savory, slow-cooked pork is luscious served in a delightful tomato gravy over noodles. It's a nice change from regular pork roast. I serve it with broccoli or green beans on the side.
—Connie McDowell, Greenwood, DE

- -

Prep: 20 min. • **Cook:** 3 hours
Makes: 2 servings

1   pork tenderloin (¾ lb.)
⅛   tsp. salt
⅛   tsp. pepper
1   Tbsp. cornstarch
¾   cup canned crushed tomatoes, divided
1   Tbsp. chopped sun-dried tomatoes (not packed in oil)
1¼   tsp. dried savory
1½   cups sliced fresh mushrooms

EASY LEMON-ROSEMARY CHICKEN

This slow cooker chicken is perfect for special gatherings. It pairs well with a variety of sides, too. Plus, the slow cooker does most of the work!
—Courtney Stultz, Weir, KS

- -

Prep: 10 min. • **Cook:** 4 hours + standing
Makes: 6 servings

- 1 **broiler/fryer chicken (3 to 4 lbs.)**
- 2 **celery ribs, cut into 1-in. pieces**
- 1 **medium onion, chopped**
- 1 **medium apple, sliced**
- 1 **Tbsp. olive oil**
- 1 **Tbsp. minced fresh rosemary or 1 tsp. dried rosemary, crushed**
- 2 **tsp. sea salt**
- 1½ **tsp. minced fresh thyme or ½ tsp. dried thyme**
- 1½ **tsp. paprika**
- 1 **garlic clove, minced**
- 1 **tsp. pepper**
- 1 **medium lemon, sliced**

1. Fill chicken cavity with celery, onion and apple. Tuck wings under chicken; tie drumsticks together. Place in a 6-qt. slow cooker, breast side up. Rub chicken with oil; rub with rosemary, salt, thyme, paprika, garlic and pepper. Top with the lemon slices.

2. Cook chicken, covered, on low until a thermometer inserted in thickest part of thigh reads at least 170°-175°, 4-5 hours. Remove chicken from slow cooker; tent with foil. Discard the vegetables and apple. Let chicken stand 15 minutes before carving.

5 oz. cooked chicken: 318 cal., 19g fat (5g sat. fat), 104mg chol., 730mg sod., 1g carb. (0 sugars, 0 fiber), 33g pro.

ALFREDO CHICKEN
& BISCUITS

ALFREDO CHICKEN & BISCUITS

For a cute potpie presentation, I like to dish out this comforting creamy chicken in ramekins, topping each with a biscuit. I sometimes serve it over hot linguine, too.
—Faith Cromwell, San Francisco, CA

Prep: 40 min. • **Cook:** 3 hours
Makes: 10 servings

- 2 jars (16 oz. each) Alfredo sauce
- 2 cans (15¼ oz. each) whole kernel corn, drained
- 2 cups frozen peas, thawed
- 2 jars (4½ oz. each) sliced mushrooms, drained
- 1 medium onion, chopped
- 1 cup water
- 1 tsp. garlic salt
- ½ tsp. pepper
- 2 Tbsp. canola oil
- 8 boneless skinless chicken breast halves (6 oz. each)
- 1 tube (12 oz.) refrigerated buttermilk biscuits
- 3 Tbsp. grated Parmesan cheese

1. In a large bowl, combine the first 8 ingredients. Pour half of the Alfredo mixture into a 6-qt. slow cooker.
2. In a large skillet, heat the oil over medium-high heat. Brown chicken in batches on both sides. Transfer chicken to slow cooker.
3. Pour the remaining Alfredo mixture over chicken. Cook, covered, on low 3-4 hours or until chicken is tender (a thermometer inserted in chicken should read at least 165°).
4. Arrange biscuits on an ungreased baking sheet; sprinkle with cheese. Bake according to package directions.
5. Remove chicken from slow cooker. Shred with 2 forks; return to slow cooker. Serve chicken mixture in ramekins or shallow bowls topped with a biscuit.

1 serving: 480 cal., 20g fat (9g sat. fat), 102mg chol., 1305mg sod., 36g carb. (10g sugars, 5g fiber), 37g pro.

PEAR & POMEGRANATE
LAMB TAGINE

PEAR & POMEGRANATE LAMB TAGINE

Pomegranate, pear and orange go together so well that I decided to use them to prepare a Middle Eastern-themed tagine with lamb. This tastes delicious served over couscous, polenta or cauliflower mashed with some feta cheese.
—Arlene Erlbach, Morton Grove, IL

- -

Prep: 20 min. • **Cook:** 6 hours
Makes: 4 servings

2½ **lbs. lamb shanks**
2 **large pears, finely chopped**
3 **cups thinly sliced shallots**
½ **cup orange juice, divided**
½ **cup pomegranate juice, divided**
1 **Tbsp. honey**
1½ **tsp. ground cinnamon**
1 **tsp. salt**
1 **tsp. ground allspice**
1 **tsp. ground cardamom**
¼ **cup pomegranate seeds**
¼ **cup minced fresh parsley**
  Cooked couscous, optional

1. Place lamb in a 5- or 6-qt. oval slow cooker. Add pears and shallots. Combine ¼ cup orange juice, ¼ cup pomegranate juice, honey and seasonings; add to slow cooker.
2. Cook, covered, on low until meat is tender, 6-8 hours. Remove lamb to a rimmed serving platter; keep warm. Stir remaining orange and pomegranate juices into cooking liquid; pour over lamb. Sprinkle with pomegranate seeds and parsley. If desired, serve over couscous.
½ lamb shank with 1 cup shallot mixture: 438 cal., 13g fat (5g sat. fat), 99mg chol., 680mg sod., 52g carb. (28g sugars, 5g fiber), 31g pro.

CHICKEN-CRANBERRY
HOT DISH

CHICKEN-CRANBERRY HOT DISH

In my family, we never eat chicken without cranberry sauce! This chicken is fall-off-the-bone tender; the sauce is divine with mashed potatoes.
—Lorraine Caland, Shuniah, ON

- -

Prep: 30 min. • **Cook:** 4 hours
Makes: 4 servings (2 cups sauce)

2 **Tbsp. canola oil**
1 **broiler/fryer chicken (4 lbs.), cut up**
½ **tsp. salt**
¼ **tsp. pepper**
1 **medium onion, chopped**
1 **celery rib, chopped**
1 **cup whole-berry cranberry sauce**
½ **cup chili sauce**
2 **Tbsp. brown sugar**
1 **Tbsp. grated lemon zest**
1 **Tbsp. balsamic vinegar**
1 **Tbsp. A.1. steak sauce**
1 **Tbsp. Dijon mustard**

1. In a large skillet, heat the oil over medium-high heat. Brown the chicken on both sides in batches; sprinkle with the salt and pepper. Transfer to a 4-qt. slow cooker.
2. Add the onion and celery to skillet; saute over medium-high heat until tender, 3-4 minutes. Stir in remaining ingredients. Pour over chicken.
3. Cook, covered, on low until chicken is tender, 4-5 hours. Skim fat from cooking juices; serve with chicken.
1 serving with ½ cup sauce: 829 cal., 41g fat (10g sat. fat), 209mg chol., 1140mg sod., 46g carb. (33g sugars, 2g fiber), 66g pro. (5g sugars, 3g fiber), 32g pro.

SIDES

NO-FUSS DRESSING

NO-FUSS DRESSING

Here's an easy dressing that's perfect for holiday get-togethers. Once it's in the slow cooker, you're free to turn your attention to the other dishes.
—Rita Nodland, Bismarck, ND

Prep: 15 min. • **Cook:** 3 hours
Makes: 8 servings

- 2 Tbsp. olive oil
- 1 medium celery rib, chopped
- 1 small onion, chopped
- 8 cups unseasoned stuffing cubes
- 1 tsp. poultry seasoning
- ¼ tsp. salt
- ¼ tsp. pepper
- 2 cups reduced-sodium chicken broth

1. In a large skillet, heat oil over medium-high heat; saute celery and onion until tender. Place stuffing cubes, celery mixture and seasonings in a large bowl; toss to combine. Gradually stir in broth.
2. Transfer to a greased 5-qt. slow cooker. Cook, covered, on low until heated through, 3-4 hours.
½ cup: 226 cal., 5g fat (0 sat. fat), 0 chol., 635mg sod., 40g carb. (3g sugars, 3g fiber), 8g pro.

SLOW-COOKER SECRETS
Turn this side into a main by stirring some cooked and cubed chicken or turkey into the dressing during the last hour of cooking. Add a bit more broth if desired.

SLOW-COOKED
MAC & CHEESE

SLOW-COOKED MAC & CHEESE

Slow-cooked mac and cheese—the words alone are enough to make mouths water. This is comfort food at its best: rich and extra cheesy. And the slow cooker makes it so easy.
—Shelby Molina, Whitewater, WI

Prep: 25 min. • **Cook:** 2½ hours
Makes: 9 servings

- 2 cups uncooked elbow macaroni
- 1 can (12 oz.) evaporated milk
- 1½ cups whole milk
- 2 large eggs
- ¼ cup butter, melted
- 1 tsp. salt
- 2½ cups shredded cheddar cheese
- 2½ cups shredded sharp cheddar cheese, divided

1. Cook macaroni according to the package directions; drain and rinse in cold water. In a large bowl, combine the evaporated milk, milk, eggs, butter and salt. Stir in cheddar cheese, 2 cups sharp cheddar cheese and macaroni.
2. Transfer to a greased 3-qt. slow cooker. Cover and cook on low for 2½-3 hours or until center is set, stirring once. Sprinkle with the remaining sharp cheddar cheese.
¾ cup: 415 cal., 28g fat (20g sat. fat), 143mg chol., 745mg sod., 20g carb. (6g sugars, 1g fiber), 21g pro.

GOOEY OLD-FASHIONED STEAMED MOLASSES BREAD

While I was growing up, the smell of this bread often greeted me as I walked in the door from school. I thought that everyone baked bread in a slow cooker. My grandmother, my mother and I—and now my daughters—all bake this. It's so tasty and comforting!
—Bonnie Geavaras-Bootz, Chandler, AZ

- -

Prep: 20 min. • **Cook:** 3 hours + cooling
Makes: 16 servings

2	**cups All-Bran**
1	**cup all-purpose flour**
1	**cup whole wheat flour**
1	**cup dried cranberries**
1½	**tsp. baking powder**
1	**tsp. baking soda**
1	**tsp. salt**
½	**tsp. ground cinnamon**
1	**large egg, room temperature**
1¾	**cups buttermilk**
½	**cup molasses**
2	**Tbsp. honey**

1. Layer two 24-in. pieces of foil. Starting with a long side, roll up foil to make a 1-in.-wide strip; shape into a coil. Place on bottom of a 5-qt. slow cooker to make a rack.
2. Combine bran, flours, cranberries, baking powder, baking soda, salt and cinnamon. In another bowl, beat egg, buttermilk, molasses and honey. Stir into flour mixture just until blended (do not overbeat). Pour into a greased and floured 2-qt. baking dish. Tightly cover with lightly greased foil. Place in the prepared slow cooker. Cook, covered, on high about 3 hours, until a thermometer reads 190-200°.
3. Remove dish to a wire rack; cool 10 minutes before inverting loaf onto the rack. Serve warm or cold.
Note: To substitute for each cup of buttermilk, use 1 Tbsp. white vinegar or lemon juice plus enough milk to measure 1 cup. Stir, then let stand 5 min. Or, use 1 cup plain yogurt or 1¾ tsp. cream of tartar plus 1 cup milk.
1 wedge: 157 cal., 1g fat (0 sat. fat), 13mg chol., 351mg sod., 36g carb. (19g sugars, 4g fiber), 4g pro.

GOOEY OLD-FASHIONED STEAMED MOLASSES BREAD

CHEESY SLOW-COOKED CORN

Even those who usually don't eat much corn will ask for a second helping of this creamy, cheesy side dish. Folks love the flavor, but I love how simple it is to make with ingredients I usually have on hand.

—Mary Ann Truitt, Wichita, KS

Prep: 5 min. • **Cook:** 3 hours
Makes: 12 servings

- 9½ cups (48 oz.) **frozen corn**
- 11 oz. **cream cheese, softened**
- ¼ cup **butter, cubed**
- 3 Tbsp. **water**
- 3 Tbsp. **2% milk**
- 2 Tbsp. **sugar**
- 6 slices **American cheese, cut into small pieces**

In a 4- or 5-qt. slow cooker, combine all ingredients. Cook, covered, on low, until heated through and cheese is melted, 3-4 hours, stirring once.

1 cup: 265 cal., 16g fat (9g sat. fat), 39mg chol., 227mg sod., 27g carb. (6g sugars, 2g fiber), 7g pro.

BLACK-EYED PEAS WITH HAM

Here's a regional favorite I grew to love after moving to the South. Serve the dish as a side with poultry, or make it your main course and round out the meal with greens and cornbread.
—Tammie Merrill, Wake Forest, NC

Prep: 10 min. + soaking • **Cook:** 8 hours
Makes: 10 servings

- 1 **pkg. (16 oz.) dried black-eyed peas**
- 1 **cup cubed fully cooked ham**
- 1 **medium onion, finely chopped**
- 3 **garlic cloves, minced**
- 2 **tsp. seasoned salt**
- 1 **tsp. pepper**
- 4 **cups water**
  Thinly sliced green onions, optional

Rinse and sort black-eyed peas; soak according to package directions. Drain and rinse the peas, discarding liquid. Transfer peas to a 4-qt. slow cooker. Stir in the next 6 ingredients. Cook, covered, on low 8-10 hours or until peas are tender. Serve with a slotted spoon. Sprinkle with green onions if desired.
¾ cup: 76 cal., 1g fat (0 sat. fat), 8mg chol., 476mg sod., 11g carb. (2g sugars, 3g fiber), 7g pro.

CREAMY CHEESE POTATOES

CREAMY CHEESE POTATOES

This easy potato dish is a comfort food classic. It's popular at winter dinners.
—Greg Christiansen, Parker, KS

Prep: 10 min. • **Cook:** 3¼ hours
Makes: 10 servings

- 1 **can (10¾ oz.) condensed cream of chicken soup, undiluted**
- 1 **can (10¾ oz.) condensed cream of mushroom soup, undiluted**
- 3 **Tbsp. butter, melted**
- 1 **pkg. (30 oz.) frozen shredded hash brown potatoes, thawed**
- 2 **cups shredded cheddar cheese**
- 1 **cup sour cream**
  Minced fresh parsley, optional

1. In a 3-qt. slow cooker coated with cooking spray, combine the soups and butter. Stir in potatoes.
2. Cover and cook on low for 3-4 hours or until the potatoes are tender. Stir in cheese and sour cream. Cover and cook 15-30 minutes longer or until heated through. If desired, top with additional shredded cheddar cheese and minced fresh parsley.
¾ cup: 278 cal., 17g fat (10g sat. fat), 52mg chol., 614mg sod., 21g carb. (2g sugars, 2g fiber), 9g pro.

SLOW-COOKER MONKEY BREAD

I often take this monkey bread to church potlucks—children and adults love it! The rum extract is optional.
—Lisa Leaper, Worthington, OH

- -

Prep: 20 min. • **Cook:** 2½ hours
Makes: 10 servings

1 cup sugar
¾ cup packed brown sugar
2 tsp. ground cinnamon
½ tsp. ground allspice
4 tubes (6 oz. each) refrigerated buttermilk biscuits, quartered
¾ cup butter, melted
½ cup apple juice
1 tsp. vanilla extract
1 tsp. rum extract
  Toasted chopped pecans, optional

1. Line a 5-qt. slow cooker with a piece of aluminum foil, letting ends extend up the sides. Grease foil.
2. Combine the sugars, cinnamon and allspice in a large bowl; sprinkle 3 Tbsp. sugar mixture in bottom of prepared slow cooker. Add biscuit pieces to bowl; toss to coat. Transfer coated biscuits to slow cooker; sprinkle any remaining sugar mixture over biscuits.
3. Stir together butter, apple juice and extracts; pour over biscuits.
4. Cook, covered, on low 2½-3 hours. Remove lid and let stand for 10 minutes. Carefully invert onto serving platter. If desired, sprinkle with pecans.

8 biscuit pieces: 473 cal., 22g fat (12g sat. fat), 37mg chol., 675mg sod., 68g carb. (41g sugars, 0 fiber), 4g pro.

> **READER RAVE...**
> *"I made this while on a recent RV trip with friends. We all really enjoyed it—I did not have any leftovers. I will be making this often!"*
> —XXCSKIER, TASTEOFHOME.COM

SLOW-COOKER MONKEY BREAD

SIMPLY INCREDIBLE GRITS

SIMPLY INCREDIBLE GRITS

Since moving to the South, I have come to love grits! I also adore my slow cooker, and I worked to find a way to make perfect grits without stirring on the stovetop. I knew this recipe was a winner when my mother-in-law overheard someone say at a church potluck that it just wasn't right that a Midwesterner could make such delicious grits!
—Tacy Fleury, Clinton, SC

- -

Prep: 10 min. • **Cook:** 2½ hours
Makes: 6 servings

2⅔ **cups water**
1½ **cups uncooked**
　　old-fashioned grits
1½ **cups 2% milk**
3 **Tbsp. butter, cubed**
2 **tsp. chicken bouillon granules**
½ **tsp. salt**
1 **cup shredded cheddar cheese**
⅓ **cup grated Parmesan cheese**

Combine the first 6 ingredients in a greased 3-qt. slow cooker. Cook, covered, on low until liquid is absorbed and grits are tender, 2½-3 hours, stirring every 45 minutes. Stir in the cheeses until melted. Serve the grits immediately.
¾ cup: 334 cal., 15g fat (9g sat. fat), 43mg chol., 755mg sod., 38g carb. (3g sugars, 2g fiber), 11g pro.

PINEAPPLE SWEET POTATOES

PINEAPPLE SWEET POTATOES

Pineapple and pecans make a pretty topping for this versatile side dish. It's light, tasty and not too sweet, and making it in the slow cooker leaves extra space in the oven for other dishes.
—Bette Fulcher, Lexington, TX

- -

Prep: 15 min. • **Cook:** 4 hours
Makes: 12 servings

4 **large eggs, lightly beaten**
6 **to 6½ cups mashed**
　　sweet potatoes
　　(without added milk or butter)
1 **cup 2% milk**
½ **cup butter, melted**
1 **tsp. salt**
1 **tsp. ground cinnamon**
1 **tsp. vanilla extract**
½ **tsp. ground nutmeg**
½ **tsp. lemon extract**
1 **can (8 oz.) sliced**
　　pineapple, drained
¼ **cup chopped pecans**

1. In a large bowl, mix the first 9 ingredients. Transfer to a greased 3-qt. slow cooker. Top with pineapple and pecans.
2. Cook, covered, on low until a thermometer reads 160°, 4-5 hours.
¾ cup: 262 cal., 10g fat (5g sat. fat), 81mg chol., 281mg sod., 38g carb. (19g sugars, 3g fiber), 5g pro.

GARLIC-ROSEMARY CAULIFLOWER PUREE

I love this delicious fake take on mashed potatoes, and it doesn't heat up my kitchen! Treat leftovers as you would leftover mashed potatoes and make mock potato pancakes.
—Sharon Gibson, Hendersonville, NC

Prep: 15 min. • **Cook:** 3 hours
Makes: 6 servings

- 2 Tbsp. butter, melted
- 1 medium onion, chopped
- 1 large head cauliflower, cut into florets
- 1 pkg. (6½ oz.) spreadable garlic and herb cheese
- ½ cup grated Parmesan cheese
- ½ tsp. Montreal steak seasoning
- ¼ tsp. pepper
- 1 tsp. minced fresh rosemary or ½ tsp. dried rosemary, crushed
- ¼ cup heavy cream, warmed
  Optional: Additional minced fresh rosemary and pepper

1. Place melted butter and onion in a 4- or 5-qt. slow cooker. Add cauliflower; cook, covered, on high until cauliflower is tender, 3-4 hours.
2. Process in batches in food processor to desired consistency. Add the next 6 ingredients and process until blended. If desired, serve puree with additional rosemary and pepper.

⅔ cup: 245 cal., 20g fat (12g sat. fat), 54mg chol., 386mg sod., 11g carb. (5g sugars, 3g fiber), 6g pro.

SLOW-COOKED SPINACH & RICE

SLOW-COOKED SPINACH & RICE

I started making this in the slow cooker to save oven space during the holidays. It's so convenient that I no longer reserve it for special occasions!
—Erica Polly, Sun Prairie, WI

Prep: 20 min. • **Cook:** 3 hours + standing
Makes: 8 servings

- 2 **Tbsp. butter**
- 1 **medium onion, finely chopped**
- 2 **garlic cloves, minced**
- ¼ **tsp. dried thyme**
- 4 **cups reduced-sodium chicken broth**
- 2 **pkg. (10 oz. each) frozen chopped spinach, thawed and squeezed dry**
- 1 **pkg. (8 oz.) cream cheese, softened**
- 1 **tsp. salt**
- 1 **tsp. pepper**
- 2 **cups uncooked converted rice**
- 2 **cups shredded cheddar cheese**
- ½ **cup panko bread crumbs**
- ¼ **cup grated Parmesan cheese**

1. In a large saucepan, melt butter over medium heat. Add onion; cook and stir 4-6 minutes or until tender. Add garlic and thyme; cook 1 minute longer. Add broth; bring to a simmer. Remove from heat. Stir in spinach, cream cheese, salt and pepper until blended. Transfer to a 4-qt. slow cooker. Stir in rice.
2. Cook, covered, 3-4 hours or until rice is tender and liquid is absorbed, stirring halfway through cooking. Remove insert; top with cheddar cheese. Let stand, covered, 20 minutes. Top with bread crumbs and Parmesan cheese.
1 serving: 488 cal., 25g fat (14g sat. fat), 71mg chol., 1016mg sod., 48g carb. (3g sugars, 3g fiber), 19g pro.

SLOW-COOKER SECRETS
Be sure to remove as much liquid as possible from the spinach before adding it to the slow cooker. Because steam can't escape from a slow cooker, it's important to remove any unneeded liquid before cooking begins.

CHEESY SPOON BREAD CASSEROLE

I love this spoon bread casserole because it's creamy with a little southwestern kick. This is comfort food at its finest and is a vivid way to add a unique dish to the usual holiday lineup. Sometimes we scoop chili on top.

—Barbara Miller, Oakdale, MN

Prep: 20 min. • **Cook:** 4 hours
Makes: 8 servings

- **2   cups shredded cheddar cheese**
- **1   can (15¼ oz.) whole kernel corn, drained**
- **1   can (14½ oz.) diced tomatoes, drained**
- **1   cup sour cream**
- **⅔ cup all-purpose flour**
- **½ cup yellow cornmeal**
- **½ cup butter, melted**
- **3   Tbsp. sugar**
- **2   Tbsp. taco seasoning**
- **2½ tsp. baking powder**
- **½ tsp. salt**
  Optional toppings: Chopped green onions and minced fresh cilantro

Combine the first 11 ingredients in a greased 3-qt. slow cooker. Cook, covered, on low until a toothpick inserted in the center comes out clean, 4-5 hours. If desired, top with green onions and cilantro.

1 serving: 412 cal., 28g fat (16g sat. fat), 66mg chol., 1028mg sod., 31g carb. (11g sugars, 3g fiber), 11g pro.

BROCCOLI-CHEDDAR
HASH BROWNS

BROCCOLI-CHEDDAR HASH BROWNS

Need a new go-to? These hash browns will fit the bill. This wonderfully gooey combination of tender potatoes and broccoli pairs well with a wide variety of entrees.

—Deborah Biggs, Omaha, NE

Prep: 20 min. • **Cook:** 4½ hours
Makes: 8 servings

- **1   pkg. (30 oz.) frozen shredded hash brown potatoes**
- **2   cups frozen broccoli florets**
- **1¼ cups shredded sharp cheddar cheese, divided**
- **2   green onions, chopped**
- **2   Tbsp. butter**
- **2   Tbsp. all-purpose flour**
- **½ cup whole milk**
- **1   can (10¾ oz.) condensed cream of broccoli soup, undiluted**
- **½ tsp. salt**
- **½ tsp. Dijon mustard**

1. In a greased 4- or 5-qt. slow cooker, combine the hash browns, broccoli, ¾ cup cheese and onions.

2. In a small saucepan, melt butter. Stir in flour until smooth; gradually add milk. Bring to a boil; cook and stir for 1 minute or until thickened. Stir in the soup, salt and mustard. Pour over potato mixture; stir to combine.

3. Cover and cook on low for 4-5 hours or until potatoes are tender. Sprinkle with remaining cheese. Cover and cook 30 minutes longer or until the cheese is melted.

¾ cup: 224 cal., 10g fat (6g sat. fat), 29mg chol., 544mg sod., 26g carb. (3g sugars, 2g fiber), 8g pro.

MUSHROOMS MARSALA WITH BARLEY

This vegetarian recipe is a tasty mashup of chicken Marsala and mushroom barley soup. It's terrific as a main dish, but it can also be served, with or without the barley, as a side.
—Arlene Erlbach, Morton Grove, IL

- -

Prep: 20 min. • **Cook:** 4¼ hours
Makes: 6 servings

1½ lbs. baby portobello mushrooms, cut into ¾-in. chunks
1 cup thinly sliced shallots
3 Tbsp. olive oil
½ tsp. minced fresh thyme
¾ cup Marsala wine, divided
3 Tbsp. reduced-fat sour cream
2 Tbsp. all-purpose flour
1½ tsp. grated lemon zest
¼ tsp. salt
¼ cup crumbled goat cheese
¼ cup minced fresh parsley
2½ cups cooked barley

1. In a 4- or 5-qt. slow cooker, combine mushrooms, shallots, olive oil and thyme. Add ¼ cup Marsala wine. Cook, covered, on low about 4 hours, until vegetables are tender.
2. Stir in the sour cream, flour, lemon zest, salt and remaining Marsala. Cook, covered, on low for 15 minutes longer. Sprinkle with goat cheese and parsley. Serve with hot cooked barley.
¾ cup: 235 cal., 9g fat (2g sat. fat), 7mg chol., 139mg sod., 31g carb. (6g sugars, 5g fiber), 7g pro. **Diabetic exchanges:** 2 starch, 2 fat, 1 vegetable..

SLOW-COOKER SECRETS

Marsala is an Italian wine fortified with alcohol. Its distinctive flavor is found in many Italian desserts, entrees and side dishes. You can substitute red or white wine, beer or broth for the Marsala wine. Doing so, however, will change the flavor dramatically, particularly in slow-cooked dishes.

MUSHROOMS MARSALA WITH BARLEY

NICOLE'S
SLOW-COOKER BROCCOLI

TRULY TASTY TURNIPS WITH GREENS

These savory greens are a hit at every church dinner I take them to. Adjust the seasonings as you please to make this recipe your own.
—Amy Inman, Hiddenite, NC

- -

Prep: 20 min. • **Cook:** 5 hours
Makes: 14 servings

- 2¾ lbs. turnips, peeled and cut into ½-in. cubes
- 1 bunch fresh turnip greens (about 12 oz.), chopped
- 8 oz. cubed fully cooked country ham or 2 smoked ham hocks (about 1½ lbs.)
- 1 medium onion, chopped
- 3 Tbsp. sugar
- 1½ tsp. coarsely ground pepper
- 1¼ tsp. salt
- 2 cartons (32 oz. each) chicken broth

In a greased 6- or 7-qt. slow cooker, combine all ingredients. Cook, covered, on low 5-6 hours or until vegetables are tender, stirring once. If using ham hocks, remove meat from bones when cool enough to handle; cut ham into small pieces and return to slow cooker. Serve with a slotted spoon.

¾ cup: 58 cal., 1g fat (0 sat. fat), 9mg chol., 514mg sod., 9g carb. (6g sugars, 2g fiber), 5g pro. **Diabetic exchanges:** 1 vegetable, 1 lean meat.

NICOLE'S SLOW-COOKER BROCCOLI

My sister is a huge inspiration to me and an amazing force behind who I have become. This is one of her favorite dishes. It's a tasty side. Typically, little to none of it is ever left over!
—Toni Ann Moschello, Manahawkin, NJ

- -

Prep: 10 min. • **Cook:** 3 hours
Makes: 6 servings

- 2 pkg. (12 oz. each) frozen broccoli with cheese sauce, thawed
- 1 can (10½ oz.) condensed cream of celery soup, undiluted
- 2 cups shredded cheddar cheese
- ½ cup chopped onion
- 2 tsp. coarsely ground pepper
- 1 tsp. Worcestershire sauce
- 16 Ritz crackers, crushed
- 2 Tbsp. butter, cubed

Mix first 6 ingredients. Transfer to a greased 3-qt. slow cooker. Sprinkle with crackers; dot with butter. Cook, covered, on low until the broccoli is tender, 3-4 hours.

¾ cup: 326 cal., 23g fat (12g sat. fat), 54mg chol., 951mg sod., 18g carb. (4g sugars, 3g fiber), 11g pro.

TRULY TASTY
TURNIPS WITH GREENS

SAVORY SAUSAGE STUFFING

I used to make the same old dressing every year for Thanksgiving. About 10 years ago, I decided to jazz up my recipe by adding pork sausage. Now everyone requests this dish for all our holiday meals.
—Ursula Hernandez, Waltham, MN

- -

Prep: 30 min. • **Cook:** 2 hours
Makes: 16 servings

- 1 **lb. sage pork sausage**
- ½ **cup butter, cubed**
- ½ **lb. fresh mushrooms, finely chopped**
- 6 **celery ribs, finely chopped**
- 2 **small onions, finely chopped**
- 2 **garlic cloves, minced**
- 1 **loaf (13 oz.) French bread, cut into ½-in. cubes (about 17 cups)**
- 4 **cups cubed multigrain bread (½ in.)**
- 1 **Tbsp. rubbed sage**
- 1 **cup chicken stock**
- ½ **cup white wine or chicken stock**
- 1 **cup dried cranberries**
- ½ **cup sunflower kernels, optional**

1. In a large skillet, cook sausage over medium heat 4-6 minutes or until no longer pink, breaking it into crumbles; drain. In a stockpot, melt butter over medium heat. Add mushrooms, celery and onions; cook and stir 3-4 minutes or until tender. Add garlic; cook 1 minute longer. Remove from heat.

2. Stir in sausage. Add the bread cubes and sage; toss to combine. Add chicken stock and wine. Stir in cranberries and, if desired, sunflower kernels. Transfer to a greased 6-qt. slow cooker. Cook, covered, on low 2-3 hours or until heated through, stirring once.
¾ cup: 261 cal., 13g fat (6g sat. fat), 31mg chol., 446mg sod., 28g carb. (10g sugars, 2g fiber), 8g pro.

READER RAVE...

"For decades I have been searching for stuffing with a wow factor. This is it! My family loved it, and the recipe allowed me to easily customize based on what I had on hand (cubing extra garlic bread left over from the night before). And there were no leftovers—that told me what I needed to know!"
—DAWNEPAFFORD, TASTEOFHOME.COM

SAVORY SAUSAGE STUFFING

SLOW-COOKED WILD RICE

This recipe has become such a family heirloom that I asked permission from my mother before passing it along. It has traveled to weddings, baptisms, landmark birthdays and wedding anniversaries—and it always makes people happy.
—Janet Mahowald, Rice Lake, WI

- -

Prep: 15 min. • **Cook:** 4 hours
Makes: 8 cups

- 1 **lb. bulk pork sausage**
- 4 **celery ribs, chopped**
- 1 **small onion, chopped**
- 1 **can (10¾ oz.) condensed cream of mushroom soup, undiluted**
- 1 **can (10¾ oz.) condensed cream of chicken soup, undiluted**
- 1 **cup uncooked wild rice**
- 1 **can (4 oz.) mushroom stems and pieces, drained**
- 3 **cups chicken broth**

1. In a large skillet, cook and crumble sausage with celery and onion over medium heat until the sausage is no longer pink and vegetables are tender, 6-8 minutes; drain. Transfer to a 3-qt. slow cooker. Add the soups, rice and mushrooms. Stir in broth.
2. Cook, covered, on low until rice is tender, 4-5 hours.

¾ cup: 236 cal., 14g fat (4g sat. fat), 30mg chol., 1059mg sod., 19g carb. (2g sugars, 2g fiber), 9g pro.

DESSERTS

PUMPKIN LATTE CUSTARD

PUMPKIN LATTE CUSTARD

Here is a traditional slow-cooker pumpkin custard with some espresso powder for a latte effect.
—Shelly Bevington, Hermiston, OR

- -

Prep: 10 min. • **Cook:** 6 hours
Makes: 8 servings

1 **can (29 oz.) pumpkin**
1½ **cups sugar**
1 **can (12 oz.) evaporated milk**
4 **large eggs, lightly beaten**
1 **Tbsp. pumpkin pie spice**
1 **Tbsp. instant espresso powder**
1 **tsp. salt**
Gingersnap cookies, crushed
Whipped cream, optional

1. Pour 1 in. water into a 6-qt. slow cooker. Layer two 24-in. pieces of foil; roll up lengthwise to make a 1-in.-thick roll. Shape into a ring; place in slow cooker to make a rack.
2. Whisk together first 7 ingredients. Transfer to a greased 2-qt. baking dish; set aside. Fold an 18x12-in. piece of foil lengthwise into thirds, making a sling. Use sling to lower the baking dish onto foil rack, not allowing sides to touch slow cooker. Cover slow cooker with a double layer of white paper towels; place lid securely over towels.
3. Cook, covered, on low 6-7 hours or until a thermometer reads 160°. Remove baking dish from slow cooker using sling. Top servings with crushed gingersnap cookies and, if desired, whipped cream.
1 serving: 280 cal., 6g fat (3g sat. fat), 108mg chol., 381mg sod., 52g carb. (46g sugars, 3g fiber), 7g pro.

CHOCOLATE ESPRESSO LAVA CAKE

CHOCOLATE ESPRESSO LAVA CAKE

My aunt inspired this cake, which can satisfy even the strongest chocolate craving. It's gooey and saucy but not crazy sweet—and it's potluck-perfect.
—Lisa Renshaw, Kansas City, MO

- -

Prep: 15 min. • **Cook:** 3 hours + standing
Makes: 16 servings

1 **pkg. chocolate fudge cake mix (regular size)**
1 **Tbsp. instant espresso powder**
3 **cups 2% milk**
1 **pkg. (3.9 oz.) instant chocolate pudding mix**
1 **cup semisweet chocolate chips**
1 **cup white baking chips**

1. Prepare cake mix batter according to package directions, adding espresso powder before mixing. Transfer to a greased 4-qt. slow cooker.
2. In a small bowl, whisk milk and pudding mix 2 minutes. Let stand until soft-set, about 2 minutes. Pour over the batter. Cook, covered, on low 3-3½ hours or until a toothpick inserted in the cake portion comes out with moist crumbs.
3. Sprinkle top with chocolate chips and baking chips. Turn off slow cooker; remove insert. Let stand, uncovered, until chips are softened, 15-30 minutes. Serve warm.
⅔ cup: 327 cal., 15g fat (6g sat. fat), 41mg chol., 317mg sod., 45g carb. (29g sugars, 2g fiber), 5g pro.

FUDGY CHOCOLATE-ALMOND SLOW-COOKER BROWNIES

When the heating element in my oven broke, I knew I would have to think of another way to make the brownies I had promised to take to a potluck that evening. But without an oven, how could I make the promised brownies? The solution equaled these divine slow-cooker brownies.
—Marion Karlin, Waterloo, IA

- -

Prep: 30 min. • **Cook:** 2 hours
Makes: 8 servings

- ½ cup butter, softened
- 1 cup sugar
- 4 large eggs, room temperature
- 2 cups chocolate syrup
- 1 tsp. vanilla extract
- 1 cup all-purpose flour
- ½ tsp. baking powder
- 1 cup chopped almonds
- 8 half-pint jars and lids
- 3 cups hot water

GANACHE
- ½ cup refrigerated nondairy creamer
- 6 oz. white candy coating, chopped
- ⅓ cup sliced almonds

1. In large bowl, cream butter and sugar until light and fluffy, 5-7 minutes. Add eggs, 1 at a time, beating well after each addition. Beat in chocolate syrup and vanilla. Add flour and baking powder, stirring just until moistened. Stir in chopped almonds.

2. Spoon the mixture into 8 greased half-pint jars. Center lids on jars and screw on bands until fingertip tight. Add hot water to a 7-qt. oval slow cooker; place jars in slow cooker. Cook, covered, on high until a toothpick inserted in the center of brownies comes out clean, 2-3 hours. Remove jars from slow cooker to wire racks to cool completely.

3. Meanwhile, bring creamer to a boil in a small saucepan over high heat. Stir in candy coating until melted. Remove from heat; cool to room temperature. Spread ganache over cooled brownies. Sprinkle with the sliced almonds.

1 serving: 743 cal., 32g fat (16g sat. fat), 124mg chol., 198mg sod., 107g carb. (82g sugars, 5g fiber), 11g pro.

**FUDGY CHOCOLATE-ALMOND
SLOW-COOKER BROWNIES**

BUTTERSCOTCH APPLE CRISP

Here's a cozy way to warm up winter nights. Apple crisp gets a sweet surprise with the yummy addition of butterscotch. Your house will smell marvelous as this dessert simmers!
—Jolanthe Erb, Harrisonburg, VA

- -

Prep: 10 min. • **Cook:** 5 hours
Makes: 6 servings

- 6 **cups sliced peeled tart apples
  (about 5 large)**
- ¾ **cup packed brown sugar**
- ½ **cup all-purpose flour**
- ½ **cup quick-cooking oats**
- 1 **pkg. (3½ oz.) cook-and-serve
  butterscotch pudding mix**
- 1 **tsp. ground cinnamon**
- ½ **cup cold butter, cubed
  Vanilla ice cream, optional**

1. Place apples in a 3-qt. slow cooker. In a large bowl, combine brown sugar, flour, oats, pudding mix and cinnamon. Cut in butter until mixture resembles coarse crumbs. Sprinkle over apples.
2. Cover and cook on low for 5-6 hours or until apples are tender. Serve with ice cream if desired.

1 cup: 422 cal., 16g fat (10g sat. fat), 41mg chol., 248mg sod., 71g carb. (53g sugars, 3g fiber), 2g pro.

GINGERED PEARS

My slow cooker allows me to serve a special dessert without much effort. These tender pears feature a surprise filling of candied ginger and pecans.
—Catherine Mueller, St. Paul, MN

Prep: 35 min. • **Cook:** 4 hours
Makes: 6 servings

- ½   cup finely chopped crystallized ginger
- ¼   cup packed brown sugar
- ¼   cup chopped pecans
- 1½ tsp. grated lemon zest
- 6   medium Bartlett or Anjou pears
- 2   Tbsp. butter, cubed
   Optional: Vanilla ice cream and caramel ice cream topping

1. In a small bowl, combine the ginger, brown sugar, pecans and lemon zest. Using a melon baller or long-handled spoon, core pears to within ¼ in. of bottom. Spoon ginger mixture into the center of each.
2. Place pears upright in a 5-qt. slow cooker. Top each with butter. Cover and cook on low for 4-5 hours or until tender. Serve with ice cream and caramel topping if desired.
1 serving: 263 cal., 8g fat (3g sat. fat), 10mg chol., 43mg sod., 52g carb. (32g sugars, 6g fiber), 1g pro.

APPLE-NUT
BREAD PUDDING

APPLE-NUT BREAD PUDDING

Traditional bread pudding gives way to winter's influences in this comforting dessert. I add apples and pecans to my slow-cooked version, then top warm servings with ice cream.
—Lori Fox, Menomonee Falls, WI

Prep: 10 min. • **Cook:** 3 hours
Makes: 8 servings

- 8   slices cinnamon-raisin bread, cubed
- 2   medium tart apples, peeled and sliced
- 1   cup chopped pecans, toasted
- 1   cup sugar
- 1   tsp. ground cinnamon
- ½ tsp. ground nutmeg
- 3   large eggs, lightly beaten
- 2   cups half-and-half cream
- ¼ cup apple juice
- ¼ cup butter, melted
   Vanilla ice cream

Place bread cubes, apples and pecans in a greased 3-qt. slow cooker. In a bowl, combine the sugar, cinnamon and nutmeg. Add the eggs, cream, apple juice and butter; mix well. Pour over bread mixture. Cover and cook on low for 3-4 hours or until a knife inserted in the center comes out clean. Serve with ice cream.
1 serving: 440 cal., 24g fat (9g sat. fat), 115mg chol., 173mg sod., 49g carb. (35g sugars, 4g fiber), 9g pro.

SLOW-COOKED FLAN IN A JAR

Spoil yourself or the people you love with these delightful portable custards. They're a cute and fun take on the Mexican dessert classic. Tuck a jar into your lunchbox for a sweet treat.
—Megumi Garcia, Milwaukee, WI

Prep: 25 min. • **Cook:** 2 hours + chilling
Makes: 6 servings

SLOW-COOKED
FLAN IN A JAR

½ cup sugar
1 Tbsp. plus 3 cups
   hot water (110°-115°)
1 cup coconut or whole milk
⅓ cup whole milk
⅓ cup sweetened condensed milk
2 large eggs plus 1 large egg yolk,
   room temperature, lightly beaten
   Pinch salt
1 tsp. vanilla extract
1 tsp. dark rum, optional

1. In a small heavy saucepan, spread the sugar; cook, without stirring, over medium-low heat until it begins to melt. Gently drag melted sugar to center of pan so sugar melts evenly. Cook, stirring constantly, until the melted sugar turns a deep amber color, about 2 minutes. Immediately remove from heat and carefully stir in 1 Tbsp. hot water. Quickly ladle hot mixture into 6 hot 4-oz. jars.

2. In a small saucepan, heat coconut milk and whole milk until bubbles form around sides of pan; remove from heat. In a large bowl, whisk condensed milk, eggs, egg yolk and salt until blended but not foamy. Slowly stir in hot milk; stir in vanilla and, if desired, rum. Strain through a fine sieve. Pour egg mixture into prepared jars. Center lids on jars; screw on bands until fingertip tight.

3. Add remaining hot water to a 6-qt. slow cooker; place jars in slow cooker. Cook, covered, on high 2 hours or until centers are set. Cool 10 minutes on a wire rack. Remove jars to a 13x9-in. baking pan filled halfway with ice water; cool 10 minutes. Refrigerate until cold, about 1 hour. Run a knife around sides of jars; invert flans onto dessert plates.

⅓ cup: 224 cal., 10g fat (8g sat. fat), 100mg chol., 87mg sod., 28g carb. (27g sugars, 0 fiber), 5g pro.

SLOW-COOKER SECRETS
You can use rum extract in place of the dark rum.

PINEAPPLE UPSIDE-DOWN
DUMP CAKE

PINEAPPLE UPSIDE-DOWN DUMP CAKE

No matter what the season, this lovely cake recipe is wonderful! It works well with gluten-free and sugar-free cake mixes, too.
—Karin Gatewood, Dallas, TX

Prep: 10 min. • **Cook:** 2 hours + standing
Makes: 10 servings

- ¾ cup butter, divided
- ⅔ cup packed brown sugar
- 1 jar (6 oz.) maraschino cherries, drained
- ½ cup chopped pecans, toasted
- 1 can (20 oz.) unsweetened pineapple tidbits or crushed pineapple, undrained
- 1 pkg. yellow cake mix (regular size)
  Vanilla ice cream, optional

1. In a microwave, melt ½ cup butter; stir in brown sugar. Spread evenly onto bottom of a greased 5-qt. slow cooker. Top with cherries, pecans and pineapple. Sprinkle with dry cake mix. Melt remaining butter; drizzle over top.
2. Cook, covered, on high for about 2 hours, until fruit mixture is bubbly. (To avoid scorching, be sure to rotate slow-cooker insert a half turn midway through cooking, lifting carefully with oven mitts.)
3. Turn off slow cooker; let stand, uncovered, 30 minutes before serving. If desired, serve with ice cream.
Note: To toast nuts, bake in a shallow pan in a 350° oven for 5-10 minutes or cook in a skillet over low heat until lightly browned, stirring occasionally.
½ cup: 455 cal., 22g fat (10g sat. fat), 37mg chol., 418mg sod., 66g carb. (47g sugars, 1g fiber), 3g pro.

CINNAMON ROLL CASSEROLE

CINNAMON ROLL CASSEROLE

Because we love cinnamon rolls, I created a slow-cooker recipe to have as a weekend breakfast or brunch. This is a delicious, simple, no-fuss dish that is perfect for company and family.
—Joan Hallford,
North Richland Hills, TX

Prep: 20 min. • **Cook:** 2½ hours
Makes: 10 servings

- 2 tubes (12.4 oz. each) refrigerated cinnamon rolls with icing, cut into quarters
- ½ cup chopped toasted pecans, divided
- ½ cup miniature semisweet chocolate chips, divided
- ½ cup evaporated milk
- 3 Tbsp. maple syrup
- 2 tsp. vanilla extract
- 1 tsp. ground cinnamon
- ½ cup all-purpose flour
- ½ cup packed brown sugar
- ¼ tsp. pumpkin pie spice
- ½ cup cold butter, cubed

1. Place half the cinnamon roll pieces in a greased 4- or 5-qt. slow cooker. Sprinkle with ¼ cup pecans and ¼ cup chocolate chips. In a small bowl, whisk the milk, syrup, vanilla and cinnamon until blended; pour over rolls. Top with remaining cinnamon roll pieces and remaining chocolate chips. Top with 1 packet of icing.
2. For topping, mix flour, brown sugar and pie spice; cut in butter until crumbly. Stir in remaining pecans. Sprinkle over icing. Cook, covered, on low 2½-3 hours or until rolls are set. Remove insert to a cooling rack and top with remaining icing. Serve warm.
1 serving: 492 cal., 25g fat (11g sat. fat), 28mg chol., 638mg sod., 65g carb. (36g sugars, 2g fiber), 5g pro.

COMMON CUTTING AND CHOPPING TECHNIQUES

Mincing and Chopping

Holding the handle of a chef's knife with one hand, rest the fingers of your other hand on the top of the blade near the tip. Using the handle to guide and apply pressure, move knife in an arc across the food with a rocking motion until pieces of food are the desired size. Mincing results in pieces no larger than ⅛ inch, and chopping produces ¼- to ½-inch pieces.

Dicing and Cubing

Using a utility knife, trim each side of the vegetable, squaring it off. Cut lengthwise into evenly spaced strips. The narrower the strips, the smaller the pieces will be. Stack the strips and cut lengthwise into uniformly sized strips. Arrange the square-shaped strips into a pile and cut widthwise into uniform cubes.

Making Bias or Diagonal Cuts

Holding a chef's knife at an angle to the length of the food, slice as thick or thin as desired. This technique is often used in stir-fry recipes.

Making Julienne Strips

Using a utility knife, cut a thin strip from one side of vegetable. Turn so flat side is down. Cut into 2-inch lengths, then cut each piece lengthwise into thin strips. Stack the strips and cut lengthwise into thinner strips.

Cutting Wedges

Using a chef's knife or serrated knife, cut the produce in half from stem end to the blossom end. Lay halves cut side down on a cutting board. Set knife at the center of one the halves and cut in half vertically. Repeat with the other half.

Zesting

Pull a citrus zester across limes, lemons or oranges, being careful not to remove the bitter white pith. Chop zest strips into fine pieces if desired.

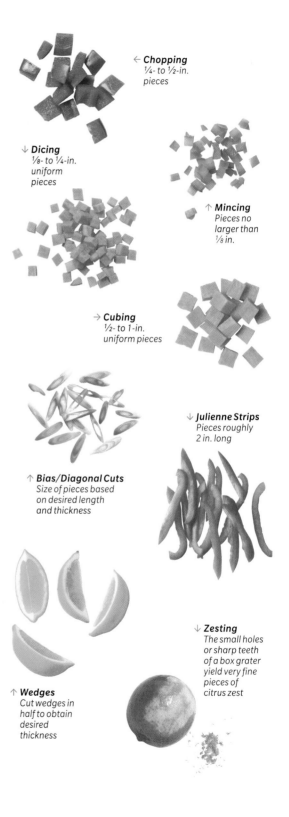

← *Chopping*
¼- to ½-in. pieces

↓ *Dicing*
⅛- to ¼-in. uniform pieces

↑ *Mincing*
Pieces no larger than ⅛ in.

→ *Cubing*
½- to 1-in. uniform pieces

↓ *Julienne Strips*
Pieces roughly 2 in. long

↑ *Bias/Diagonal Cuts*
Size of pieces based on desired length and thickness

↓ *Zesting*
The small holes or sharp teeth of a box grater yield very fine pieces of citrus zest

↑ *Wedges*
Cut wedges in half to obtain desired thickness

EQUIVALENT MEASURES

3 TEASPOONS	= 1 tablespoon	**16 TABLESPOONS**	= 1 cup
4 TABLESPOONS	= ¼ cup	**2 CUPS**	= 1 pint
5⅓ TABLESPOONS	= ⅓ cup	**4 CUPS**	= 1 quart
8 TABLESPOONS	= ½ cup	**4 QUARTS**	= 1 gallon

FOOD EQUIVALENTS

MACARONI	1 cup (3½ ounces) uncooked	= 2½ cups cooked
NOODLES, MEDIUM	3 cups (4 ounces) uncooked	= 4 cups cooked
POPCORN	3 cups (4 ounces) uncooked	= 8 cups popped
RICE, LONG GRAIN	1 cup uncooked	= 3 cups cooked
RICE, QUICK-COOKING	1 cup uncooked	= 2 cups cooked
SPAGHETTI	1 cup uncooked	= 4 cups cooked
BREAD	1 slice	= ¾ cup soft crumbs, ¼ cup fine dry crumbs
GRAHAM CRACKERS	7 squares	= ½ cup finely crushed
BUTTERY ROUND CRACKERS	12 crackers	= ½ cup finely crushed
SALTINE CRACKERS	14 crackers	= ½ cup finely crushed
BANANAS	1 medium	= ⅓ cup mashed
LEMONS	1 medium	= 3 tablespoons juice, 2 teaspoons grated zest
LIMES	1 medium	= 2 tablespoons juice, 1½ teaspoons grated zest
ORANGES	1 medium	= ¼–⅓ cup juice, 4 teaspoons grated zest

CABBAGE	1 head = 5 cups shredded	**GREEN PEPPER**	1 large = 1 cup chopped	
CARROTS	1 pound = 3 cups shredded	**MUSHROOMS**	½ pound = 3 cups sliced	
CELERY	1 rib = ½ cup chopped	**ONIONS**	1 medium = ½ cup chopped	
CORN	1 ear fresh = ⅔ cup kernels	**POTATOES**	3 medium = 2 cups cubed	
ALMONDS	1 pound = 3 cups chopped	**PECAN HALVES**	1 pound = 4½ cups chopped	
GROUND NUTS	3¾ ounces = 1 cup	**WALNUTS**	1 pound = 3¾ cups chopped	

EASY SUBSTITUTIONS

WHEN YOU NEED...		USE...
BAKING POWDER	1 teaspoon	½ teaspoon cream of tartar + ¼ teaspoon baking soda
BUTTERMILK	1 cup	1 tablespoon lemon juice or vinegar + enough milk to measure 1 cup (let stand 5 minutes before using)
CORNSTARCH	1 tablespoon	2 tablespoons all-purpose flour
HONEY	1 cup	1¼ cups sugar + ¼ cup water
HALF-AND-HALF CREAM	1 cup	1 tablespoon melted butter + enough whole milk to measure 1 cup
ONION	1 small, chopped (⅓ cup)	1 teaspoon onion powder or 1 tablespoon dried minced onion
TOMATO JUICE	1 cup	½ cup tomato sauce + ½ cup water
TOMATO SAUCE	2 cups	¾ cup tomato paste + 1 cup water
UNSWEETENED CHOCOLATE	1 square (1 ounce)	3 tablespoons baking cocoa + 1 tablespoon shortening or oil
WHOLE MILK	1 cup	½ cup evaporated milk + ½ cup water

INDEX